European Wet Grassland

Guidelines for management and restoration

European Wet Grassland

Guidelines for management and restoration

Phil Benstead, Paul José, Chris Joyce and Max Wade

Citation

For bibliographic purposes this book should be referred to as Benstead, P J, José, P V, Joyce, C B and Wade, P M (1999) *European Wet Grassland. Guidelines for management and restoration*. RSPB, Sandy.

The techniques described or referred to in this book do not necessarily reflect the policies of the RSPB or individuals involved in its production. A great deal of the information presented originates from the experiences of individual managers and must therefore be considered on a site-specific basis.

No responsibility can be accepted for any loss, damage or unsatisfactory results arising from the implementation of any of the recommendations in this book.

The authors

Max Wade works at the University of Hertfordshire as a researcher and teacher in the Department of Environmental Sciences in which he is the Professor in Ecology.

Dr Chris Joyce is a lecturer in Environmental Geography at the University of Brighton.

Dr Paul José is the RSPB's UK Wetlands Adviser and is a specialist in the ecology, hydrology and water quality dynamics of floodplain waterbodies, as well as co-author of several conservation management handbooks.

Phil Benstead is the RSPB's Wetlands Project Officer and involved in the production of RSPB literature on wetland-related topics.

Published by

The Royal Society for the Protection of Birds, The Lodge, Sandy, Bedfordshire SG19 2DL, UK

Typesetting and page design by

Barry Tucker, Maythyme Creative

Figures by

Rob Burns, Drawing Attention

Printed by

McCorquodale Confidential Print

RSPB Ref: 24/535/98-9

ISBN: 1 901930 01 7

Cover photographs:

Haymaking in Poland – David Woodfall (Woodfall Wild Images)

Great burnet – Andrew N Gagg (Photoflora)

Corncrake – Mike Lane (RSPB Images)

Marsh fritillary – Richard Revels (RSPB Images)

Endorsements

The following organisations have endorsed the
production of this guide:

Contents

Appendices

Acknowledgments

The authors thank Kevin Standring (RSPB) and Laurence Rose (RSPB) for participating in the Project Scoping and Steering Groups and also Sylvia Sullivan (RSPB) for her editorial input.

We also thank the following who freely gave information and advice and drafted or reviewed case studies: Malcolm Ausden (RSPB), Piotr Banaszuk (National Foundation for Environmental Protection), Jean-Jacques Blanchon (LPO), Harry Bowell (Norfolk Wildlife Trust), Tim Callaway (RSPB), Cliff Carson (RSPB), Catherine Casey (BirdWatch Ireland), Hugo Coops (RIZA), Nicola Crockford (RSPB), Frank de Roder (Staatsbosbeheer), Clive Doarks (English Nature), Andrew Dodd (RSPB), Alison Duncan (LPO), Deborah Dunsford (Broads Authority), Chris Durdin (RSPB), Andrzej Dyrcz (Wroclaw University), Philip Eckersley (Eurosite), C Egreteau (LPO), Jaanus Elts (EOS), David Evans (Loughborough University), Mike Evans (BirdLife International), Harry Fabritius (Staatsbosbeheer), Martin Flade, Sarah Fowler (RSPB), Roman Guziak (ProNatura), Mel Heath (BirdLife International), Tomas Hertzman (Swedish EPA), Stephen Hare (RSPB), Carl Hawke (RSPB), Quentin Hill (FRCA), Graham Hirons (RSPB), Nigel Holmes (Alconbury Environmental Consultants), Martin Janes (River Restoration Centre), Richard Jefferson (English Nature), Hein Korevaar (AB-DLO), Alexander Kozulin (NASB), Alex Lotman (Matsalu Nature Reserve), Jane Madgwick (WWF), Klaus Markgraf-Maué (NABU), Clive Mellon (RSPB), Mogens Bjørn Nielsen (County of Sønderjylland), Sarah Niemann (RSPB), Petr Obrdlik (WWF-Auen Institut), Thies Oomes (AB-DLO), Otars Opermanis (Museum of Zoology, University of Latvia), Eduard Osieck (Vogelbescherming), Oran O'Sullivan (BirdWatch Ireland), Ole Ottosen (County of Sønderjylland), Karel Prach (University of South Bohemia), Elle Puurmann (West Estonian Archipelago Biosphere Reserve), Bernd Raab (Landesbund für Vogelschutz), Tiit Randla (West Estonian Archipelago Biosphere Reserve), Norbert Schäffer (RSPB), Bob Scott (RSPB), Jan Seffer (Daphne Centre for Applied Ecology), John Sharpe (RSPB), Rikke Schultz (County of Sønderjylland), Viera Stanova (Daphne Centre for Applied Ecology), Jana Straškrabová (Agricultural University, Prague), J J Terrisse (LPO), Sandie Tolhurst (Broads Authority), Laimi Truus (Institute of Ecology, Tallinn), Peter Veen (Veen Ecology), Zoltán Waliczky (BirdLife International), Gwyn Williams (RSPB), Johanna Winkelman (Vogelbescherming) and Henk Zingstra (Wetlands International).

Max Wade and Chris Joyce acknowledge the financial assistance of the Darwin Initiative which supported the production of several of the case studies through its funding of wet grassland resource surveys in the Czech Republic and Estonia, co-ordinated by the Department of Geography at Loughborough University.

Finally, these guidelines owe a great debt to the authors of its 'parent' publication *The Wet Grassland Guide*, namely Jo Treweek, Owen Mountford (ITE), Martin Drake (English Nature) and Chris Newbold (English Nature).

Foreword

Throughout Europe, historical demands to protect people and property from flooding have resulted in a legacy of insensitive land management and flood defence activity. This has led to a substantial decline in wet grassland biodiversity. River engineering and the subsequent isolation of floodplain wetlands have exacerbated problems of eutrophication, water shortages and flooding. Paradoxically, many semi-natural wet grasslands in the Baltic States and Central Europe also face a different kind of threat – neglect owing to the cessation of traditional agricultural management.

In the early 1980s, the Council of Europe carried out a campaign on 'The Water's Edge', stressing the high value for wildlife of wet grasslands and other riverine habitats. New political initiatives are being developed by signatories of the Convention on Biological Diversity to reinforce wetland/biodiversity conservation. Within the countries of the EU acknowledgment of the need for the wise use of floodplains has resulted in the drafting of the Water Framework Directive. This legislation aims to introduce integrated river basin planning. Meeting the objectives of this legislation will involve floodplain restoration and the improvement of existing management practices. Integrated land and water management is seen as essential to resolving Europe's water problems. Ultimately, the fate of biological diversity in Europe will rely on full integration of biodiversity conservation in all spheres of economic activity.

Conservation of floodplain wetlands is no longer regarded as an 'add-on' with benefits for wildlife but as an essential process with important social and economic benefits. These factors are recognised in the Pan-European Biological and Landscape Diversity Strategy and underpin the philosophy behind the development of the European agri-environment schemes.

The future of wet grassland in Europe is intimately linked with the future of traditional, low-intensity pasture and meadow management, and the steady improvement of agri-environment schemes will be vital in the maintenance of wet grassland biodiversity.

The Guidelines bring together examples of wet grassland management from around North-west and Central Europe and are extremely timely as European attention turns to best practice management and restoration of floodplain wetland biotopes. Currently, wet grassland wildlife in Europe faces an uncertain future and to ensure its survival it will be necessary to encourage proper management of existing areas as well as the expansion of the resource by restoration. These Guidelines are a welcome step in providing site managers with information to manage and restore wet grasslands and further the aims of the Pan-European Biological and Landscape Diversity Strategy, and will promote wise use of floodplain areas.

Finally, the Guidelines are also an excellent example of international collaboration and co-operation, and the Council of Europe would like to congratulate all those involved in the production of this valuable contribution to the preservation of our biodiversity. Wet grasslands have indeed an extraordinary biological interest and form superb landscapes. They deserve all our attention.

Eladio Fernández-Galiano, Head a.i. of Environment Conservation and Management and Regional Planning Division, Council of Europe, Strasbourg.

Preface

Background

Maintaining wet grassland biotopes throughout Europe is pivotal to the maintenance of biodiversity in the region. Ultimately, conservation of this biological capital will rely on further extension of the existing resource, as well as changes in current policies regarding floodplain basin land use. Reinstating wet grassland will also restore wider functions with valuable benefits to society. These important facts are recognised by the signatories of the recent Pan-European Biological and Landscape Biodiversity Strategy, which provides the framework for the Convention on Biological Diversity in Europe.

Strategy implementation is not only dependent on policy mechanisms and appropriate funding but also on practical management and restoration action. These guidelines therefore aim to enable wet grassland managers to implement best management practice by providing information on the practical aspects of wet grassland management and restoration in northern and central Europe. The guidelines largely comprise case studies from the region and aim to:

- share practical management and restoration experience

- present alternative management and restoration options

- describe the functions of wet grassland (as well as biodiversity conservation), eg flood storage and nutrient removal.

The guidelines are designed to be practical and are aimed at everyone with an interest in wet grassland management and restoration.

Structure of this book

The guidelines comprise four main sections:

Part 1 defines wet grassland and emphasises its importance for European biodiversity conservation, as well as detailing the threats the biotope faces and speculating on the future.

Part 2 highlights the importance of planning for management and restoration. This section considers what should be done once the potential to rehabilitate a site or create new wet grassland has been identified. It explains how to evaluate a site and examines the range of physical, chemical, wildlife and legal factors that may influence management decisions.

Part 3 summarises the main management techniques practised in European wet grasslands. Individual sections deal with grassland management, water management, the management of associated biotopes, restoration techniques and management for specific wildlife. The grassland management section takes an overview of the two main techniques; mowing and grazing. The water management section examines the importance of natural hydrological processes, water level management on regulated sites as well as factors influencing water quality. Management of associated biotopes deals with the management of the important features, such as drainage channels and hedgerows, that occur alongside and within more intensively regulated/managed wet grassland sites. The following sections look at the most important techniques that can be used to restore wet grassland, management for specific target wildlife groups and monitoring.

Part 4 comprises the bulk of the guidelines and consists of 16 case studies – taken from northern and central Europe – that represent a cross-section of the main types of wet grassland within the region. The nature of wet grasslands varies across Europe from highly regulated grasslands in the UK and the Netherlands (Case Studies 3 and 6), to near natural systems such as the floodplains of the Biebrza in Poland (Case Study 1) and Pripyat in Belarus (Case Study 2). Similarly, approaches to management techniques and available resources differ throughout the region which results in a range of management scenarios. The case studies have also been selected to reflect these differences.

Throughout the guidelines the use of jargon has been avoided where possible but a glossary is included for those possibly unfamiliar terms which remain (Appendix 1). Abbreviations used in the text are given in full in Appendix 2.

Throughout the guidelines all costings are given in Euros (€) at the relevant exchange rates for the given currency on 10 March 1999. At that time the € was roughly equivalent to the US$, being valued at US$1.09.

Part 1
Introduction to European wet grassland

1.1 Wet grassland

Wet grasslands in northern and central Europe provide valuable habitat for indigenous plants, birds and invertebrates, particularly in the lowlands where semi-natural biotopes are often limited. Wet grasslands are typically characterised by:

- an abundance of low-growing grasses

- periodic but not continuous flooding with fresh or brackish water, or a high water table at or near the soil surface for much of the year

- regular management, usually mowing (cutting) or grazing.

Wet grasslands can include *Carex* dominated biotopes but not reedbeds of *Phragmites australis*.

Aside from their importance for wildlife and biodiversity conservation, wet grasslands are important for other reasons. In recent years there has been increasing awareness of the value of the hydrological and chemical functions of wetlands. Wet grasslands can perform the following functions:

- flood alleviation – wet grasslands can contain floodwater.

- groundwater recharge – wet grasslands retain water within a watershed enabling groundwater to be replenished.

- water quality improvement – riparian wet grasslands retain nutrients, toxic substances and sediment, preventing them from entering watercourses.

Economic benefits accrue from the functions described above, and when they are lost through the destruction of wet grassland they often have to be replaced at enormous financial cost. These benefits include:

- water supply; wet grasslands can influence both water quantity and quality

- the health of freshwater fisheries

- agriculture; floodplains provide some of the most fertile agricultural land in Europe

- recreation and tourism opportunities.

Wet grassland types

Some European wet grasslands are natural in origin, such as ice-governed meadows in Sweden, and spring-fed *Carex* grasslands in central and western Spain. However, most wet grasslands have developed as a result of human activity through the clearance of forests and drainage of bogs, marshes and saltmarshes in order to convert river floodplains, lake margins and coastal marshes to low-intensity grassland production. Most European wet grasslands are found in the lowlands and are often termed lowland wet grasslands. This general label covers a number of terms used to identify and describe different types of wet grasslands in Europe, including:

- river floodplain meadows and pastures (Plate 1)

- lakeside flood meadows and pastures (Plate 2)

- washlands, ie extensive semi-natural areas adjacent to rivers created as flood storage areas (Plate 3)

- polders and coastal grazing marshes behind a seawall, ie wet grassland areas claimed from saltmarshes or the sea (Plate 4)

Plate 1
River floodplain meadows in May, along the Lužnice River, Czech Republic. The pools are natural ox-bows.

Chris Joyce

Plate 2
Lakeside wet grassland is an important feature of many wetland areas in Europe.

RSPB

Plate 3
The Ouse Washes is the largest man-made flood storage area in the UK, containing 1900 ha of wet grassland.

Chris Joyce

Plate 4
Typical UK coastal grazing marsh behind the sea defences at Gibraltar Point, UK.

Chris Joyce

Plate 5
Natural sea-shore grassland is an important conservation feature of the Baltic coast.

Chris Joyce

- natural sea-shore grasslands, forming part of a transitional sequence from marine to terrestrial habitats (Plate 5).

This handbook uses the CORINE vegetation classification, and communities included within the definition 'wet grassland' are outlined in Figure 1.1. A glance at these wet grassland types reveals the importance of management to the majority of grassland ecosystems. Different management systems (Figure 1.2) create different types of grassland. Low-intensity, low-input agriculture produces the most diverse and important wet grasslands from a conservation perspective and is a sustainable process. Encouraging such management is increasingly the focus of agricultural incentive schemes throughout the region which aim to enhance biological and landscape values.

Most wet grasslands of nature conservation value in Europe therefore exhibit most or all of the following attributes:

- appropriate flooding and/or water regime

- regular mowing or grazing

- no or low inputs of fertiliser

- no use of herbicides and/or other pesticides

- no re-seeding

- maintenance of a range of associated biotopes, eg secondary channels, ox-bows and temporary pools and drainage channels.

These conditions are characteristic of the traditional management of wet grasslands as part of a low-intensity agricultural system but conflict with modern intensive agricultural practice (Table 1.1). This is one of the main reasons why wet grasslands have declined both in extent and wildlife value particularly in the last 50 years (Figure 1.3). The intensification process rapidly changes the competitive relations between plant species; a few, often grasses, becoming dominant at the expense of a number of other species, especially forbs. This dominance is usually a result of increased nutrient availability and lower water table.

European wet grasslands have also been lost and degraded by flood defence and river regulation, urban and industrial development, mineral extraction and pollution, particularly eutrophication, and modifications brought on by navigation and hydro-electric schemes.

Figure 1.1
CORINE classification of European wet grassland plant communities.

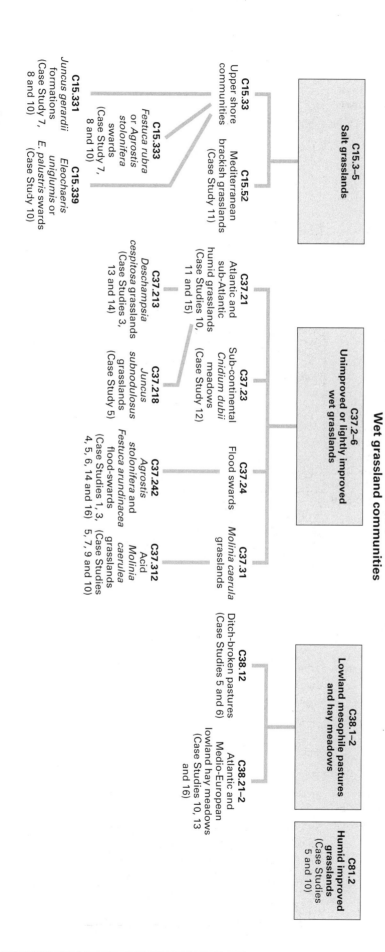

Wet grassland communities

C15.3-5
Salt grasslands

C37.2-6
Unimproved or lightly improved wet grasslands

C38.1-2
Lowland mesophile pastures and hay meadows

C81.2
Humid improved grasslands
(Case Studies 5 and 10)

C15.33
Upper shore communities

C15.52
Mediterranean brackish grasslands
(Case Study 11)

C15.333
Festuca rubra or *Agrostis stolonifera* swards
(Case Study 7, 8 and 10)

C15.331
Juncus gerardii formations
(Case Study 7, 8 and 10)

C15.339
Eleocharis uniglumis or *E. palustris* swards
(Case Study 10)

C37.21
Atlantic and sub-Atlantic humid grasslands
(Case Studies 10, 11 and 15)

C37.213
Deschampsia cespitosa grasslands
(Case Studies 3, 13 and 14)

C37.218
Juncus subnodulosus grasslands
(Case Study 5)

C37.23
Sub-continental *Cnidium dubii* meadows
(Case Study 12)

C37.24
Flood swards

C37.242
Agrostis stolonifera and *Festuca arundinacea* flood-swards
(Case Studies 1, 3, 4, 5, 6, 14 and 16)

C37.31
Molinia caerula grasslands

C37.312
Acid *Molinia caerulea* grasslands
(Case Studies 5, 7, 9 and 10)

C38.12
Ditch-broken pastures
(Case Studies 5 and 6)

C38.21-2
Atlantic and Medio-European lowland hay meadows
(Case Studies 10, 13 and 16)

Additional communities intimately associated with wet grassland include:

- pioneer salt mud and saltmarsh communities **(C15.1-2)** (Case Study 10)
- generally dry, free-draining grasslands eg alluvial Mesobromium **(C34.324)** (Case Study 16) and siliceous sandy grasslands **(C35.22)** (Case Study 10)
- *Filipendula ulmaria* and related tall herb communities **(C37.1)** (Case Study 10)
- swamp communities, including stands of *Phragmites* **(C53.1)** (Case Studies 1, 2 and 6), *Scirpus* **(C53.12)**; (Case Studies 1 and 6), *Typha* **(C53.13)**, *Glyceria maxima* **(C53.15)** (Case Studies 1 and 4) and *Phalaris arundinacea* **(C53.16)** (Case Studies 1, 2, 4, 8 and 13)
- beds of large *Carex* **(C53.21)** (Case Studies 1, 2, 7, 8, 13 and 14)
- fens **(C54.2)** (Case Study 4), including tall herb fens **(C54.21)** (Case Study 1)
- acidic fens **(C54.5)** and mires **(C54.5)**

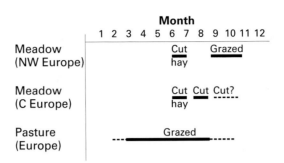

Table 1.1 Typical characteristics of traditional and modern wet grassland management in Europe.

Characteristic	Traditional	Modern
Hydrology		
Flooding	Largely unregulated	Highly regulated
Water table	High	Low
Vegetation management		
Cutting frequency	Low (but regular)	High
Livestock density	Low	High
Use of artificial fertilisers	None	High
Use of other agri-chemicals (eg herbicides)	None	High
Associated biotopes	Many and varied	Few and uniform

1.2 Biodiversity

Biodiversity (or biological diversity) encompasses the range of variation in living organisms at genetic, species and ecosystem level. It means the variety of life. European wet grasslands support considerable biodiversity comprising rare and threatened plant and animal species and communities, including nationally and internationally important bird populations, and a range of mammals, invertebrates, reptiles and amphibians (Table 1.2).

The biodiversity value of wet grassland is often greatly enhanced when it occurs in association with other wetland biotopes (Figure 1.4) and features such as floodplain backwaters (secondary channel, river arms, oxbows, etc), appropriately managed artificial drainage channels, temporary pools and hedgerows (Figure 1.5). Diversity is particularly high where two biotopes meet (known as the ecotone), for example where reedbed grades into wet grassland.

Wet grassland plants

Wet grasslands support a range of plant communities maintained by a regime of grazing and/or cutting, and natural processes in some cases. Botanical diversity can be high (Table 1.3, Case Studies 12 and 13) and a number of globally threatened and declining plant species are associated with wet grasslands in Europe including *Apium repens*, *Selinum carvifolia* and *Scorzonera humilis* (Jefferson and Grice 1998) (Tables 1.4 and 1.5). Some plant communities have become very restricted; eg the *Alopecurus pratensis-Sanguisorba officinalis* flood meadow (C38.2) and the central European *Cnidium dubium* association (C37.23) (Case Study 12), such that they are specially protected by the European Union (EU) (Council of the European Communities 1992).

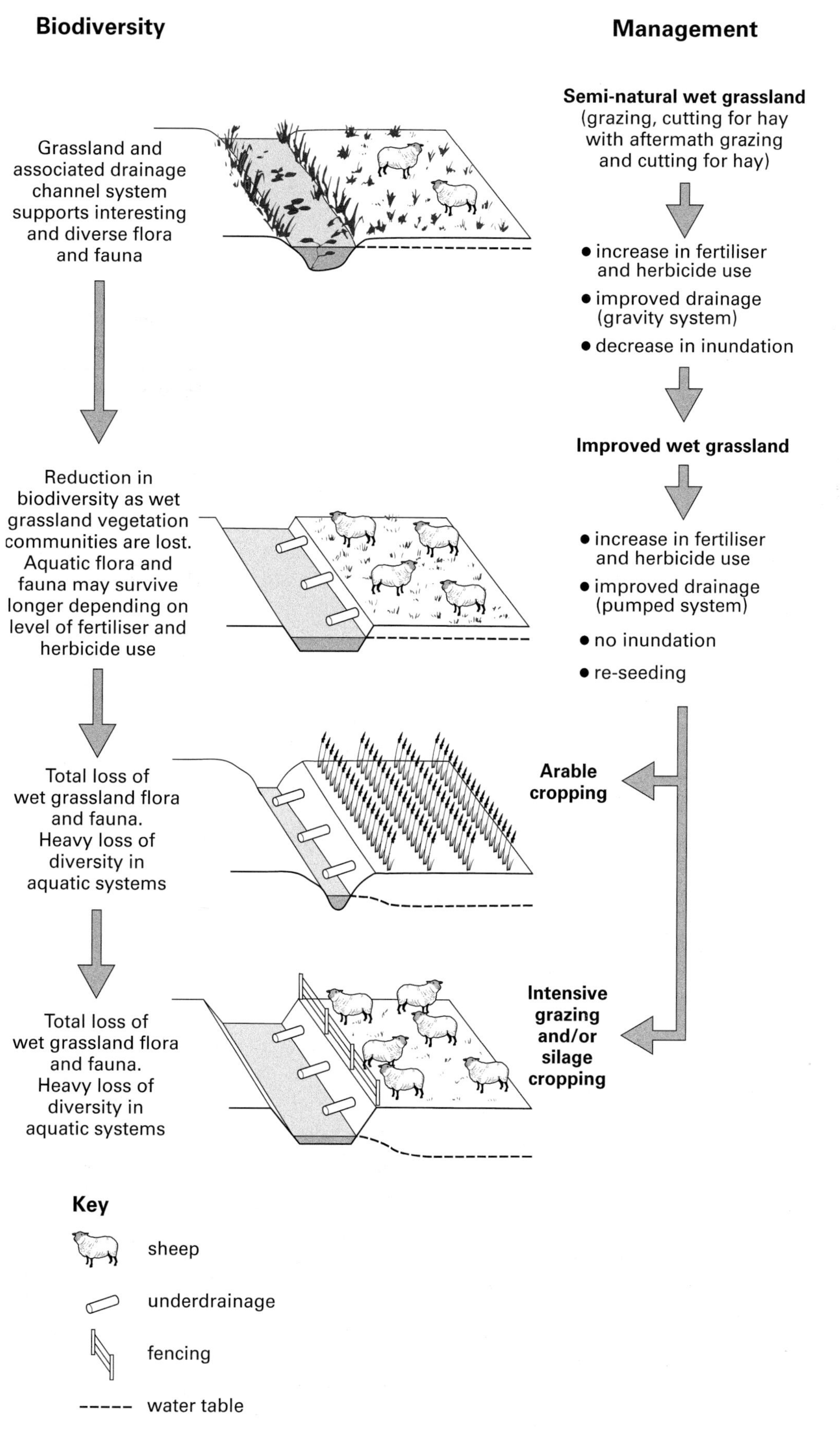

Biodiversity

Management

**Figure 1.3
Process of
agricultural
intensification.**

Semi-natural wet grassland
(grazing, cutting for hay
with aftermath grazing
and cutting for hay)

Grassland and
associated drainage
channel system
supports interesting
and diverse flora
and fauna

- increase in fertiliser
  and herbicide use
- improved drainage
  (gravity system)
- decrease in inundation

Improved wet grassland

Reduction in
biodiversity as wet
grassland vegetation
communities are lost.
Aquatic flora and
fauna may survive
longer depending on
level of fertiliser and
herbicide use

- increase in fertiliser
  and herbicide use
- improved drainage
  (pumped system)
- no inundation
- re-seeding

Total loss of
wet grassland flora
and fauna.
Heavy loss of
diversity in
aquatic systems

**Arable
cropping**

Total loss of
wet grassland flora
and fauna.
Heavy loss of
diversity in
aquatic systems

**Intensive
grazing
and/or
silage
cropping**

Key

sheep

underdrainage

fencing

----- water table

Table 1.2 Examples of rare and threatened species that utilise wet grassland in Europe.

Chiroptera
Rhinolophus blasii, Rhinolophus ferrumequinum, Rhinolophus hipposideros, Rhinolophus mehelyi, Myotis emarginatus and *Myotis myotis* [The presence of bats feeding over wet grassland depends on the proximity of suitable roosting and nursery sites]

Rodentia
Microtus cabrarae

Carnivora
Canis lupis and *Lutra lutra*

Reptiles
Elaphe quatuorlineata, Elaphe situla and *Vipera ursinii*

Amphibians
Bombina bombina and *Bombina variegata*

Lepidoptera
Coenonympha oedippus, Euphydryas aurinia, Maculinea nausithous and *Maculinea teleius*

Odonata
Coenagrion mercuriale [The extent to which adult riverine and still-water dragonfly species utilise adjacent habit for feeding is unknown. Good quality, diverse wet grassland may be very important feeding areas for this group]

Gastropoda
Vertigo angustior

Figure 1.4 Plant communities often associated with wet grassland. Association with these communities greatly enhances biodiversity within wet grassland.

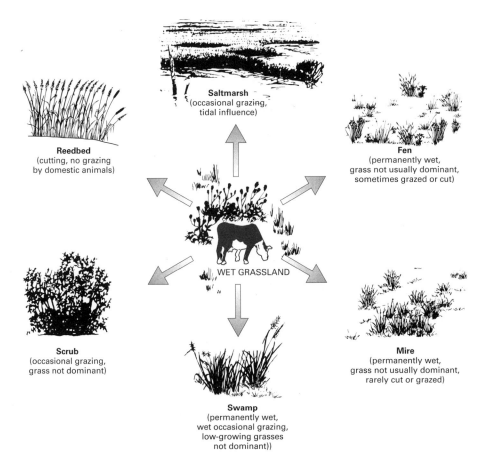

Saltmarsh
(occasional grazing, tidal influence)

Reedbed
(cutting, no grazing by domestic animals)

Fen
(permanently wet, grass not usually dominant, sometimes grazed or cut)

Scrub
(occasional grazing, grass not dominant)

WET GRASSLAND

Mire
(permanently wet, grass not usually dominant, rarely cut or grazed)

Swamp
(permanently wet, wet occasional grazing, low-growing grasses not dominant))

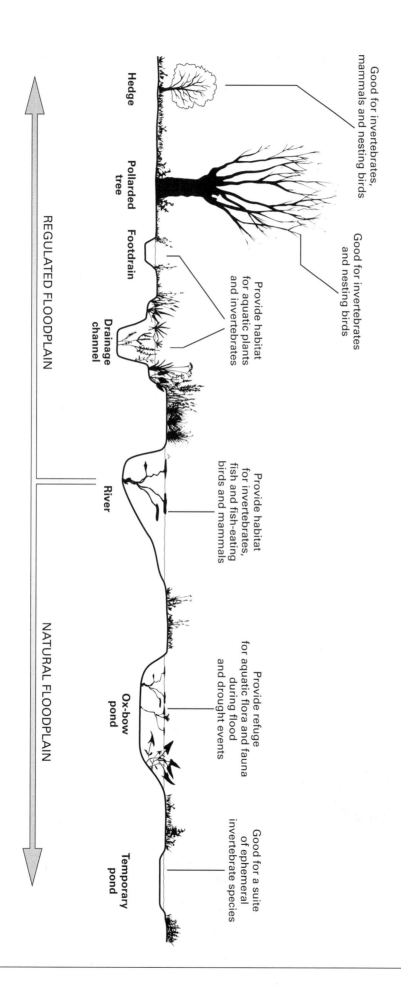

Figure 1.5
Wet grassland exists within a matrix of associated biotopes, the presence of which enhance biodiversity.

REGULATED FLOODPLAIN

NATURAL FLOODPLAIN

Hedge

Pollarded tree

Footdrain

Drainage channel

River

Ox-bow pond

Temporary pond

Good for invertebrates, mammals and nesting birds

Good for invertebrates and nesting birds

Provide habitat for aquatic plants and invertebrates

Provide habitat for invertebrates, fish and fish-eating birds and mammals

Provide refuge for aquatic flora and fauna during flood and drought events

Good for a suite of ephemeral invertebrate species

Table 1.3 Examples of plant biodiversity for European wet grasslands.

Country	Plant diversity indicator
Czech Republic	• 80 vascular species along a 150 m transect in the Lužnice river floodplain[1] (Case Study 13)
Denmark	• 150 vascular plant species (12% of the flora of Denmark) found along a 1.4 km (50 m wide) transect of the riparian zone of the upper River Gudenå[2]
Estonia	• Islands support over 15 different coastal wet grassland communities[3] (Case Studies 7 and 8) • 20% of the rare species of the Baltic region are found in wet floodplain biotopes[4] (Case Study 8)
France	• Over 20 vascular species in a 20 m transect of wet coastal grassland[5] (Case Study 11) • 655 species in a 500 m reach of the Adour river floodplain[6]
Netherlands	• 55 species per 100 m^2 in an *Arrhenatherum elatius* wet grassland[7]
Poland	• 24 vascular species per m^2 in an alluvial meadow[8]
Slovakia	• Over 540 species in the Morava river floodplain, of which 12% are nationally rare[9] (Case Study 12)
Spain	• 37 species in 100 m^2 in wet meadows in central Spain[10]
Sweden	• An average of 29 species per m^2 (and 46 in 2.25 m^2) in *Deschampsia caespitosa* wet grassland[11] (Case Study 14)
UK	• 20 nationally rare or scarce vascular species present in English wet grasslands, including seven in coastal grazing marsh[12]

References: [1] Prach and Straškrabová (1996); [2] Baattrup-Pedersen *et al* (in prep), [3] Nilson *et al* (1997); [4] Truus (1998); [5] Muller *et al* (1998); [6] Décamps and Tabacchi (1994); [7] Oomes and Mooi (1981); [8] Pasternak-Kuśmierska (1984); [9] Ružička(1994); [10] Rey Benayas and Scheiner (1993); [11] Berlin (1998); and [12] Jefferson and Grice (1998).

Table 1.4 Rare plant species associated with floodplain grasslands in Estonia (Truus and Tõnisson 1998).

Status	Example of species
Nationally endangered	*Angelica palustris, Carex ligerica, Isoetes setacea* and *Silene tatarica*
Nationally vulnerable	*Carex pediformis rhizodes, Crepis mollis, Lepidotis inundata, Ligularia sibirica, Nuphar pumila, Sanguisorba officinalis* and *Selaginella selaginoides*
Nationally rare	*Elatine hydropiper* and *Gladiolus imbricatus*
Rare/scarce in the Baltic region	*Angelica sylvestris, Blysmus compressus, Blysmus rufus, Calla palustris, Cyperus fuscus, Iris sibirica, Pinguicula vulgaris, Saussurea alpina esthonica, Schoenus ferrugineus, Scorzonera humilis, Succisa pratensis* and *Valeriana officinalis.*

Table 1.5 Rare plant species associated with wet grasslands in England (Jefferson and Grice 1998).

Status	Biotope		
	Coastal grazing marsh	Fen meadows and *Juncus* pasture	Inland wet grassland
Nationally rare (ie occurrence in ≤15 10 km squares)		*Erica vagans, Lobelia urens**, *Selinum carvifolia** and *Scorzonera humilis**	*Apium repens**
Nationally scarce (ie occurring in 16–100 10 km squares)	*Alopecurus bulbosus, Althaea officinalis, Bupleurum tenuissimum, Carex divisa, Cyperus longus, Lepidium latifolium* and *Trifolium squamosum*	*Gentiana pneumonanthe, Hypericum undulatum, Lathyrus palustris* and *Peucedanum palustre*	*Carex elongata, Carex filiformis, Fritillaria meleagris* and *Oenanthe silaifolia*

* Globally threatened species.

Wet grassland birds

Wet grasslands provide breeding or wintering habitat or migratory stop-over sites for a number of bird species, particularly wading birds (waders) and wildfowl. Estimates of populations of waders breeding in the countries of the EU revealed that more than half of all the waders in the region bred on wet grasslands (Hötker 1991). In the UK, over 40 bird species of conservation concern are dependent or partly dependent on wet grasslands, including globally endangered species such as *Crex crex* and internationally important populations of other species, eg *Cygnus columbianus, Anser fabalis* and *Anas acuta* (Benstead *et al* 1997). Appendix 3 lists birds which utilise wet grassland in northern and central Europe and are of European conservation concern.

Breeding waders are a good indicator of the intensity of management of a site (Table 1.6, Section 3.5.2). Wildfowl are also a major bird group characteristic of wet grassland and similarly require low-intensity, high water table agricultural management (Section 3.5.2). Other species make use of wet grassland too, some preferring rank unmanaged areas for feeding (eg *Tyto alba, Asio flammeus* and *Circus cyaneus*). *Motacilla flava* makes use of tussocky, cattle-grazed fields for breeding. Large numbers of wintering birds attract hunting birds of prey, eg *Falco peregrinus* and *Falco columbarius*. Associated swamp biotopes support *Porzana* species and provide early season cover for *Crex crex* (Case Study 4).

Table 1.6 Vulnerability of waders to intensification of wet grassland. The last two species may be favoured by grassland intensification (adapted from Beintema 1983).

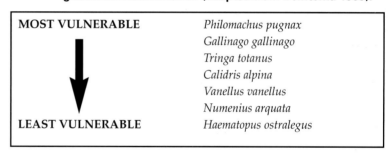

MOST VULNERABLE	*Philomachus pugnax*
	Gallinago gallinago
	Tringa totanus
	Calidris alpina
	Vanellus vanellus
	Numenius arquata
LEAST VULNERABLE	*Haematopus ostralegus*

Landscape scale dictates the suitability of a grassland area for a given species. For example, scrub encroachment into large open grasslands in Poland and the Baltic States has had a harmful effect on wintering goose populations but benefited breeding *Grus grus*.

Wet grassland invertebrates

Wet grasslands can support a high diversity of invertebrates although in the UK relatively few species appear to be dependent on the grassland itself (Drake 1998). Invertebrate diversity and the number of rare species tend to be associated with environmental heterogeneity in the wet grassland landscape which is increased by the presence of biotopes such as damp hollows and temporary pools, channels and old trees. Invertebrates are also an important food source for breeding wildfowl and waders.

Some internationally rare invertebrates are

associated with wet grasslands in Europe, including the butterfly *Eurodryas aurinia* which is globally threatened. A study of the wet meadows of a Hungarian nature reserve found 21 species of Orthoptera (Table 1.7). Brackish marshes are the stronghold for many coastal Coleoptera, and coastal grasslands in Estonia serve as corridors for migrating Lepidoptera and Odonata (Leibak and Lutsar 1996).

Table 1.7 Species of Orthopteroid insect found in wet grasslands in the Bátorliget Nature Reserves in north-east Hungary (Nagy 1990).

Orthoptera
Phaneroptera falcata, Conocephalus discolor, Conocephalus dorsalis, Ruspoilia nitidula, Tettigonia viridissima, Metrioptera roeseli, Pteronemobius concolor, Gryllotalpa gryllotalpa, Xya variegata, Xya pfaendleri, Tetrix subulata, Tetratetrix nutans, Odontopodisma rubripes, Mecosthetus grossus, Parapleurus alliaceus, Chrysocraon dispar, Omocestus ventralis, Gomphocerripus rufus, Chorthippus albomarginatus, Chorthippus dorsatus, and Chorthippus parallelus.

Blattodea
Ectobius laponicus

Dermaptera
Forficula auricularia

Wet grasslands and fish

Backwaters, ditches and other open water habitats within wet grassland areas are important for the well-being of river fisheries (Cowx and Welcomme 1998). Lateral habitat diversity across the floodplain is important for the maintenance and development of fish communities. Backwaters from continuously flowing side channels to partially abandoned river side arms, ox-bow lakes and drainage channels provide essential breeding habitat for a range of fish species (José 1988). These lateral habitats, often characterised by low velocity areas (flow <4 cm s^{-1}), are important for the development of young-of-year fish which could be washed away in the main channel or chanellised reaches of rivers. Seasonally flooded pools in wet grassland areas provide spawning habitat for species including *Esox lucius*, while species such as *Scardinius erythropthalmus* are characteristic of side arms and pools with no or seasonal flow only.

Temporarily flooded wet grassland areas also provide feeding refuges for many species and can substantially improve fish yields following flood events. The maintenance of lateral connectivity between the river and its floodplain waterbodies/wet grassland is vital to maintaining not only productivity but also species diversity (Tockner *et al* 1999). This factor should be taken into account when restoring areas for biodiversity.

Other wildlife

Other wildlife of importance that utilises wet grasslands and their associated biotopes in Europe includes amphibians, and mammals (eg *Lutra lutra, Arvicola terrestris* and *Alces alces*) (Kminiak 1994, Bejcek and Stastný 1996, Leibak and Lutsar 1996).

Associated biotopes

Ox-bows and other floodplain waterbodies can provide a refuge from rivers, and temporary field pans provide habitat for certain types of invertebrates, eg Crustacea, which require ephemeral waterbodies. Drainage channels have been identified as being of particular significance for aquatic flora and invertebrate fauna in lowland areas with regulated river systems.

Differences in salinity across a site can create special biotopes of weakly saline (euryhaline) conditions suitable for certain scarce species, eg *Ruppia maritima* in drainage channels, and certain species of invertebrates, eg the Crustacea *Palaemonetes varians* and *Corophium* species and brackish water Coleoptera.

1.3 Threats

From an early stage in the human history of Europe rivers have been subject to modification (Table 1.8). Since Roman times rivers have been engineered and harnessed for power generation; there has also been a gradual deforestation of floodplains to create agricultural land to support a rapidly expanding population. Removal of trees resulted in destabilisation, with rapid recycling of channel form and increases in catastrophic flooding. The Industrial Revolution of the 18th Century increased pressures on rivers and set in motion the events leading to the present-day situation. Flood control, navigation, power and waste disposal needs led to intensive channel engineering, interconnection through canals, pollution and ultimately the disconnection and drainage of floodplain wetlands.

Table 1.8 Historical summary of the modification of European floodplains, adapted from Cowx and Welcomme (1998)

Period	State of floodplain
Pre-Roman	Ubiquitous; most floodplains forested and relatively stable. Small-scale establishment of floodplain grasslands for agriculture.
Roman 1–1000	Deforestation of floodplains continues in limited way, particularly in southern Europe. Deforestation of hill slopes increases siltation and subsequently alluvial deposition.
Medieval/Renaissance 1000–1700	Deforestation of floodplains ongoing and floodplain wetlands claimed for water meadows, both activities creating wet grassland areas. Groundwater levels begin to fall.
Industrial Revolution 1700–1800	Floodplain use for agriculture further intensifies, riverine forests severely reduced. Groundwater levels drop further, flooding increases leading to the advent of modern day flood control engineering.
1800–1900	Large sections of river channel regulated, disconnecting floodplain wet grasslands and other wetlands from the system.
Modern 1900–1970	Floodplain wet grassland disconnected in most European systems. Improved drainage allows floodplains to be occupied for urban and intensive agricultural use.
1970–present	Floodplains still disconnected from rivers and agricultural intensification continuing, but small-scale rehabilitation of wet grassland and other features commences.

Note: This process was mirrored in coastal and other wetland areas throughout Europe at the same time, creating many of the wet grassland areas that are found outside floodplains.

As a result, throughout Europe perhaps as much as 15 million hectares of wet grassland has been lost over the last 200 years. In the UK, for example, there has been a 40% reduction in area since the 1930s (Williams and Hall 1987). This loss of biotope has resulted in declines in the breeding populations of seven of the eight wader species using wet grassland in Europe (Hötker 1991). European wet grasslands and their associated flora and fauna continue to decline. This is being brought about by:

- changes in agricultural practices (Case Study 5), such as:

  - increased land drainage
  - increased use of fertiliser
  - change from hay-making to silage
  - re-seeding
  - herbicide use
  - conversion to arable
  - higher stocking densities
  - neglect or abandonment

- land drainage/flood defence (Case Study 15) which leads to:

  - modification of natural hydrological regimes
  - isolation of floodplains from river flows
  - early fall in water-table levels in spring
  - rapid evacuation of winter floods
  - maintenance of low water levels in drainage channels in winter
  - use of aquatic herbicides

- abstraction for drinking water and crop irrigation (a problem in the Black Fens of the Czech Republic, for example) which leads to:

  - lowered river flows and in-channel water levels
  - lowered water tables
  - exacerbation of drought-related problems

- eutrophication leading to:

  - changes in grassland plant communities. This has occurred in parts of the Baltic with *Phragmites* beds displacing wet grassland communities due to the eutrophication of the Baltic Sea coupled with the lack of grazing (Case Study 7)
  - increased sward vigour which allows higher stocking densities

- sea-level rise which is threatening coastal grasslands

- development and mineral extraction (eg peat extraction in the Parc des Marais du Cotentin et du Bessin, France, has resulted in the loss of wet grassland) leading to:

  - decline in area routinely flooded
  - increased frequency of flooding of remaining washland

- site fragmentation leading to:

  - isolation of sites threatening species restricted to wet grassland and vulnerable to extinction
  - problems with water level control and implementing agricultural management.

The threats outlined above have affected all groups of wildlife dependent on wet grassland. For specific threats to bird species of conservation concern see Table 1.9.

Intensification and neglect

Figure 1.3 summarises the changes in wet grasslands as they pass from traditional through improved to intensive management for agriculture. Farmers can achieve higher productivity and hence increased yields of milk and meat by regulating the water table (usually by lowering it) by applying fertilisers, and by controlling unwanted plants. Typically this is accompanied by a reduction in the incidence of flooding and often the re-seeding of fields with productive grasses, such as *Lolium perenne*. As the water table and drainage become regulated, for example through the installation of a pumping system, it enables arable agriculture, such as wheat or maize cropping, to be developed. This pattern of intensification is widespread in Europe. The intensification process has a rapid and negative impact on the biodiversity of wet grasslands, specifically reducing botanical and invertebrate diversity and affecting breeding wader populations (Table 1.6).

In contrast, there are also many remaining European wet grasslands of nature conservation value that are deteriorating through a lack of management with, for example, agricultural over-production and policy reform in western Europe leading to the withdrawal of marginal areas from agriculture. Many central and eastern European countries have recently undergone changes in their agricultural as well as political systems, resulting in the neglect or abandonment

Table 1.9 Threats faced by birds of conservation concern that utilise European wet grassland (adapted from Tucker and Evans 1997).

Species	Crop improvements	Pesticide use	Land abandonment	High stocking levels	Marginal habitat-loss	Afforestation	Farming operations	Recreation	Overhead structures	Increased predators	Urbanisation/roads	Drainage/flood control	Loss of hay meadows	Loss of old buildings	Pasture conversion
Ardea purpurea								✓			✓	✓			
Ciconia ciconia	✓				✓	✓			✓			✓			
Cygnus columbianus						✓		✓	✓			✓			
Cygnus cygnus						✓		✓	✓			✓			
Anser brachyrhynchus						✓		✓	✓			✓			
Anser erythropus									✓			✓			
Anas acuta			✓			✓	✓	✓				✓			
Anas querquedula			✓			✓	✓	✓				✓			
Circus cyaneus	✓			✓	✓						✓				
Falco tinnunculus	✓	✓		✓	✓	✓								✓	
Aquila pomarina		✓	✓		✓						✓	✓			
Aquila clanga		✓			✓			✓	✓			✓			
Aquila heliaca	✓	✓						✓	✓		✓				
Coturnix coturnix	✓	✓		✓			✓						✓		
Porzana porzana					✓							✓			
Crex crex	✓			✓		✓	✓			✓			✓		
Grus grus	✓								✓		✓	✓			
Calidris alpina			✓							✓		✓	✓		
Philomachus pugnax	✓		✓	✓						✓		✓			
Gallinago media	✓		✓	✓						✓		✓			
Limosa limosa	✓		✓	✓		✓	✓			✓		✓			
Numenius tenuirostris							✓					✓			
Numenius arquata	✓		✓	✓		✓	✓			✓		✓			✓
Tringa totanus	✓		✓	✓		✓	✓			✓		✓			
Chlidonias niger						✓					✓	✓			
Tyto alba	✓			✓	✓							✓	✓	✓	
Athene noctua	✓	✓			✓										
Asio flammeus	✓										✓	✓			
Alauda arvensis	✓	✓	✓	✓			✓	✓							
Anthus pratensis	✓						✓								
Saxicola rubetra	✓				✓								✓		
Saxicola torquata	✓				✓								✓		
Locustella naevia					✓							✓	✓		
Acrocephalus paludicola			✓									✓	✓		

of many areas (Case Studies 7, 8 and 13). For example, in Estonia cutting and grazing management of floodplain grasslands has almost completely ceased, due to uncertainties over land ownership and the use of intensively managed cultivated grasslands for fodder production (Truus and Tõnisson 1998). Unmanaged grasslands have a lower nature conservation value, becoming dominated by a few robust plant species at the expense of others (Oomes and Mooi 1981, Bakker 1989) (Case Study 8). They eventually succeed to scrub and forest although succession can be arrested if

plant litter (which tends to accumulate in the absence of management), high water levels or competition from the herbaceous field layer excludes woody species.

When grassland is abandoned, the floral and faunal composition alters but the impact on biodiversity is difficult to predict. For example, abandoned floodplain meadows developing into woodland may acquire a valuable invertebrate fauna and avifauna but lose the characteristic flora and fauna associated with the wet grassland.

1.4 The way forward?

Wet grassland biodiversity depends on the continuation of low-intensity agricultural management. Mechanisms that aim to deliver management for wildlife whilst maintaining agricultural production will become increasingly important. The EU's response to the decline of biodiversity as a result of the intensification of agriculture was the EU Agri-environment Regulation (2078/92), which resulted in Environmentally Sensitive Area schemes and other support mechanisms for low-intensity farming (Case Studies 4, 5 and 11).

Paradoxically, agri-environment schemes are also being advocated to combat agricultural neglect in central European and Baltic States countries (Case Studies 1, 7, 8, 12 and 13), although many of these countries have also suffered from intensification. The lessons learnt from EU experience must be heeded when designing new projects elsewhere. For example, Case Study 5 illustrates that generic prescriptions often do not deliver benefits to biodiversity; flexibility is important, allowing prescriptions to be modified to suit conditions on particular sites. Agri-environment mechanisms subject to frequent appraisal (Case Study 5) are likely to evolve and become more important for wildlife conservation.

In addition to the appropriate management of wet grassland sites of biodiversity value, conservation of wet grassland biodiversity in Europe can only be assured with a continued investment in restoration. Potential restoration

sites must therefore be safeguarded by the planning process to ensure that they remain available for restoration in the future.

It is probable that the scale of projects will need to increase to consider entire catchments, or substantial areas in a floodplain context, and the emphasis will be on restoring near-natural functions. Catchment management planning will play an important role in securing water supplies for both people and wildlife in the next millennium, ensuring the effective wise use of water. The role of wet grasslands in providing valuable functions such as flood alleviation, groundwater recharge and water quality improvement will be widely recognised and factored into resource planning processes. Natural processes and ecosystem management are likely to be embraced more widely.

Restoration ecologists must seize every opportunity. For example, sea-level rise is ongoing and whilst coastal wetlands will be threatened by marine incursion and the improvement of sea defences, there is also the opportunity for wetland restoration which will provide flood defence functions and create habitat. A task for environmentalists is to lobby and work with coastal defence bodies to ensure that flood protection and managed retreat schemes result in no net loss of wetland habitat.

Key References

Bailey, R G, José, P V and Sherwood, B R (Eds) (1988) *United Kingdom floodplains*. Westbury, West Yorkshire.

Benstead, P, Drake, M, José, P, Mountford, O, Newbold, C and Treweek, J (1997) *The wet grassland guide: managing floodplain and coastal wet grasslands for wildlife*. RSPB, Sandy.

Drake, M (1998) The important habitats and characteristic rare invertebrates of lowland wet grassland in England. In C B Joyce and P M Wade (Eds) *European wet grasslands: biodiversity, management and restoration*, pp 137–150. John Wiley, Chichester.

Tucker, G M and Evans, M I (1997) *Habitats for birds in Europe: a conservation strategy for the wider environment*. BirdLife International, Cambridge.

Tucker, G M and Heath, M F (1994) *Birds in Europe: their conservation status*. BirdLife International, Cambridge.

Part 2

Site evaluation and management planning

2.1 Introduction – setting goals and how to achieve them

This section considers how to identify the potential for maintaining, enhancing or restoring wildlife value in wet grassland and then how to ensure that appropriate management decisions are taken. As much as possible about the existing and potential wildlife value of the wet grassland site must be known so that objectives can be defined. Whatever the goal for a site, making the most of any opportunity requires careful consideration and planning.

The steps in Figure 2.1 should be followed to make the best use of management and restoration opportunities. Some wet grassland sites will have greater potential than others, depending on the factors outlined in Table 2.1. Site evaluation is important to determine current wildlife interest and identify potential for enhancement and restoration. It is also necessary to identify any legal, technical and financial factors that might constrain management options. All management undertaken should be subject to monitoring, which should be planned and adequately resourced from the outset. The ability to modify management in the light of results from monitoring is essential if any unforeseen, undesirable effects are to be reversed.

2.2 Planning for management and restoration

2.2.1 Conservation status and ownership

The starting point for any wet grassland site assessment should be to ascertain its existing conservation status. If the site is designated, it is always necessary to contact the appropriate statutory conservation agency as options for management will usually already be set. For such sites, legislation may include specific requirements, which must be considered. Relevant international legislation is presented in Appendix 4. If a site has no existing conservation interest, options for management will be less constrained.

**Figure 2.1
Steps to optimise
management.**

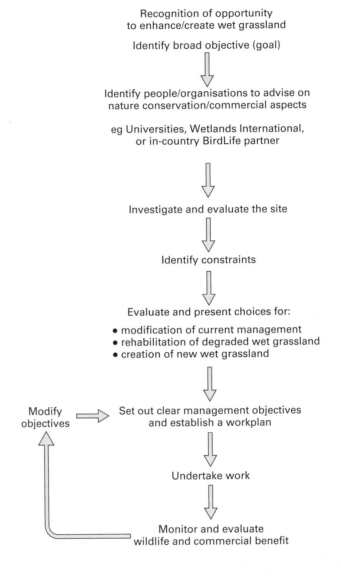

Recognition of opportunity
to enhance/create wet grassland
Identify broad objective (goal)

Identify people/organisations to advise on
nature conservation/commercial aspects

eg Universities, Wetlands International,
or in-country BirdLife partner

Investigate and evaluate the site

Identify constraints

Evaluate and present choices for:

- modification of current management
- rehabilitation of degraded wet grassland
- creation of new wet grassland

Modify objectives → Set out clear management objectives
and establish a workplan

Undertake work

Monitor and evaluate
wildlife and commercial benefit

2.2.2 Wildlife value

It is essential to establish the current value of a
wet grassland site for wildlife, so as to ensure
that any proposed changes in management will
safeguard important species, communities or
biotopes. The government conservation
agencies may be able to provide information
about the wildlife value and past/present
management of a particular wet grassland.
Non-governmental conservation organisations
may also have valuable information on wildlife
and management. Universities/research
institutes and local biological records centres
and museums may hold relevant information,
for example on species records and historical
management. For information about birds,
contact the relevant bird protection society or
Wetlands International to gain access to

national survey data. All possible sources
should be contacted; however, it should be
noted that relatively few wet grassland sites in
Europe are well recorded and it can be difficult
to assess the quality of information collected
especially when it comes from different sources.

It is advisable to complement existing
information with field surveys to assess the
current status of biotopes and species at a site
(Plate 1). Lack of knowledge can lead to
inadvertent damage to inconspicuous species
(often invertebrates, but also some plants).
Specialist help in identifying wildlife may be
sought through the government conservation
agencies, universities/research institutes, NGOs
and individual experts.

Table 2.1 Points to consider when setting objectives for wet grassland management.

Evaluate status/ownership
- Site designations
- Past and current management
- Scope for enhancement of wildlife value

Site characteristics
- Size
- Past wildlife interest
- Existing and potential wildlife value
- Vulnerable communities and species present
- Associated biotopes present, eg floodplain backwaters and drainage channels
- Proximity to other wet grasslands
- Surrounding land use/management
- Soil type
- Water supplies and infrastructure

Legal constraints
- Discuss any proposals with statutory rural planning, water management and nature conservation agencies
- Discuss any planning considerations with local authorities and other stakeholders

Management constraints
- Availability of resources/labour/equipment/skills
- Availability of stock for grazing management
- Potential problems with water excess, shortage or quality
- Access

Andrew Hay

Plate 1 Field surveys are essential to assess the current status of biotopes and species on site and add important knowledge when planning management.

For wet grasslands already supporting a diverse assemblage of wildlife and rare and threatened species, changes in management should be considered particularly carefully. Determine whether such sites sustain their nature conservation value under existing management or whether they are deteriorating and merit remedial action. If the existing management regime has led to the development of valued communities or populations, it should be retained where possible. If, in contrast, there is evidence that existing management is leading to a decline in interest, remedial action can be taken. As a general rule, changes should be implemented gradually and only over a proportion of the site. Sudden changes, even when undertaken with the best intentions, can lead to the loss of species.

Thorough surveys are expensive but can be important to determine the presence of rare and vulnerable species. It is also useful to focus on species that indicate management changes, such as declines in water levels, or deterioration in site quality (eg grassland species like *Lolium perenne* indicative of agricultural improvement, or algal domination of waterbodies indicative of eutrophication). Such surveys should also be designed to provide a suitable baseline for monitoring.

Wherever possible, quantitative measures such as species frequency or cover and population size should be obtained using standard methods, so that surveys can be repeated in future, eg in order to monitor the success of management and restoration.

2.2.3 Site size and location

Options for management are greater on larger wet grassland sites, where a range of biotopes and species and larger populations can be supported. On small sites, characteristic species and communities are more vulnerable to the detrimental effects of external influences and chance extinctions (eg edge effects, such as spray drift from nearby agricultural areas, or fire).

Site location has implications not only for management, but also the likelihood that species will colonise it spontaneously and establish viable populations. Even where large areas of wet grassland remain in Europe, they have often become increasingly isolated from potential sources of colonising species through habitat loss, fragmentation and flood control preventing diaspores being deposited. Isolation means that many desirable species may be slow to colonise even when management has created apparently appropriate conditions for them.

For species that cannot travel distances easily (some plants and many invertebrates), deliberate introductions or reintroductions may be necessary (Case Study 16). Introduction projects should be considered only as a last resort and should be well researched and fulfil the IUCN criteria for the reintroduction of species (IUCN 1998). Permission must be sought from the relevant government conservation agency for introductions on designated sites. Species distributions show inherent regional variation and species should not be introduced outside their natural ranges. Introduction of species or genotypes from other areas can have an adverse effect on the genetic viability of native populations. It is also important to ensure that management caters for species and communities appropriate to the geographic location of a site. Not all conservation objectives are applicable in all parts of Europe.

2.2.4 Site hydrology

Maintenance of natural hydrological processes should be the primary objective. However, where these have been lost, restoration of wet grassland often relies on the reinstatement of suitable hydrological conditions, eg the raising of water levels. Availability of water is therefore a crucial factor and even on wet grasslands with existing high wildlife value maintaining water supplies of a suitable quality can be a major challenge, often due to abstraction and drainage.

Liaison with staff responsible for water resources and flood defence in the appropriate water-management agency may be sufficient to give an indication of water availability. However, more detailed assessment of a site's hydrology and the calculation of water budgets is essential for major schemes (Plate 2). Estimates are necessary for inputs (eg rainfall

or in-flows from watercourses) and losses (including evapotranspiration and seepage). Seeking advice from hydrologists with expertise in this area should be considered. It is also vital to understand, where possible, the hydrological requirements of target biotopes and species (eg Newbold and Mountford 1997).

Table 2.2 shows the range of factors that may be investigated, depending upon the scale of the project and the resources available, before determining options for water management. A description of the wet grassland site, including the location of depressions, patterns of water flow and soil types is useful as a first step in characterising hydrological conditions. The need for detailed topographic survey may be reduced if it is possible to observe the sequence of flooding on a site and make a photographic record.

Dave Rees

Plate 2
Levelling surveys
provide detailed
topographic
information and aid
the understanding
of site hydrology.

2.2.5 Legal and planning considerations

Legal and planning considerations must be taken into account when certain management improvements or restoration activities are proposed. Issues likely to need consideration include water resource management, wildlife legislation, public rights of way, and planning concerns.

2.2.6 Resource constraints

From the outset, the resource implications of management proposals should be considered. The costs of feasibility studies, any necessary engineering works and subsequent management should all be examined. The following costs may be incurred:

- design and feasibility studies, for example

  - hydrological survey
  - wildlife survey

- one-off capital items, for example

  - land-forming, eg bund and drainage channel construction
  - installation of water control structures
  - machinery purchase

- ongoing management

- labour/staff costs to undertake management

- servicing/maintenance of machinery

- livestock costs, for example

  - purchase of stock
  - fencing and stock pen construction
  - animal husbandry

- ongoing survey and monitoring.

2.2.7 Management plans

Whatever the proposals for a site, it is often useful to put the background and rationale for any work in writing. This can take the form of a short project proposal or a comprehensive management plan. It is important to establish consensus among stakeholders and interested parties on proposals for any site. This can be accomplished through holding pathfinder and

Table 2.2 Possible approaches to hydrological assessment.

What to assess	Sources of information	Implications for water management
Catchment area	Maps, aerial photographs, satellite imagery	Indicates sources of water, likely directions of flow and location of low-lying areas.
Soils (concentrating on hydrological properties such as hydraulic conductivity)	Soil survey maps, field investigations (eg soil pits and auger samples)	Soil type influences type of hydrological regime which can be sustained. Grasslands on alluvial/clay soils can be managed by surface flooding. Those on peat require high water tables to stay wet.
Topography	Levelling survey. Observe extent of flooding (take photographs and examine old photographs)	Large-scale topography determines design of hydrological control system if one is required, assisting in the siting of water control structures, eg sluices.
	Observe patterns of flooding	Small-scale topography determines extent of field flooding at given water levels.
Climate/weather (especially rainfall and evapotranspiration)	Meteorological records	Influences such factors as likely availability of water and rates of evapotranspiration.
	Weather station on site	Important for calculation of water budgets and estimation of need for winter storage to supplement summer deficits.
Water sources	Gauge boards on-site to measure river/drainage channel levels and seasonal regime. Check for level of water in river/drainage channel relative to field surface and soil water table	Information on water quantity is required to determine if target hydrological regimes can be implemented. Sluice construction or pumping may be required where levels of water supply are below field surface.
	Check with water management agencies for information on availability of surface water, water quality, and pollution records	Necessary to establish water inputs and nature of potential pollution sources.
	Investigate groundwater supplies. Establish seasonality of seepage/spring flows	Groundwater can be a source of high quality/low nutrient level water, but can also be polluted (particularly in areas with intensive agriculture).
	Measure water-table heights using dipwells	If carried out regularly, should indicate problem periods of low soil water levels. *Caution:* detailed assessment of groundwater (other than simple water-table measurements) is difficult: seek expert advice.
Requirements of other water users in catchment	Catchment-wide management plans where available. Water management agencies will have details of abstractions	Water needs may have to be balanced with those of other users. This is particularly important in low rainfall/highly populated areas.
Water-management infrastructure	Establish condition of any existing drainage infrastructure (including sub-surface drainage) and water control structures. Check for leakage in bunds and check sluices are operational.	New water-management infrastructure may be required. Major, expensive engineering works may be necessary.
Other factors	Water management agencies	Potentially adverse impacts on adjacent land. Protective mechanisms such as bunding, secondary ditching may be required to protect adjacent land from flooding/raised water levels.

public meetings (Case Study 3). Ideally, management plans or project proposals should contain the following sections:

- site description

- site evaluation, including key features of nature conservation value

- aim, objectives and rationale behind site proposals

- detailed prescriptions to achieve objectives, including monitoring

- costed work plans.

Such a framework can assist with the long-term planning of resources, labour and monitoring programmes, and can enable constraints and any conflicting objectives to be identified. Much information can be collated in the form of maps, diagrams and photographs. Detailed guidance on the management planning process is available in NCC (1988) and Hirons *et al* (1995). An additional benefit of producing a management plan is that the necessary work for the period covered by the plan can be agreed with a statutory or non-governmental conservation agency facilitating funding.

2.3 Making choices

Wildlife conservation involves making choices. Limits to what can be achieved will be imposed by financial cost, practicality, legal constraints and the priorities of the managing organisation. Some species or communities, eg those that are globally threatened, will be considered more important than others. It is rarely the case that the most worthwhile wildlife management is also the cheapest to undertake. However, much can be achieved with carefully targeted management action.

The first stage in decision-making involves evaluating survey results to identify the most important aspects or areas of a site. Species or communities that are internationally or nationally important should usually have priority for conservation management. In some cases priorities for species conservation will have already been set in policy frameworks or in local or regional strategies for biodiversity, eg Biodiversity Action Plans. Priorities are likely to be ranked as follows:

1. Species/biotopes of international importance, eg *Crex crex, Cnidium dubium* flood-meadow
2. Species/biotopes of national importance, eg *Limosa limosa, Agrostis stolonifera* flood-sward
3. Species/biotopes of regional importance, eg small populations of breeding waders and associated semi-improved wet grassland
4. Species/biotopes of local importance, eg ponds and drainage channels.

It may be useful to distinguish between management for the restoration of wildlife interest where it has declined and management intended to maintain or enhance existing value. When considering a restoration project the desired end-point should be identified from historic records and/or investigation of remnant flora and fauna on the site. In extremely neglected sites, restoration may have to be introduced piecemeal to the site, so that there is a gradual change in the vegetation, allowing less mobile species to migrate and adapt to the altered conditions. Once restoration has begun to take effect, the implementation of a maintenance management regime can be considered. The time taken for restoration to be successful depends on the condition of the site at the outset and the objectives that have been set.

Table 2.3 gives examples of possible management options on wet grassland sites supporting various levels of wildlife interest. The techniques that may be employed on wet grassland sites are considered in more detail in Part 3 of this guide. It should be remembered, however, that every site is unique and while guidance can be given as to the range of management techniques available, management decisions must be closely tailored to the needs of individual wet grassland sites based on information available, the experience of the wet grassland manager and the interests of other stakeholders.

Table 2.3 Making choices: management strategies and options for European wet grasslands.

Management strategy	Management options
Area with high wildlife interest (Case Studies 1 and 2)	
Maintain existing management	Water management: ■ Always maintain natural flooding regime if still present ■ Identify existing regime by talking to previous and neighbouring land managers ■ Maintain water control infrastructure (if this exists) and implement appropriate drainage channel maintenance regime (Section 3.2.3 and 3.3.1). Grassland management: ■ Identify existing regime by talking to previous and neighbouring land managers ■ Maintain grassland management regime, especially in respect of type of grazing animal, stocking density and timing and frequency and dates of mowing (Section 3.1).
Area with moderate wildlife interest and potential for enhancement (Case Study 3)	
Improve/modify existing management	Water management: ■ Investigate possibility of return to more natural flooding regime ■ Check operation of water-control structures to ensure water-level prescriptions can be met (Sections 2.2.4 and 3.2.3) ■ Install new low-cost structures (eg flexi-pipe sluices) to improve flows while enhancing drainage channel wildlife value (Section 3.2). Grassland management: ■ Ensure cutting is delayed until after nesting (Section 3.5.2) ■ Consider cutting followed by aftermath grazing (Section 3.1.2) ■ Optimise grazing regime: consider type and density of stock and timing and duration of grazing (Section 3.1.1) ■ Stop, or at least minimise, fertiliser and herbicide applications.
Area with limited wildlife interest (eg pump-drained grassland cut for silage with wildlife restricted to drainage channels).	
Implement rehabilitation programme	Water management: ■ Consider options for reinstating water levels by repairing existing or installing new water management structures, eg dropboard and flexi-pipe sluices and windpumps (Section 3.2.3) ■ Rotationally manage existing drainage channels and consider enhancing them by re-profiling during this process. Dig new ones as necessary (Section 3.3.1) ■ Consider need for winter water storage, eg by reservoir construction or using natural waterbodies (Section 3.2.3). Grassland management: ■ Extensify management, eg introduce hay-cutting (Section 3.1.2) ■ Stop or limit applications of fertilisers, herbicides and pesticides ■ Consider options for grazing ■ Consider reintroduction of herbaceous species, eg slot-seeding, transplants (Section 3.4.1).
Area with negligible or no wildlife interest (eg land drained and under arable for many years)	
Implement restoration/creation programme (Section 3.4)	Water management: ■ Consider need for sub-irrigation/removal of under-drainage ■ Consider scope for setting back/removing floodbanks. Grassland establishment: ■ Assess/estimate condition of soil seed bank ■ Assess proximity to other sources of grassland species ■ Consider soil remediation, eg nutrient stripping, topsoil removal (Case Study 9) ■ Carefully consider spraying with herbicide to eliminate competitive weeds ■ Attempt natural regeneration on sites under arable for relatively short periods which are near suitable seed sources ■ Otherwise select and sow appropriate seed mix (Case Study 12) ■ Consider subsequent transplanting of herbaceous perennials ■ Consider follow-up management/monitoring.

Key references

Eurosite (1996) *Management plans for protected and managed semi-natural areas*. Report of Eurosite Working Group. Eurosite, Wimeraux.

Hirons, G, Goldsmith, B and Thomas, G (1995) Site management planning. In W J Sutherland and D A Hill (Eds) *Managing habitats for conservation*, pp 22–41. Cambridge University Press, Cambridge.

Mitsch, W J and Gosselink, J G (1993) *Wetlands*. 2nd Edition. Van Nostrand Reinhold, New York.

NCC (1988) *Site management plans for nature conservation – a working guide*. Nature Conservancy Council, Peterborough.

Spellerberg, I F (1992) *Evaluation and assessment for conservation: ecological guidelines for determining priorities for nature conservation*. Chapman and Hall, London.

Usher, M B (Ed) (1986) *Wildlife conservation evaluation*. Chapman and Hall, London.

Part 3
Management

Vegetation management in the form of cutting and/or grazing is necessary to maintain nearly all wet grassland in Europe, as it prevents the invasion of woody species and natural succession to woodland. Vegetation management (Section 3.1) is usually part of an agricultural system that utilises primary production to support domestic herbivores either directly through grazing (pastures) or indirectly by producing fodder (meadows). Pastures are usually grazed by cattle or sheep, a form of management prevalent on many wet grasslands (Section 3.1.1, Plate 1). Meadow management (Section 3.1.2, Plate 2) consists of mowing for a fodder crop, such as hay, on an annual basis. The re-growth or aftermath can subsequently be grazed, a common practice in western Europe, or as in many parts of central Europe cut again for further crops.

The continued existence of a wet grassland site is also dependent on the maintenance of an appropriate water regime (Section 3.2). Where possible, a near natural hydrological regime should be maintained. In intensively regulated systems it will be necessary to manipulate water levels/flooding regimes to achieve conservation and farming objectives. Management of a wet grassland site also needs to take into account other associated biotopes, eg backwaters, ox-bows, pools, trees and drainage channels (Section 3.3). Recently the creation and restoration of wet grassland has become increasingly important following alarming declines in the extent of the biotope in many countries. Restoration techniques are introduced in Section 3.4. Finally the management requirements of three key wildlife groups, namely plants, birds (breeding waders and wintering wildfowl) and invertebrates, are described in Section 3.5.

Wet grassland biodiversity is dictated by the interaction of three main environmental gradients; moisture, nutrient availability and disturbance (eg grazing and poaching), all of which are affected by management practices.

Harry Fabritius

Plate 1
Agricultural management in the form of grazing is one of the most important practices carried out on wet grasslands, creating a varied sward structure and preventing the invasion of woody species and succession to woodland.

Dieter Brandi (FLPA)

Plate 2
Mowing is another form of management that has long, traditional links with many wet grassland areas. Areas managed in this way often support botanically diverse swards as mowing tends to favour forbs at the expense of grass species.

3.1 Grassland vegetation management

Establishing or maintaining a management regime appropriate to the conservation aims of a wet grassland site while maintaining a sustainable agricultural activity is a challenge. Decisions need to be made about whether to use grazing or mowing or a combination of the two. Both require decisions about timing, technique and intensity of management. Burning is occasionally practised on wet grassland and has particular applications in restoration management (Section 3.1.4, Case Studies 10 and 14).

3.1.1 Grazing

The most natural and beneficial form of grassland management for wildlife is grazing, a process which has facilitated a wide range of different plant communities. Grazing management is beneficial because it:

- creates structural diversity

- prevents the expansion of coarse species and the invasion of woody plants.

In contrast to mowing, the effects of livestock grazing on vegetation are selective. The effects depend upon:

- type of livestock used

- season and frequency of grazing

- density of grazing.

Before introducing grazing, make sure to:

- take professional advice

- ensure training of staff in welfare and grazing skills

- establish a work relationship with a registered veterinary surgeon

- construct a strong handling pen.

A combination of livestock types is beneficial on large sites. All livestock have different (but overlapping) grazing characteristics, giving additional structural diversity at appropriate densities. Combination grazing can also reduce the density of parasites on a site and lead to better livestock health.

Type of livestock

In Europe, the most commonly used animals for grazing wet grasslands are cattle. Sheep, horses, ponies and goats are less widely used. Cattle and horses are probably best for managing wetland vegetation (see below). Consideration should be given to using breeds of livestock that have traditionally been used to graze wet grasslands (Case Study 14; Alderson and Small 1997). In many cases traditional breeds are the most suitable animals for grazing wet grassland because they have:

- a historical association – certain breeds are associated with particular regions, so using them appropriately allows continuity of management

- hardy constitutions – some breeds are adapted to harsh, wet conditions, eg Belted Galloway cattle in Scotland and Konik ponies in Poland

- an ability to thrive on relatively poor forage

- variable requirements – traditional breeds vary in their characteristics and it should be possible to find a traditional breed to suit a particular site

- variable size – size varies between breeds allowing a choice of animal to suit given conditions

- disease resistance – there is evidence that some traditional breeds are more resistant to disease, eg to foot-rot

- resistance to parasites and biting insects – traditional breeds are tough-skinned, tolerant of biting insects and display little sign of ill-health from intestinal parasites in the absence of dosing with anthelmintics

- low cost – traditional breeds are generally less expensive to buy than more commercial breeds but may not be as profitable when sold.

It should be remembered that despite claims for self-reliance, hardiness, thriftiness and disease resistance, welfare of these animals is still important.

Commercial breeds should not be ignored, however, as they are often effective on 'well managed' wet grassland and can show favourable economic returns, eg on alluvial flood-meadows. The least productive systems for livestock tend to be wet fen meadows and *Juncus* pastures and such systems ideally require traditional breeds.

Cattle

In many of the case studies in Part 4, cattle are the preferred grazing animal. This is because they are:

- more tolerant of wet conditions than sheep

- easy to contain using drainage channels as field boundaries

- cause less soil compaction and poaching than sheep due to lower stocking densities and higher hoof area/weight ratio

- relatively unselective in their grazing compared with sheep and useful for removing tall or rank vegetation and controlling invading scrub

- well suited to the conservation management of productive sites which require summer grazing as they do not graze flowers preferentially.

Cattle trample grassland vegetation and create bare areas, particularly in softer ground, creating niches for early successional plants and invertebrates. The grazing of the margins of waterbodies and drainage channels reduces the competitiveness of the tall emergent plants enabling more light to reach the water surface and increases the diversity of aquatic plants.

Cattle tend to produce a more tussocky sward, which is preferred to more uniform swards by most nesting waders and is advantageous to invertebrates. Because of their larger size, fewer cattle than sheep can be used to achieve the same grazing pressure and hence the risk of trampling to wader nests is lower. Young cattle, being more active than older animals, are probably a greater trampling threat to ground-nesting birds.

Store cattle, young stock or suckler cows are particularly well suited to wet grasslands. Dairy farming necessitates disturbance as the animals are moved on and off the fields twice a day as well as requiring special shelter and feeding facilities. Dairy cattle also require high levels of nutrition and are rarely suitable for managing semi-natural grasslands.

Sheep

Sheep are less often grazed in wet grassland than cattle owing to their relative intolerance of wet conditions. A number of serious health problems are associated with sheep grazing wet grasslands and it is particularly unsuitable for lambs. Intensive shepherding is essential for husbanding sheep, especially breeding stock. Provision for shearing and perhaps dipping is also necessary.

Sheep graze most effectively on swards maintained at 3–6 cm height, grazing closely and evenly to produce a uniform sward structure which is well suited to grazing by some wintering wildfowl, eg *Anas penelope*. However, such a uniform sward structure is not particularly suitable for breeding waders and invertebrates and may reduce botanical diversity. Sheep may be unable to graze effectively on tall, rank grassland and are generally not as useful as cattle for the early management of overgrown sites. However, sheep can be used as pioneer grazers when restoring neglected areas because they:

- are lightweight

- open up areas

- graze saplings and browse subsequent re-growth

- are easy to transport

- are effective in small areas requiring short-term grazing

- require less fresh drinking water than cattle.

Horses and ponies (equines)

Equine grazing is often wrongly considered to be damaging to species-rich grassland. As with cattle and sheep, equines have a place in wet grassland management and traditionally are often associated with this landscape (Girard 1992, Oates and Bullock 1997). However, proper management, particularly in small fields, is critical, otherwise damage will ensue from the establishment of latrine areas, overgrazing and enrichment from imported feed.

In general, equines:

- feed primarily on grass but also take a wide range of *Carex* and *Juncus* species

- are variable grazers. A plant species can be favoured in one location and avoided in another depending on botanical composition. This makes it difficult to predict the impact of equine grazing, particularly on sites with a mosaic of vegetation communities

- are capable of heavily grazing some elements of the plant community and ignoring others. Selective overgrazing alongside undergrazing can be beneficial to invertebrate diversity

- have a tendency to leave orchid spikes. Indeed, flowers are much more visible in grasslands grazed by horses in summer compared to those grazed by sheep

- will only browse woody species when there is an inadequate quantity of grass. They can assist in managing scrub by pushing through and opening up low scrub and browsing

- are very active and can cause poaching

- may require supplementary feed which can cause eutrophication of the grassland.

Equines may be the most suitable animal for year-round extensive grazing of wet grassland because:

- horses show no signs of mineral deficiency when grazed without supplementary feed

- there are often fewer legal requirements associated with keeping equines (in many countries they are not classed as an agricultural animal)

- they are able to adapt to different food types and can tolerate fluctuations in condition/weight with less ill-effect than other types of livestock.

Consideration should be given to equine herd

dynamics. Large sites being extensively grazed benefit more from the presence of breeding herds (a near natural scenario) rather than one large even-aged herd. The smaller herds will range over the whole of their territory and the net result will be better grazing coverage than the opportunistic use of optimal areas and the neglect of sub-optimal ones that often results from a large group of animals. Extensive free-range grazing is more likely to be successful on large sites with a mosaic of vegetation communities. This allows livestock to satisfy their nutritional requirements throughout the year by switching to different species, including woody browse.

Pigs

Pigs have been successfully used to graze and forage on wet grasslands, creating an early successional stage by churning up and poaching the soil surface, making suitable conditions for feeding waders and the germination of seed-bearing plants.

Dung

The dung produced by livestock provides an important niche for certain types of invertebrates (Simpson and Gee 1997). Anthelmintics to control livestock internal parasites should be avoided because they can:

- kill invertebrates including rare Coleoptera and important prey species for wader chicks

- cause a build up of dung which cannot be broken down by natural processes.

Where possible, alternative anthelmintics which have no adverse effects on terrestrial invertebrates should be used, eg those which have benzimidazoles or imidazopyrimidines as their active ingredients.

Season and frequency of grazing

Grazing regimes can be:

- seasonal, which is the predominant type of grazing on European wet grasslands. On grasslands with natural hydrological regimes grazing starts whenever the land dries out enough to support animals. On hydrologically regulated systems the start of the grazing season is usually a compromise between the grazier and the conservation manager. The grazier prefers to turn animals out as early as possible (eg in April) to make the most of the initial spring growth. The conservation manager may wish to delay grazing to avoid disturbance of nesting birds and allow plants to flower. Delaying turn-out for too long can however result in wastage of plant growth as mature growth is less palatable and animals can trample vegetation rather than eat it.

- continuous: year-round grazing at low stocking densities can produce diverse wet grassland swards with a varied structure but carries the risk of damage for both nesting birds, invertebrates and flowering plants. Low stocking levels are important to avoid such damage. Expect stock to lose 30% of their autumn weight over winter, this weight loss is swiftly corrected in spring. It may be necessary to increase stocking density in the summer in wet grasslands to prevent scrub invasion.

- rotational, ie movement of livestock around available management compartments. This can be either regular or irregular. More stable annual regimes are likely to benefit a wider range of wet grassland species. Rotational grazing can be used to produce a variety of sward structures and to ensure that sensitive life-stages are avoided on specific areas, eg flowering plants, nesting birds and larval or adult stages of Lepidoptera. Overstocking must be avoided, although rapid defoliation can be appropriate to opening up foraging areas for birds such as *Vanellus vanellus*, *Limosa limosa* and *Tringa totanus* and their broods.

Stocking density

Deciding on the correct stocking density is essential and failure to achieve this is a common factor in reducing the conservation value of wet grassland. In practice achieving a desired sward state by grazing is often done by regularly monitoring livestock and removing them at the appropriate moment. This process is, to a large extent, intuitive and subjective and it requires experience to judge grazing pressures in the autumn to achieve a desired sward structure in

the following season. There are a number of factors to be considered when making such a decision (Crofts and Jefferson 1999):

- differential grazing impact. In order to make direct comparisons between different types of livestock, stocking densities are often expressed in terms of livestock units or equivalents (Table 3.1). Suggested stocking rates for wet grassland are given in Table 3.2, Case Studies 3, 5, 10 and 11. These should be regarded only as an approximate guide as all wet grassland sites have different requirements.

- annual fodder requirements. Livestock units can be used to calculate the extent to which available wet grassland will meet the annual fodder requirements and any supplementary feed which might be needed.

- botanical composition. The sward needs to be compatible with the livestock density both in terms of palatability and conservation value.

- productivity. The annual fodder requirements are linked to wet grassland productivity.

- soil type. Soil fertility will have an important influence on botanical composition and productivity

- hydrology. Drainage and flooding regimes will determine the grazing period and hence influence fodder availability.

- climate, such as temperature and rainfall, has a significant impact on productivity.

- accessibility. The extent to which the grass can be reached by the livestock is important, as all parts of a wet grassland site are rarely equally accessible. Livestock may need to be guided to parts of the site.

- farm system. The grazing of the site needs to be integrated with the constraints imposed by the particular farm system as a whole.

Additional feed is often necessary to sustain livestock in wet grassland systems. Because this can represent an import of nutrients, extra feeding should take place on sacrificial areas where nature conservation interest is less important. Hay, bought in as feed, is also a source of seed and can result in the introduction of alien species to the site. Ideally therefore, locally grown hay should be used.

Table 3.1 Livestock unit coefficients (SAC 1990).

Stock type	Livestock unit coefficient
Cattle	
Dairy cow	1.00
Dairy bull	0.65
Beef cow	0.75
Cattle (0–1 year)	0.30
Cattle (1–2 years)	0.54
Cattle (> 2 years)	0.80
Horse	1.00
Sheep	
Ewe (light, 40 kg)	0.07
Ewe (medium, 60 kg)	0.09
Ewe (heavy, 80 kg)	0.11
Ram	0.08
Lamb	0.04–0.08

Table 3.2 Suggested medium level stocking rates for wet grasslands in the UK (after Lane 1992 and Tickner and Evans 1991).

Grazing period	Livestock unit days ha^{-1} year^{-1}
From mid-May to November, to create a mosaic of short swards and tussocks for breeding *Gallinago gallinago*, *Tringa totanus* and wildfowl	100–250
Between mid-July and October on winter-flooded areas, to create a sward 5–7 cm high for breeding *Vanellus vanellus*, *Limosa limosa* and wintering *Anas penelope*, *Cygnus columbianus* and other wildfowl	120–370
Aftermath grazing following a hay cut	50–80

Ownership of livestock

Livestock belonging to the landowner can be used for grazing, or wet grassland can be rented out to graziers who bring their livestock to graze the site. Graziers are often prepared to transport their livestock significant distances particularly for premium grazing and where a reliable grazing service is provided. Wet grasslands can provide such quality because grasses require a lot of water for maximal production. Forage intake rates of cattle using wet grassland are often high, reflecting this. Where grazing is not high quality or there is a conflict between farming and conservation grazing objectives, grazing may have to be rented at a reduced rate.

The advantages of owning livestock are:

- conservation objectives can be given priority (provided animals remain healthy)

- livestock can be used to graze less productive areas

- a profit can often be made

- traditional/rare breeds can be used.

The disadvantages of owning livestock are:

- large amounts of capital can be tied up (eg cost of constructing handling areas and buildings)

- high running costs (eg veterinary bills)

- no guarantee of return on investment

- livestock management requires time and expertise.

The labour requirements of livestock care are high; eg a breeding ewe flock requires an average of 4 hours work ewe^{-1} year^{-1}. A full-time shepherd can look after 400 ewes with lambs given additional help during lambing and shearing. Shepherding store cattle is less labour-intensive. For store cattle, out-wintered or summer grazed, the labour requirement is about 0.9 and 0.2 hours head^{-1} month^{-1} respectively. Suckler herds of cows need from about 0.9–2.9 hours head^{-1} month^{-1} depending on how many calves are suckled per cow.

Livestock care

Wet grasslands pose some particular problems for livestock health, including slow wear of feet on soft ground with potential for lameness, drowning in waterbodies, footrot in sheep, lungworm in cattle, and liver fluke infection in sheep and cattle.

The following provides a basic code of practice for managing livestock:

- all livestock must be counted and inspected daily

- all livestock must be inspected by a registered veterinary surgeon at least once every 12 months.

- livestock should be free to display most normal patterns of behaviour

- the condition of the sward being grazed must be inspected weekly and livestock removed or reduced immediately if insufficient grazing exists to maintain the

livestock in good health

- boundary fencing must be inspected at regular intervals especially where adjacent to major roads and railway lines

- all livestock must have access to fresh drinking water each day

- appropriate shelter must be provided

- the requirements of public access must be addressed where livestock are to be grazed.

Dead animals

Where possible, ie on very large sites grazed year-round, there are benefits to carrion-eating fauna to leaving dead animals unburied. Care should be taken that this does not contravene public or livestock health legislation, however.

3.1.2 Mowing

Mowing involves the cutting of standing vegetation and its subsequent removal for use as animal fodder. In contrast to grazing, mowing is non-selective and the vegetation is cut to a uniform height. Mowing is an effective wet grassland management practice in terms of nature conservation and is relatively straightforward to implement compared with grazing. Mowing should not be introduced as the only management technique on a site that was formerly grazed without consideration of the likely impact.

There is strong evidence to suggest that mowing, especially for hay, followed by grazing of the regrowth (aftermath) is important for the maintenance of high species-richness in many botanically rich meadow communities. However, large parts of the Shannon Callows (Case Study 4) and the Lužnice floodplain (Case Study 13) are mown only, and also sustain diverse plant communities and other wildlife interest. Mowing using modern machinery can be damaging to invertebrate and amphibian populations (Blake and Foster 1998, Claßen *et al* 1996), which in turn can affect bird and mammal populations.

Advantages of mowing are that it:

- does not require a range of special skills

such as those involved in livestock management

- is not labour intensive throughout the year. Mowing is carried out over only a relatively few days in the year whereas grazing demands daily labour input

- is potentially able to deplete nutrient levels in the soil, favouring a diversity of less productive plant species

- is ideal for wet grassland sites that are small, isolated and difficult to access

- is compatible with public access, whereas livestock and public access can conflict.

However, mowing is based on the assumption that there is a value in the mown grass either for use on the site or for sale in the form of hay or silage. Other disadvantages of mowing are:

- mowing may not be cost-effective on large wet grassland sites especially if there is no market for the crop

- although mowing itself is not labour intensive, hay and silage-making are. On average, making hay or one cut of silage requires about 12 tractor-hours ha^{-1}. A second silage cut takes about 9 tractor hours ha^{-1}

- silage-making can be damaging to wildlife conservation. It usually takes place earlier in the year than haying and therefore can kill ground-nesting birds, and prevents seed ripening and the completion of invertebrate life-cycles.

Frequency and time of mowing

There are no strict guidelines on when and how often to mow. There are, however, two viewpoints from which decisions need to be made: those of the farmer and the conservation manager. From the farmer's perspective, the following factors are important:

- the nutritional value of hay or silage is generally greater the earlier in the season the cut is taken

- improving drainage generally encourages earlier onset of vegetative growth and increases the load-bearing capacity of the soil allowing areas to be cut by machinery earlier in the year.

Grassland management for nature conservation does not to have to conflict with agricultural aims. For example, flood-meadows mown annually at a similar time each year support valuable species-rich swards. Diverse wet grasslands are also the result of irregular regimes with mowing at different times of the year or, in some years, not at all. However, mowing for nature conservation is usually undertaken in July or August but can be varied to:

- allow important species to complete critical phases of their life-cycle, eg ground-nesting birds rearing broods, the hatching of adult Lepidoptera, and flowering plants setting seed

- manage for tall-growing plant species by mowing late, eg topping in September

- manage for lower growing and vernal species by earlier mowing, eg in June

- optimise species diversity, eg in the Netherlands a September cut on less productive grasslands enhanced species diversity whereas an earlier cut (in July) was more effective on more productive sites (Bakker 1989)

- control rank growth or competitive species which would otherwise dominate the vegetation.

Removal of mown vegetation

Mown wet grassland vegetation should always be removed as this:

- can open up the sward for seed germination

- reduces nutrient levels in the soil where mowing and harvesting is annual, benefiting the agriculturally less productive grasses (eg *Anthoxanthum odoratum* and *Festuca rubra*) and promoting sward diversity.

Failure to remove cut vegetation can:

- lead to nutrient enrichment

- contribute to the development of a mat of litter which prevents seeds from reaching the soil

- reduce light levels at the soil surface interfering with germination and suppressing seedlings and mosses

- expose livestock using the grassland for aftermath grazing to poisonous plants, eg *Senecio aquaticus* remains highly toxic but is more palatable to livestock when cut. Grazing should not take place for at least six weeks after cutting if toxic plants are present and the cuttings are not removed.

3.1.3 Topping

Topping consists of mechanical cutting aimed at removing coarse or excessive vegetation often in wet grasslands which have been grazed or to control weeds, eg *Cirsium* species. Invariably, cutting machinery is set higher than when the same machinery is used to harvest a fodder crop. Topping is therefore slightly more selective than mowing. Topping can benefit grazing birds, eg Anatidae, but where there is no particular need for topping it should be avoided as it can reduce invertebrate diversity.

3.1.4 Burning

Burning is a convenient, cost-effective method for removing large volumes of coarse vegetation from neglected wet grassland sites prior to the re-establishment of more sympathetic grazing or mowing regimes (Case Studies 10 and 14). It can however be damaging, especially to invertebrate interest. Burning is a skilled task and should not be tackled by the inexperienced. Burning during January and February is potentially least damaging to the conservation interest of wet grasslands.

3.2 Water management

The maintenance of an appropriate water regime to meet the requirements of key target species is an essential prerequisite to successful wet grassland management. Typically, this should aim towards a natural and sustainable flooding/water-level management regime. Natural flood regimes are rare as a result of human activity particularly for agricultural intensification and flood defence. Rivers have been channelised (deepened and straightened), embanked and associated floodplain wetlands drained. This process accelerated towards the end of the 19th Century and by the 1950s few unmodified rivers and wetlands were left in north-west Europe (Cowx and Welcomme 1998).

It is widely recognised that some degree of flooding is important for the maintenance of wet grassland biodiversity. Such conditions influence soil wetness, affecting the floristic composition of the grassland and the suitability of a site for breeding waders during the spring period. Winter flooding flushes out food material, making it available to wintering birds. Floods affect systems by overbank sedimentation and lateral erosion, which results in the creation of new habitat features. Such disturbance sustains habitats for pioneer plant species and early successional stages. Without such natural processes, more intensive water-level management with artificial structures becomes an inevitable, and expensive, consequence of maintaining wet grassland systems.

This section examines the factors influencing water regime on a site and focuses on measures that can be taken to artificially reinstate flooding/water level management on degraded sites.

Wherever natural processes can be retained, they should be, for they can result in significant savings in management costs and constitute the most sustainable option for the maintenance of wet grassland site biodiversity.

Water regime describes the timing, duration and degree (area and depth) of flooding. The water regime of a wet grassland may be influenced by both management and environmental factors. These include:

- competitive water demands in the catchment
- drainage infrastructure on site
- factors such as catchment area, rainfall, evapotranspiration, surface flows, soil type, topography and groundwater flows.

The maintenance of an appropriate water regime can be usefully divided into factors influencing water supply and distribution to wet grasslands, and methods for controlling water levels on degraded sites.

3.2.1 Water supply

A critical factor for the maintenance of wet grassland is an adequate water supply. In a natural state, this comes from surface water flooding and/or groundwater and both are influenced by climatic conditions. Water supplies have, however, been altered greatly by human activity (Section 1.3). The extent to which water supply can be managed varies between sites according to:

- seasonal differences; evapotranspiration will be highest in summer when water inputs will be at their lowest

- type of water source (eg river, groundwater and precipitation)

- competition with other user interests

- losses from site (eg evapotranspiration, seepage and abstraction).

Water supply can be increased by:

- storing excess water during the winter and redistributing this during the summer. This practice has traditionally been carried out in some areas, eg washlands, both as a flood protection measure and as a source of water for agriculture. Installing water storage systems can, however, be deleterious to existing biotopes, damaging both the grassland flora and its invertebrate fauna where water stands for long periods.

- diverting water, usually from a river, onto the site. This is a traditional system used to maintain high water-table levels for grass growth and watering livestock. Pumping may be necessary to raise the water onto the site, especially on highly regulated river systems.

3.2.2 Water distribution

Water distribution or movement through a wet grassland site is influenced by:

- topography, which creates a variety of wetness regimes influencing plant community composition

- surface flows, often controlled by a system of channels constructed to both drain and irrigate the site depending on the position of the water table relative to drainage channel levels. Sluices and other such control structures along drainage channels can regulate the movement of water through the site

- groundwater, knowledge of which can be important, particularly when creating new wet grassland. Specialist advice from a hydrologist or hydrogeologist is usually needed

- soil type and structure, which influence the ability to manage water levels on a site. Generally, clay/silt soils depend on surface flooding to maintain wetness, whereas water table levels in peat soils can be influenced by lateral movement of water (Figure 3.1).

**Figure 3.1
Examples of management of field water tables on wet grassland on two substrates – peat and clay (Self *et al* 1994).**

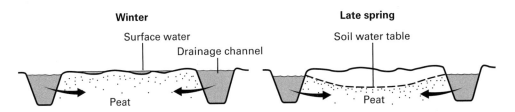

(a) Moderately permeable soil, high drainage channel water levels all year. Soil water table maintained at or near field surface level by lateral movement through the soil.

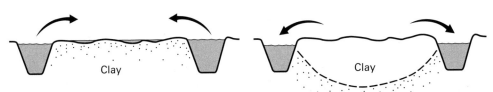

(b) Low permeability soil, eg clay, high drainage channel water levels. Drainage channels have little influence on field conditions except when they overflow

3.2.3 Water level control

The water levels of a wet grassland are controlled by the rate at which water enters and leaves the site. In a site with a natural hydrological regime they will be governed by seasonal events such as winter and spring flooding. They are influenced by natural factors linked to climate and seasonality and on regulated sites are typically managed using a range of structures and techniques:

- **Bunds or levees** are low earth banks keyed into the substrate that retain floodwater or water pumped into the site. The stored water can be used to make up spring and/or summer deficits. The water can be stored:
  - across the site as a whole, or in part(s) of the site. Such controlled flooding is temporary, the water receding as the seasons progress
  - in a reservoir or lagoon strategically located within or adjacent to the site.
  (Both strategies can also be used to control flooding within or downstream of the site. Bunds should be set well back from the edges of channels to prevent slumping and reduce leakage. The gradient of the bund should allow cutting of the vegetation. Grazing of the bunds is possible but there is a risk that livestock will damage the profile or structure, reducing its water retention capacity.)

- **Dams** can be constructed in drainage channels in order to retain water and isolate hydrological units. Use of dams can enable rotational flooding in winter. Dam construction is easier in areas with loamy or clay soils, whereas peat will only make satisfactory dams if well compacted

- **Sluices** are used to perform the same function as dams but are designed to regulate water levels by controlling through-flow. There are four main types:
  - flexi-pipe sluices consisting of a flexible ribbed plastic pipe (approx. 25 cm in diameter) incorporated into an earth bund (Figure 3.2)
  - dropboard sluices, a simple structure comprising a series of boards that drop into a grooved spillway (Plate 3). Water levels are adjusted by inserting

or removing boards.
  - lifting gate sluices, a more complex structure (Plate 4) in which the gate is raised. Precise water level control is difficult to achieve.
  - tilting-weir or drawbridge sluices consisting of a hinged weir that can be adjusted to give precise water level control. They are, however, expensive.
  (Where flooding of adjacent land must be prevented and sluices are not large enough to take predicted storm flows, a spillway must be incorporated.)

- **Pumps** are required to move water against prevailing hydraulic gradients and are often used where more water is required than can be supplied by inflowing streams, groundwater or precipitation. Pumps can be fixed or mobile and powered by wind, electricity or diesel. The following points need to be considered:
  - volume of water and rate of delivery required
  - vertical difference between input and output levels
  - distance between intake and discharge points
  - proximity to electrical supply (where relevant)
  - whether a licence to abstract water is required.

- **Surface irrigation** is usually based on systems of footdrains, which are small spade-sized channels (30–60 cm in width and up to 50 cm deep) running across the field surface and connected to the drainage channel system (Plate 5). They have several advantages, being:
  - a biotope with their own wildlife interest
  - good for creating linear pools in summer
  - useful on clay and silt where soil permeability is poor
  - useful for rapidly creating shallow floods for wintering wildfowl
  - valuable feeding areas when wet for breeding *Vanellus vanellus* and *Tringa totanus*.

Disadvantages include being:

- impractical for transporting water in summer as it is rapidly lost into the soil and through evaporation
- a hazard for machinery, eg during mowing
- higher than maximum drainage channel level in summer, water may have to be pumped from the drainage channel into the footdrain.

- **Sub-surface irrigation** relies on existing under-drainage piping or mole drains which are used to raise water tables by raising the water level in the drainage channels; the drainage system then works in reverse. However, care must be taken to ensure drainage-channel water levels remain high otherwise drainage will occur. Under no circumstances should pipes be installed for this purpose.

Figure 3.2
A flexi-pipe sluice

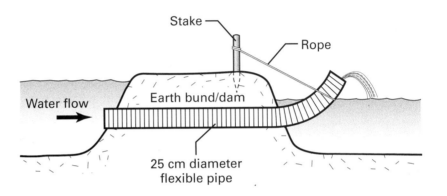

Plate 3
A steel-frame dropboard sluice set in a dam constructed of trench-sheets.

Paul José

Plate 4
Lifting gate sluices are unpopular on wet grassland nature reserves as precise water level control is difficult to achieve.

Owen Mountford

Plate 5
Cutting footdrains can create habitat for wildlife and ease winter flooding on some wet grasslands.

Dave Barratt

3.2.4 Maintenance of water quality

Determining the quality of the water associated with a wet grassland may involve chemical analyses by local or national government agencies. Alternatively the plant and/or invertebrate communities of the watercourses can be used as indicators of water quality (eg Palmer *et al* 1992).

Common water quality factors affecting wet grasslands and their associated biotopes are:

- eutrophication, which is the excessive input of nutrients and results from fertiliser run-off, sewage effluent, livestock slurry and silage. The altered balance of nutrients disrupts the competitive interactions between plant species both in the sward and in associated biotopes, eg ponds and drainage channels, and can severely damage nature conservation interest. Nutrients can be imported into a grassland site either dissolved in the drainage water, in water abstracted into the system, or as sediment deposited during winter flooding.

- salinity is a potential problem particularly in reclaimed coastal grasslands through saline intrusion into the drainage system, seepage from estuaries or the sea through outcropping peat, or sea spray. Plants and invertebrates have a restricted range of tolerance to salinity and excessive fluctuations can be detrimental.

- iron and sulphur toxicity, which can occur particularly in areas of deep-drained peat soils. The formation of ochre and associated toxicity can occur where drainage channels are dug exposing iron-rich peat and can also lead to significant increases in the acidity of surface waters.

Water quality problems in wet grasslands can be avoided by:

- exercising caution about where and when water is abstracted into a system, eg not taking water from eutrophicated rivers in the first flood after a protracted dry period as this could result in excessively high nutrient loads as material is flushed from the catchment

- abstracting eutrophic river water just after the peak of a flood to avoid high sediment loads

- keeping sluices and tidal outlets in good condition which reduces saline and eutrophic water incursions

- diluting with fresh water where saline intrusion occurs particularly in artificially embanked coastal grazing marsh which has been reclaimed from saltmarsh (eg polders)

- isolating the wet grassland system from highly eutrophic waters, eg by the use of bunds and sluices. This has the disadvantage of disrupting natural hydrological processes, however, and may adversely affect the water budget of a site.

- using buffer strips, reedbeds or other natural techniques to minimise the amount of nutrients entering the system (Haycock *et al* 1997)

- taking a precautionary approach when planning and digging new drainage channels to avoid ochre deposits and nutrient flushes.

3.3 Management of associated biotopes

Several biotopes are often associated with a wet grassland site in addition to the grassland sward. Appropriate management of these biotopes can significantly enhance the biodiversity value of a site. The main types of associated biotopes in Europe are:

- permanent waterbodies, eg ox-bows and secondary channels and other backwaters, which are very important features for a range of wildlife. Where ox-bows still exist they are often highly valued geomorphological features and may be protected by law. Care should be taken when planning management to avoid damage to these features. When creating permanent waterbodies, eg a reservoir (which may be considered on hydrologically isolated sites to provide water storage to meet potential deficits), incorporate a deep area for fish and invertebrates when water levels are low in summer; a shelf for marginal and emergent plants; and islands planted with vegetation. If the waterbody is physically isolated from other similar biotopes, consideration should be given to introducing local indigenous flora and fauna to accelerate the establishment phase.

- temporary waterbodies, eg field pans in which specialised types of Amphibia, Insecta and Crustacea can pass rapidly through their life-cycles. Maintaining the water levels in the site, not only to create such biotopes but to ensure that they function effectively, is important.

- drainage channels, which can be of particular significance for aquatic flora and invertebrate fauna. The most diverse biota are found on sites with:
  - extensive networks of drainage channels
  - a wide range of drainage channel type
  - a range of drainage channels at different seral stages, representing biotopes from open water to dense emergent vegetation
  - appropriate drainage channel maintenance regimes (the maintenance of drainage channels to sustain biodiversity is summarised in Section 3.3.1).

- springs and seepages, for example seepages through a river wall, are often botanically interesting and valuable for a specialised insect fauna. Springs and seepages need to be kept open by light grazing or trampling. Shading, eg by *Juncus* spp, will reduce their value.

- trees, scrub and hedges are a traditional component of many wet grassland landscapes, and their presence can greatly enhance the biodiversity of a wet grassland area. Both fauna and flora are supported, the former ranging from invertebrates (eg *Aromia moschata*) to birds (eg nesting *Turdus philomelos*).

- tracks and lanes used for access to the wet grassland require mowing with removal of the cuttings where possible. The timing of the cut and the number of cuts per year can be manipulated to optimise the biotope for invertebrates and flora. Leaving a strip approximately 1 m from the edge of the track to revert to rough grassland diversifies the range of biotopes and can benefit different birds, invertebrates (especially Lepidoptera) and mammals such as mice, voles and bats.

Wet grassland sites may merge into a neighbouring biotope, eg fen, reedbed, saltmarsh and scrub (Figure 1.4) or may exhibit a mosaic of such biotopes. Natural gradations (ecotones) into other habitats often support exceptional biodiversity and should be managed sensitively. Maintenance should be aimed at preserving the ecological gradients and the extent over which they occur. Reference to books and manuals dealing with these other biotopes can be useful in the management of these systems, eg reedbeds (Hawke and José 1996).

3.3.1 Drainage channel management

Cleaning out drainage channels prevents them choking up with plant material and accumulated silt. It is desirable to have a diversity of seral stages at any one site, ranging from open water to channels with emergent abundant vegetation, as each stage has its own particular plant and invertebrate species. This variety can be maintained by adopting a regular rotational cleaning regime which:

- allows a full range of successional stages to develop

- permits less mobile species to escape catastrophic effects

- may require specific intervention to control weeds.

In the UK the highest species diversity of aquatic plants has been noted in freshwater

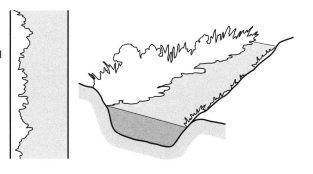

Clear the drainage channel from only one side (if it is wide) or for only half its length in any particular year.

**Figure 3.3
Sympathetic options for drainage channel management (after Newbold *et al* 1989).**

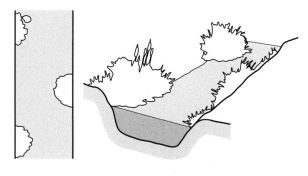

Use a sinuous dredging route or scallop the vegetation to create meanders.

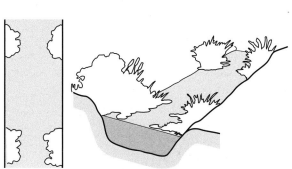

Leave 10 m blocks of vegetation every 30 m or so.

drainage channels managed every three to five years (Thomas *et al* 1981, Wolsey *et al* 1984), although it must be stressed that every stage, from open water to choked stretches that have not been cleaned for more than 20 years, is important in contributing to overall biodiversity.

The key to drainage channel maintenance for wildlife is to introduce structural variety in terms of depth, width, and profile during the operation, thereby providing habitat for a diverse range of species. In order to conserve particular species, sympathetic drainage channel cleaning methods can be adopted (Figure 3.3).

3.3.2 Scrub, tree and hedge management

Scrub is to be encouraged in discrete patches in the wet grassland landscape as it provides valuable habitat for amphibians, invertebrates, mammals such as *Vulpes vulpes*, *Lutra lutra* and *Mustela erminea*, and birds including nesting *Remiz pendulinus*, *Erithacus rubecula* and *Luscinia svecica*. The presence of nesting birds can attract avian predators such as *Accipiter nisus*. Trees and scrub, however, also provide perches and nesting sites for other predatory birds, eg *Corvus corone* and *Buteo buteo*, which may prey on breeding wader populations. Likewise, scrub areas can attract predatory mammals.

Hedgerows and pollarded trees must be managed to maintain their wildlife interest, ideally on a regular rotation.

3.4 Restoration management

Conservation of wet grassland species and communities in Europe cannot rely solely on the management of existing sites. The expansion of the resource through restoration is essential because:

- as a result of the loss of hydrological connectivity between sites due to river regulation remaining wet grassland sites are becoming increasingly isolated making it difficult or impossible for species to move from one area to another

- extending the area of an existing wet grassland site increases its carrying capacity which might enable a species not previously present on the site to establish a population, eg *Circus aeruginosus*, or allow a species already established to increase its population size and hence be better able to withstand damaging events, eg drought and disease.

Restoration should not be used as a substitute for the *in situ* protection of an existing semi-natural wet grassland biotope or to mitigate loss of such habitat.

The need to ensure that restoration is undertaken is starting to appear in the legislation of European countries and is an important factor in initiating and implementing projects. Mechanisms for funding are also part of this process. In Denmark, for example, the Nature Protection Act (1992) provides both an obligation and opportunity to promote restoration, stating that:

'The objectives of this Act are, in particular to: 1) protect nature, with its stock of wild animals and plants and their habitats, as well as its scenic, historical, natural science and educational values; 2) improve, restore or create areas of significance for wild animals and plants and for landscape and historical interests; and 3) provide public access to nature and to improve the opportunities for open-air recreation.'

Also, since 1983, the Danish Act on Watercourses has provided certain possibilities for the rehabilitation of watercourses (Case Study 15). It is important to identify those administrative units at state and regional levels, which are responsible for wetland restoration projects and are to an increasing degree now also experienced in managing them.

Restoration projects demand significant commitment in time and money, and careful consideration should be given before commencing a project. Tables 3.3 and 3.4 list a set of practical criteria and factors to take into account when deciding whether or not to proceed with a proposed restoration project.

The aims of any proposed restoration scheme should be the subject of careful consideration and could include:

- restoration of a site to an earlier state including all elements of flora and fauna

- restoration of certain site characteristics, eg water table or mowing regime, such that certain communities or species can re-establish

- rehabilitation of a site by returning it to a wet grassland condition, eg by scrub removal, but not seeking or expecting to restore previous plant and/or animal communities

- focusing on restoring a single species or number of species, eg *Fritillaria meleagris* or *Eurodryas aurinia*.

The stated aims of a wet grassland restoration project will govern subsequent management, and this should be considered from the outset. The steps to take when planning restoration management are outlined in Figure 3.4.

As with any form of management, setting clear objectives allows the success of the project to be evaluated. Evaluation criteria could include:

- temporal aspects, eg achieving a certain level in the water table after a pre-determined number of years

- a quantification of success, eg the re-establishment of a target population of *Tringa totanus*

- aspects of quality, eg to achieve breeding for particular bird species.

Table 3.3 Criteria for selection of sites for restoration

- The status of the area from an agricultural point of view (ie marginal land versus more fertile soils).

- The economic aspects of the project – relatively low prices for land purchase and compensation to landowners as well as low running costs for management of the area is preferred. Cost-effectiveness aspects are important!

- The ecological aspects of the project – status of the area today and expected development of the future biotope with reference to the establishment of plants and animals including threatened species, eutrophication, disturbance etc.

- Are there environmental benefits, ie reduction of eutrophication and/or preservation of groundwater resources?

- Is there a positive regional and local interest in realisation of the project, ie in the county, municipality and the local community?

- Are there possibilities for recreation and use of the restored area for educational purposes?

- Are there aspects relating to archaeological and cultural history, ie conservation of antiquities?

- Will it improve scenic value?

- Fulfilment of international obligations concerning nature conservation, eg the Ramsar Convention, the Helsinki Convention and the EU Birds Directive and Habitats Directive (Appendix 4).

Table 3.4 Checklist for a wet grassland restoration project

Introduction
- Basis of the restoration project and description of the site to be restored
- Aim or aims of the project
- Statement of objectives

Description of existing conditions
- General description of the locality and site (eg location, topography, soils and water quality)
- Conservation and regional planning constraints, eg conservation designations and planning status at local, national and international levels
- Land use (eg agricultural or recreational)
- Fauna and flora (collation of existing knowledge/reports and data from contemporary surveys)
- Evaluation of environmental processes (eg patterns of flooding and sedimentation, functioning of wildlife corridors and immigration)
- Quality objectives particularly with respect to water quality (eg pollution status)
- Drainage conditions (eg water levels, catchment size and character, groundwater conditions, and legislation)
- Soil conditions including information on special conditions (eg potential ochre problems and contamination by heavy metals) and legislation relating to movement of contaminated soils and sediments
- Location of services and other installations, eg cables and pipes, roads, footpaths and other crossings, masts, structures (weirs and dams), overflows and inlets
- Ownership (eg private or public)

Design and implementation
- Design of project in relation to aims
- Undertake an impact assessment:

Table 3.4 Checklist for a wet grassland restoration project (continued)

- predict future conditions, including water levels, water quality, flora and fauna
- assess consequences for land use
- Plan future ownership
- Implementation of pilot project or projects (if necessary)
- Detailed description of the planned restoration in relation to specific objectives
- Call for tenders
- Implementation of project including engineering, re-establishment of vegetation (eg planting or re-seeding), fencing, construction of walkways/bridges and footpaths
- Undertake post-project monitoring

Documents and legislation
- Review of the property entries in the land registry to determine ownership
- Ensure that registered rights and easements are not violated
- Take into account the possible rights of third parties, eg agricultural leasehold agreements
- Ask the owner about such rights and enter into an agreement clarifying who is to cover losses caused by restoration work, eg a leaseholders crop losses

Timetable
- Pilot project or projects (if necessary)
- Preliminary discussions with landowners
- Consider political dimension
- Public participation
- Clarification of financing
- Necessary approvals including appeal periods
- Implementation phase
- Follow-up, including updating land registry and deciding future division of maintenance obligations and responsibilities
- Project appraisal and associated monitoring

Economic aspects
- Assessment of site value
- Precise budget estimate and a summary of financing
- Compensation payment to landowners or leaseholders
- Financial benefits – direct and indirect

Supporting plans and documentation
- Outline maps in scale 1:10 000 and 1:25 000
- Old maps of the area
- Survey and survey maps
- Planning conditions
- Existing longitudinal and cross-sectional profiles/transects
- Water level fluctuations
- Present ownership
- Present land use
- Measures planned in the project
- Proposed longitudinal and cross-sectional profiles/transects
- Miscellaneous detailed drawings
- Future ownership
- Future land use.

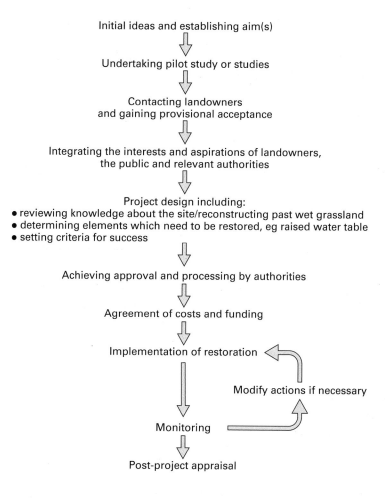

Initial ideas and establishing aim(s)

Undertaking pilot study or studies

Contacting landowners
and gaining provisional acceptance

Integrating the interests and aspirations of landowners,
the public and relevant authorities

Project design including:
• reviewing knowledge about the site/reconstructing past wet grassland
• determining elements which need to be restored, eg raised water table
• setting criteria for success

Achieving approval and processing by authorities

Agreement of costs and funding

Implementation of restoration

Modify actions if necessary

Monitoring

Post-project appraisal

**Figure 3.4
The stages of a wet
grassland restoration
project.**

If a restoration project fails, then a frank appraisal will highlight what prevented certain success criteria being met, and inform future restoration projects.

Damage to wet grasslands, through intensification or neglect, may be reversible although it may take many years for a characteristic wet grassland community to recover (Case Studies 12, 13 and 16). Restoration can be a relatively simple process where only the reinstatement of former management practices to a neglected area is required (Case Study 13) or it can be very problematic as in the re-creation of wet grassland after intensive agricultural use (Case Study 9). Care must be taken to evaluate an abandoned wet grassland as it could have developed wildlife of significant value. For example, removal of wooded areas from a floodplain could have adverse impacts on biodiversity.

Restoration of an abandoned site may necessitate:

- removing scrub and trees (Case Study 10)

- reinstating mowing (Case Study 13) or grazing (Case Study 7)

- reinstating former water regime (Case Study 11)

- returning associated biotopes to an early stage in their succession, eg dredging out drainage channels and ponds, or pollarding willows

For example, five years after reinstating cutting management to a wet grassland in the Lužnice river floodplain (Czech Republic) plant species diversity and composition were restored to a quality comparable with adjacent grasslands that had received uninterrupted management (Case Study 13). A similar time span was found for the restoration of grazing pasture in 1991 on a nature reserve in the North Kent Marshes, UK (Benstead *et al* 1997). An increase in the number of waders breeding on the site was observed within three years (Table 3.5). The project involved manipulating the sward either by re-seeding or through allowing natural

Table 3.5 Numbers of pairs of breeding waders at Northward Hill, North Kent Marshes, UK after restoration in 1991.

Species	Breeding population – pairs							
	1991	**1992**	**1993**	**1994**	**1995**	**1996**	**1997**	**1998**
Vanellus vanellus	3	2	16	35	56	26	15	26
Gallinago gallinago	0	0	2	0	0	0	0	1
Tringa totanus	1	1	5	27	35	5	10	32
Avosetta recurvirostra	0	0	0	5	33	26	14	20

regeneration and by raising water levels in the drainage channels using sluices, the creation of bunds and blocking off underfield drainage pipes. The site was grazed by sheep (April–December) owned by grazing tenants, and subsequently topped.

Reversion of arable to wet grassland can be difficult because the sites may have:

- high nutrient availability

- impoverished seed banks

- altered hydrological regimes

- few or no associated biotopes.

For example, in the Drenthe Aa area of the Netherlands, the mean number of plant species increased from 18 to 26 (per field of 500 m^2) within 16 years after the cessation of fertiliser application (Bakker 1989). However, these fields were adjacent to diverse unimproved meadow communities so that colonisation from these populations could occur. In addition to stopping fertilising, a decline in productivity can be caused by mowing and hay removal and in extreme circumstances by stripping off topsoil. However, reduction in productivity alone cannot guarantee successful restoration of species-rich meadows. Although significant reductions can be achieved in nitrogen, phosphorous and potassium levels, the eventual proportions of these three key elements could be very different from that found in the wet grassland before agricultural intensification (Case Study 9).

In the Upper Thames Tributaries Environmentally Sensitive Area, UK, ex-arable sites have been shown to take many years to restore a characteristic vegetation type relying on natural regeneration, whereas sowing seed mixtures resulted in a significantly greater number of species in the sward (Manchester *et al* 1998).

Restoration after arable agriculture is therefore more likely to succeed on sites:

- under cultivation for a short time

- adjacent to existing semi-natural grassland which can act as a seed source

- where appropriate hydrological conditions can be re-established (Case Study 9).

The stages which typically make up a restoration project are shown in Figure 3.4. The timescale for achieving wet grassland restoration will depend upon a number of factors:

- how degraded the site is

- how hydrologically and ecologically isolated the site is

- the ability to use the site for low-intensity agricultural purposes, eg renting the grazing to a neighbouring farmer or selling the hay crop

- climatic factors, eg low rainfall will delay restoration, and dry conditions will encourage invasion of weedy plant species, eg *Cirsium.*

- the extent and knowledge of the land drainage system, eg length and location of under-drainage

- nature of adjoining land use, eg back flooding on a neighbour's arable fields would not be acceptable.

Table 3.4 provides a useful checklist for undertaking a restoration project.

Restoration of desirable hydrological conditions can be achieved by reinstating riverine flooding to produce a more natural hydrological regime or simply by restoring channelised rivers by re-meandering and bed raising, which raises the water table (Case Study 15). Water-quality aspects should be taken into consideration when restoring the hydrological regime of highly eutrophic (ie effluent affected) lowland floodplain rivers. For example, parts of the Rhine floodplain, currently hydrologically isolated from the river, are now groundwater-fed and are predominantly oligotrophic. Flooding of these polders with eutrophic water would alter the existing flora significantly. Such constraints, however, should not preclude consideration of major floodplain grassland restoration initiatives, which may ultimately deliver much greater biodiversity, flood storage and water quality benefits.

3.4.1 Restoration of flora and fauna

A number of techniques can be used to encourage species to re-colonise a wet grassland site:

- regular flooding, which brings allochthonous material including:

  - wet grassland plant diaspores, eg seeds and rhizome fragments
  - aquatic biota, which can re-colonise associated biotopes such as drainage channels and ponds

- spreading the material mown, or collected by hand (Case Study 16), from an existing wet grassland site onto the site being restored thereby introducing seed material and invertebrates

- sowing seeds, using container-grown plants and turf transfer (Case Study 16). Introducing species in this way has been shown to increase the number of desired species in the restored sward (Manchester *et al* 1998)

- moving livestock from an existing wet grassland site to a site which is being restored. Livestock transport both diaspores and invertebrates between sites. Sheep are considered to be better than other livestock: in a study of a German grassland, 8500 diaspores of 85 plant species and 13 species of Orthoptera were transported by just one sheep (Fischer *et al* 1996).

3.4.2 Restoration of associated biotopes

When deciding the aims and objectives for the restoration of a wet grassland site, consideration should also be given to the restoration or creation of associated biotopes (Section 3.3). The presence of many wet grassland species depends on the quality of the associated biotopes. Odonata are a classic example: they require suitable aquatic habitat for egg-laying and larval development, emergent vegetation for emergence, and good feeding habitat in close proximity to water for the flying adult stage. Creating areas of open water, reprofiling drainage channels and planting trees can therefore add significantly to the value of wet grassland sites. Such restoration in a river floodplain, for example, will strengthen the corridor effect (Figure 3.5), creating:

- permanent waterbodies, which provide habitat for diving ducks (eg *Aythya fuligula* and *Aythya ferina*), *Fulica atra*, dabbling ducks (eg *Anas crecca* and *Anas clypeata*) and fish-eating species (eg *Podiceps cristatus*, *Mergus merganser*, *Ardea cinerea* and *Phalacrocorax carbo*)

- gravel banks, shoals and sand banks, which may have been lost as a result of river regulation (eg Upper Rhine). These biotopes are important for nesting birds (eg *Sterna albifrons*, *Sterna hirundo*, *Burhinus oedicnemus*, *Charadrius dubius* and *Riparia riparia*) and invertebrates (Dister *et al* 1990)

- different bank profiles in drainage channels encourages a range of different plant and animal communities (Newbold *et al* 1989).

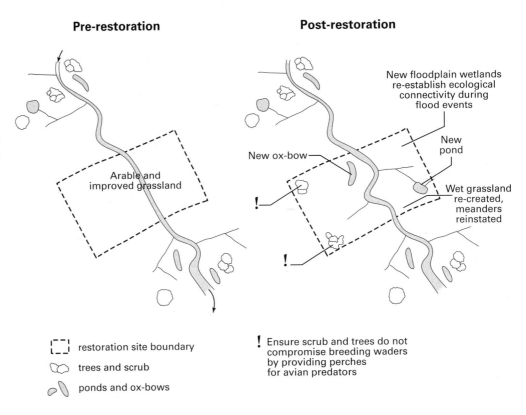

Pre-restoration **Post-restoration**

Figure 3.5
Restoration of associated biotopes such as waterbodies optimises biodiversity on a site and allows ecological re-connection of floodplain features

New floodplain wetlands re-establish ecological connectivity during flood events

New pond

Wet grassland re-created, meanders reinstated

New ox-bow

Arable and improved grassland

⌐ ¬ restoration site boundary
⌙ _⌡

◯◯ trees and scrub

◌◖ ponds and ox-bows

! Ensure scrub and trees do not compromise breeding waders by providing perches for avian predators

3.5 Management for wildlife

3.5.1 Management for botanical diversity

Diverse swards are associated with wet soils with a low nutrient availability. In nutrient-rich soils relatively few, often agricultural grass, species out-compete other flora and become dominant. Even low applications of inorganic fertiliser can cause damage to botanical interest. Highly eutrophic floodwater can also have a similar effect.

Wet grassland plant communities are profoundly influenced by water regimes. Each plant species is adapted to survive in different soil water conditions (Newbold and Mountford 1997). Soil wetness and water availability can have a considerable influence on the competitive balance between species depending on their relative tolerances.

Regular vegetation management (Section 3.1) is important for conserving nearly all botanically rich wet grasslands as it:

- removes plant material and therefore nutrients

- prevents succession to coarser grassland and/or scrub and woodland

- favours a diversity of less competitive species.

Traditional wet grassland management techniques, such as extensive grazing or mowing for hay, can create very diverse plant communities and careful consideration should be given before altering such a regime. Community structure and composition is influenced by management regime. Grazing, for example, can favour many plants, especially smaller ones, by opening up the sward to light, creating conditions suitable for seed germination and plant growth. Many valuable plant communities have also developed under a hay cutting with aftermath grazing regime. A relatively late hay cut allows plants to flower and set seed, and aftermath grazing diversifies sward structure.

The timing of management with respect to key plant life-stages is important. Grazing/mowing can prevent flowering or seeding of some species, reducing their reproductive capacity. Although many wet grassland species are perennial, knowledge of plant regeneration strategies is important when trying to conserve important plant species and communities.

3.5.2 Management for birds

Management for breeding waders

Wet grassland in Europe provides breeding habitat for several wader species, most of which are declining in numbers. *Vanellus vanellus, Gallinago gallinago, Numenius arquata, Limosa limosa, Philomachus pugnax* and *Tringa totanus* are widespread breeders on wet grassland throughout the region. Additionally, the rarer *Gallinago media* and *Xenus cinereus* utilise the more pristine wet grassland systems of central Europe.

Waders are ground-nesting and raise a single brood per year. Most species will lay a replacement clutch if the first fails and conditions remain suitable. Breeding wader distribution and success are linked to a number of factors:

- water table depth and soil type. A high soil water table during the breeding period (mid-March to end of June) is the single most important factor. It ensures that soil invertebrate prey, mainly Lumbricidae and Tipulidae larvae, remains close to the soil surface and increases the biomass available to birds.

- amount of flooding/surface water in early spring. Surface water and muddy channel and pool margins are important feeding areas for adult and young waders. Ephemeral waterbodies provide suitable conditions for colonisation by high biomass pioneer invertebrate communities (dominated by Chironomidae). These are important food sources for young waders.

- vegetation structure. Preferred vegetation structure varies from long vegetation, which attracts *Gallinago gallinago*, to short, intensively grazed swards suitable for *Vanellus vanellus*.

- predation. The presence of trees and hedgerows, which provide observation points for predatory birds greatly reduces productivity

- loss of nests through trampling by livestock and agricultural operations. During the early part of the breeding season (ie before mid-June) grazing should be at extremely low densities (<0.75 cow ha^{-1}) and agricultural operations such as rolling should not be carried out.

Management for wintering waterfowl

In milder parts of Northern and Central Europe wintering wildfowl can often be found in large concentrations where suitable feeding and roosting conditions exist in areas free from disturbance. River management activities have probably had a lesser impact on wintering birds than on breeding populations. This is because, even in well regulated systems, some degree of winter flooding can still occur.

Shallow flooding in winter is the most important requirement, providing feeding opportunities and secure roost sites (Thomas 1982). Large areas of surface water with an average depth <50 cm are required by the majority of species, providing:

- food by releasing seeds and invertebrates from vegetation

- security from ground predators

- secure roost sites.

Creating disturbance-free winter refuges for roosting is an important role of nature reserves, allowing surrounding agricultural land to support feeding wildfowl. This may negatively affect surrounding farmland, however, and the potential for conflict should be recognised.

Different species have different requirements.

A mosaic of grassland vegetation with flooded and unflooded areas is required to attract a diverse range of wildfowl. Wintering wildfowl can be split into three main groups:

- Grazing wildfowl such as *Cygnus* spp, *Anser* spp and *Anas penelope* which feed on open grassland. Vegetation composition and structure are both important to these species. Many grazing species prefer to feed on young, grassy swards composed of 'soft' grasses, such as *Agrostis stolonifera*, typical of grazed areas subject to regular temporary inundation. Coarse grass species such as *Phalaris arundinacea* tend to be completely ignored. Most species prefer a sward of 5–15 cm in height but this varies with species.

- Dabbling (or surface-feeding) ducks prefer shallow open water, feeding on seeds and invertebrates released by floodwater. Depth preferences vary with species size. Some seed-eating species, eg *Anas crecca* and *Anas clypeata*, require the presence of suitable seed sources, such as large areas of *Juncus* spp. Management should aim to create a succession of surface water areas or slowly draw-down water to ensure a steady supply of food throughout the winter.

- Diving ducks, eg *Aythya* spp, are scarce on wet grassland because they require deep water (>2 m) with high densities of invertebrates in the sediment. These conditions are usually only found in wide, deep channels on larger sites.

3.5.3 Management for invertebrates

Wet grassland and associated aquatic biotopes provide habitat for a variety of grassland and aquatic invertebrates (Figure 3.6). Many invertebrates are highly specialised, with precise habitat requirements, and are very sensitive to change, particularly as a result of management (Table 3.6).

Table 3.6 Reasons for invertebrate sensitivity to environmental change.

- Most have annual life-cycles and lack long-term resting stages. Disruption of the annual cycle can cause a species to disappear from a site.

- Life-cycles are often complex and requirements vary for different stages.

- Many species are highly specialised.

- Many species are dependent on apparently insignificant site features which they are able to exploit because of their small size.

- Many species are physically or behaviourally ill-adapted to dispersal.

When managing wet grasslands and associated biotopes for invertebrates the following general principles should be observed.

- Maintain habitat continuity and variety of vegetation structure.

- Constant small-scale management is best for keeping vegetation structure varied.

- Rotational management provides habitat continuity and structural variety allowing mobile species to evade catastrophic management practices such as cutting. Care should be taken when assigning management compartments (Case Study 3) to ensure that entire communities or populations of species are not isolated in one compartment.

- Management should not normally be undertaken just to benefit one species.

Wet grassland invertebrates

Wet grassland biotopes support a generalist invertebrate fauna, as well as the adult forms of many species with aquatic larvae (eg Odonata). The invertebrate interest of grassland tends to be lower than that of associated aquatic biotopes (Drake 1998).

Vegetation structure and composition affect the number and range of species likely to be present in a wet grassland. Structure is particularly important, as relatively few species (most notably various Lepidoptera) are reliant on single food plants. Vegetation influences the micro-climate at ground level and provides the physical habitat for invertebrates. There is no ideal structure that will suit all species. Many invertebrates require a mixture of sward

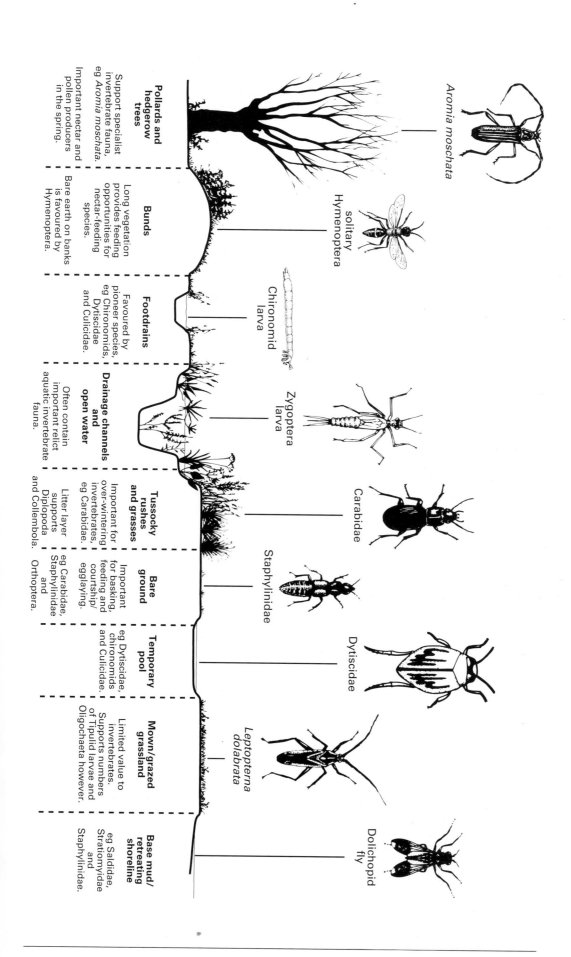

Figure 3.6
Wet grassland micro-habitats and characteristic invertebrates (after Benstead *et al* 1997).

heights in close proximity to provide suitable habitat during different stages of their life-cycle. Large wet grassland sites with a varied micro-topography and range of management offer a greater potential for variation in vegetation structure and therefore the potential to support a more diverse invertebrate fauna (Table 3.7).

The more varied the vegetation structure the better. Tussocky grassland is especially valuable. Continuity of management is also important, even short periods of adverse conditions can be damaging for species with exacting requirements.

Many wet grassland and semi-aquatic invertebrates are dependent on bare ground and exposed mud for feeding, courtship and egg-laying. Management should aim to create suitable bare areas either by drawdown of waterbodies or through poaching by grazing animals.

The litter layer is also an important component of wet grassland for many species, eg Oligochaeta and Collembola. A damp litter layer also acts as a thermal buffer during extremes of temperature.

The timing, duration and rate at which wet grassland sites are flooded affect invertebrate fauna. Some important groups, eg Tipulidae, remain active in October so flooding before then will prevent such species from egg-laying in muddy margins. Managed flooding should therefore be left until November at the earliest, when the average temperature is low enough to have reduced activity and stimulated most species to find overwintering sites. Most invertebrates are inactive during the winter.

However, prolonged winter flooding (November to March) can kill or expel invertebrates overwintering in soil or litter if not adapted to prolonged submersion. Some groups tolerate temporary flooding, for example the Carabidae have several species typical of winter-flooded washlands. Shallow flooding is less likely to be damaging than deep flooding because individual invertebrates may survive in tussocks protruding above water level. Flooding during summer, when warmer water temperatures cause a rapid build-up of anoxic conditions, can be very damaging to the terrestrial invertebrate fauna of a wet grassland.

Regularly flooded grasslands have a 'terrestrial' invertebrate fauna able to survive temporary inundation. Where sites are returned to regular flooding (eg in restored sites), the existing 'dry' invertebrate fauna is likely to be eliminated but re-colonisation by a flood-tolerant fauna may take many years (especially for Oligochaeta). This may affect food supplies for breeding waders.

Aquatic invertebrates

Waterbodies associated with wet grassland support a high number of aquatic invertebrate species and these are generally of greater conservation value than those on surrounding grassland. These waterbodies often support relict species from natural wetlands that existed prior to human utilisation of the site.

Shallow water (<30 cm) generally provides better habitat for aquatic invertebrates than deep water because it has higher water temperatures and oxygen availability. Temporary waterbodies are an important invertebrate habitat and are used by species with rapid larval development, eg Chironomidae.

Drainage channels make up a large proportion of available aquatic habitat in the less natural wet grasslands. Drainage channels exhibit a marked sequential change in their invertebrate species composition as they undergo vegetation succession following clearing (Figure 3.7).

Good water quality is essential for high invertebrate diversity and for many of the rarest invertebrates, eg aquatic molluscs such as *Segmentina nitida*. Saline influences create conditions suitable for a range of species adapted to brackish conditions, eg some Dytiscidae. Irregular inundation by brackish or saline water is, however, damaging. Water chemistry is influenced by soil type. Drainage channels cut into peat tend to support more diverse invertebrate faunas than those in clay.

Relatively few aquatic invertebrates eat living plants. Predators, parasites and detritivores far outnumber herbivores whose principal food is algae rather than macrophytes. Aquatic macrophytes provide physical habitat for invertebrates: a diverse variety and structure of vegetation is therefore beneficial for invertebrate diversity. Therefore, management that enhances structural variety will enhance invertebrate diversity. However, there are some swamp monocultures (eg *Bolboschoenus* *maritimus* and *Phragmites australis* stands) that support rich and unusual invertebrate communities despite limited structural diversity.

Table 3.7 Vegetation requirements of invertebrates on wet grassland (after Benstead *et al* 1997).

Vegetation feature	Benefit	Invertebrate groups benefiting
Suitable plant species	Provide food.	Suitable plant in correct condition and position required by herbivores, eg Lepidoptera larvae, root herbivores, seed feeders and flower visitors.
Tussocks	Provide shelter and refuge from cold, predators and flooding.	Needed year-round, but especially in winter, by ground-dwelling predators such as Caribidae and Staphylinidae and terrestrial litter-feeders eg Tipulidae and Stratiomyidae larvae.
Sward height	Mosaic of sward heights required. Sward height also controls micro-climate and food-plant condition for herbivores.	Mosaics benefit ground-dwelling predators such as Caribidae. Tall ungrazed or unmown swards are required by seed-feeders, eg Tephritidae and Curculionidae.
Tall emergent plants	Provide shelter, foodplants and emergence sites.	Important as emergence sites and perches for Odonata and Asilidae and water-margin predators such as Saldidae and Dolichopodidae. Food plants for herbivores, eg Chrysomelidae larvae and seed feeders. Provide good litter layer for water-edge litter feeders.
Flowers	Provide nectar, pollen and seed.	Used as perches and as bait for prey by flying predators. Oviposition sites and larval food for seed-feeders. Food for flower visitors, eg Syrphidae, from spring to autumn.
Hedges, bushes and trees	Provide shelter, food (dead and alive), litter source and perches.	Used as hunting stations by flying predators. Food plants for herbivores, eg *Gonepteryx rhamni* caterpillars. Litter supply for terrestrial litter feeders.

**Figure 3.7
The main stages of
drainage channel
succession and their
associated
invertebrate fauna
(after Benstead *et al*
1997)**

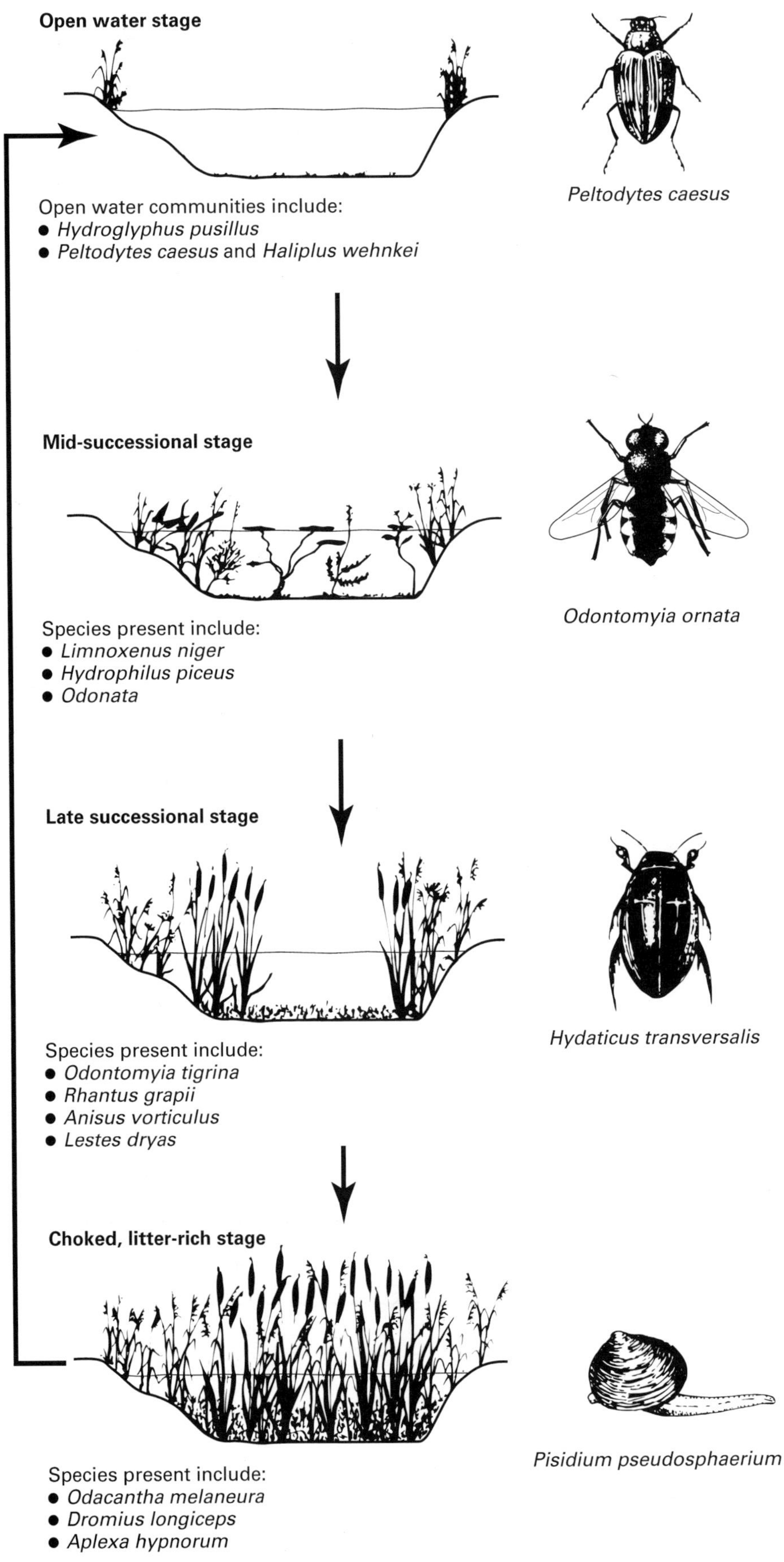

Open water stage

Open water communities include:
- *Hydroglyphus pusillus*
- *Peltodytes caesus* and *Haliplus wehnkei*

Peltodytes caesus

Mid-successional stage

Species present include:
- *Limnoxenus niger*
- *Hydrophilus piceus*
- *Odonata*

Odontomyia ornata

Late successional stage

Species present include:
- *Odontomyia tigrina*
- *Rhantus grapii*
- *Anisus vorticulus*
- *Lestes dryas*

Hydaticus transversalis

Choked, litter-rich stage

Species present include:
- *Odacantha melaneura*
- *Dromius longiceps*
- *Aplexa hypnorum*

Pisidium pseudosphaerium

3.6 Monitoring species, biotopes and projects

Monitoring forms an essential part of conservation management activities. Without monitoring, the effectiveness of management or restoration cannot be assessed. Adequate planning and the allocation of resources are necessary as monitoring, can be time-consuming and expensive (section 2.2.7). Monitoring, which follows on from initial surveys, provides essential feedback, which can be used to adjust management if necessary to ensure that objectives are being met.

When designing a site-monitoring system several key questions must be considered (Hellawell 1991):

- What are the objectives of the monitoring system?

- What should be monitored? Selecting key indicator species and groups is essential (Table 3.8)

- What is the baseline to be?

- What methodologies should be employed?

Table 3.8 Monitoring techniques for groups of taxa and management

Monitoring of:	Techniques
Vegetation communities	Line intercept, point count, quadrats, cover maps, aerial photographs, satellite images and photo stations. If national vegetation classification systems exist use these to categorise vegetation communities.
Aquatic flora and drainage channel vegetation	Aquatic flora are excellent indicators of water quality. Record species presence along fixed sections or areas of waterbodies.
Aquatic invertebrates	Pond netting.
Terrestrial invertebrates	Pitfall traps, sweep netting, water traps, interception traps. Large flying invertebrates such as Odonata and Lepidoptera can be monitored using transects
Birds	Monitor breeding and wintering birds using standardised techniques. Techniques and timing of counting methodologies may vary according to species.
Management	Regularly record all management undertaken, eg mowing dates, grazing pressure and water levels.

Key references

Alcock, M R and Palmer, M A (1985) *A standard method for the survey of ditch vegetation*. Chief Scientist Team (CST) Notes 37. Nature Conservancy Council, Peterborough.

Ausden, M and Treweek, J (1995) Grassland. In W J Sutherland and D A Hill (Eds) *Managing habitats for conservation*, pp 197-229. Cambridge University Press, Cambridge.

Bakker, J P (1989) *Nature management by grazing and cutting*. Kluwer Academic, Dordrecht.

Benstead, P, Drake, M, José, P, Mountford, O, Newbold, C and Treweek, J (1997) *The wet grassland guide: managing floodplain and coastal wet grasslands for wildlife*. RSPB, Sandy.

Brooks, A (1980) *Hedging: a practical conservation handbook*. 2nd Edition. British Trust for Conservation Volunteers, Reading.

Brooks, A and Agate, E (1997) *Waterways and wetlands: a practical handbook*. 3rd Edition. British Trust for Conservation Volunteers, Wallingford.

Crofts, A and Jefferson, R G (Eds) (1999) *The Lowland Grassland Management Handbook*. 2nd Edition. English Nature/The Wildlife Trusts.

Gilbert, G, Gibbons, D W and Evans, J (1998) *Bird monitoring methods: a manual of techniques for key UK species*. RSPB, Sandy.

Girard, N (1992) *Extensive rearing of horses for the management of nature reserves*. Office National Chase, Paris. [In French]

Hellawell, J M (1991) Development of a rationale for monitoring. In F B Goldsmith (Ed) *Monitoring for conservation and ecology*, pp 1–14. Chapman and Hall, London.

Kirby, P (1992) *Habitat management for invertebrates: a practical handbook*. RSPB, Sandy.

Newbold, C, Honnor, J and Buckley, K (1989) *Nature conservation and the management of drainage channels*. The Association of Drainage Authorities and the Nature Conservancy Council, Peterborough.

Oates, M and Bullock, D (1997) Browsers and grazers. *Enact* 5 (4): 15–18.

Pollard, E and Yates, T J (1993) *Monitoring butterflies for ecology and conservation*. Chapman and Hall, London.

Smith, I R, Wells, D A and Welsh, P (1985) *Botanical survey and monitoring methods for grasslands*. Focus on Nature Conservation No 10. Nature Conservancy Council, Peterborough.

Welch, H (Ed)(1996) *Managing water – conservation techniques for lowland wetlands*. RSPB, Sandy.

Part 4
Case studies
Contents

Introduction

This section contains 16 case studies that illustrate different aspects of wet grassland management and restoration. Sites have been selected from throughout Northern and Central Europe (Figure 4.1) to demonstrate a wide range of approaches and techniques.

The case studies follow a standard format:

- main management objectives – provides details of main conservation objectives for the site

- general information – including site name, location, area, wet grassland type (including CORINE plant communities present; see also Figure 1.3), soil, hydrology, climate, designations[1], tenure/ownership, and mechanisms

- background – provides background information about the site

- techniques – describes in detail the implementation of the chosen management technique(s) highlighted in the case study

- benefits – describes the wildlife benefits of the management undertaken and socio-economic benefits where appropriate

- a references and further reading list.

---

[1] Under DESIGNATIONS the following IUCN categories are used to describe the status of local designations:

I   Strict Nature Reserve/Scientific Reserve
To protect nature and maintain natural processes in an undisturbed state

IV   Managed Nature Reserve/Wildlife Sanctuary
To assure the natural conditions necessary to protect nationally significant species, groups of species, biotic communities, or physical features of the environment where these may require specific human manipulation for their perpetuation.

V   Protected Landscapes and Seascapes
To maintain nationally significant natural landscapes which are characteristic of the harmonious interaction of humans and the land while providing opportunities for public enjoyment through recreation and tourism within the normal life style and economic activity of these areas.

IX   Biosphere Reserve
To conserve for present and future use the diversity and integrity of biotic communities of plants and animals within natural ecosystems.

Additionally nearly all of the sites are listed as Important Bird Areas (IBA), which are sites that require effective protection in order to safeguard the birds of Europe (Grimmett and Jones 1989). IBAs are designated under one or more of four categories:

- sites for migratory species which congregate in important numbers

- sites for globally threatened species

- sites for species and sub-species which are threatened throughout all or large parts of their range in Europe

- sites for species which have relatively small total world ranges with important populations in Europe.

**Figure 4.1
Location of case
study sites**

Key

1 Biebrzanski Park Narodowy
(Biebrza National Park), Poland

2 Srednyaya Pripyat
(Floodplain of Mid Pripyat River),
Belarus

3 Pulborough Brooks, UK

4 The Shannon Callows,
Republic of Ireland

5 The Broads Grazing Marshes,
UK

6 Eilandspolder and Polder Mijzen,
Netherlands

7 Hullo ja Sviby Laht,
(Hullo and Sviby Bays) Vormsi,
Estonia

8 Matsalu, Estonia

9 De Veenkampen,
Netherlands

10 Vecdaugava, Latvia

11 Marais de la Vacherie, France

12 Alúvium Rieky Moravy
(Morava River Floodplain),
Slovakia

13 Niva Reky Lužnice
(Lužnice River Floodplain),
Czech Republic

14 Hornborgasjön
(Lake Hornborga), Sweden

15 River Brede floodplain,
Denmark

16 Donauaue bei Platter
(Floodplain of River Danube),
Germany

Biebrzanski Park Narodowy

(Biebrza National Park), Poland

Techniques

Natural processes

Low-intensity management

Main management objectives

- To protect existing high-value biodiversity and habitats

- To maintain natural ecosystems.

Location

50 km north-west of Bialystok, in north-east Poland. 52°21' to 53°41'N, 22°28' to 23°32'E.

Area

Area of Biebrza National Park: 59 233 ha (with a buffer zone of 66 824 ha).

Total grassland area: 62 609 ha, of which 42 225 ha is semi-natural wet grassland and 8731 ha is managed wet grassland.

Wet grassland type

Carex-dominated meadows cover 50% of the National Park. Thirty-six plant associations have been identified including:

- swamp and marsh communities dominated by *Scirpus* spp, *Phragmites australis*, *Glyceria maxima*, *Phalaris arundinacea* (C53.1) and *Carex* spp (C53.21)

- a range of wet grassland and fen communities such as flood-swards (C37.242), tall herb fens (C54.21) and communities described by *Calamagrostis neglecta*, *Agrostis canina* with *Festuca rubra*, and *Poa palustris* with *Alopecurus pratensis* (Palczynski 1984).

The inundation communities present are relatively stable due to the maintenance of a natural hydrological regime and the absence of damage to the system as a result of land-drainage activities.

Soil

Fen peat.

Hydrology

The Biebrza River is 156 km long and is the second largest tributary of the Narew River (Figure 1). The headwaters are at an altitude of 162 m asl and the confluence with the Narew River is at 102.5 m. River channel width varies from 10 to 80 m. Spring flooding after the snow melt in April extends for many kilometres down the Biebrza valley and high water levels remain throughout the early summer, especially in the lower parts of the system (Figure 2). An appreciable inflow of groundwater also occurs from surrounding upland moraine. Attempts have been made to drain the area but, although some have succeeded in lowering the water table in limited areas, few agricultural benefits have resulted (Plate 1). Drained areas are characterised by poor, xerophilous grassland, severe oxidation of peat and associated water-quality problems (ie ochre deposition).

Plate 1 Intensification can create conditions that are initially favourable to birds but breeding productivity is invariably affected by agricultural operations, such as early mowing.

Figure 1 Map showing the three basins of the
Biebrza marshes and the extent of the
National Park.

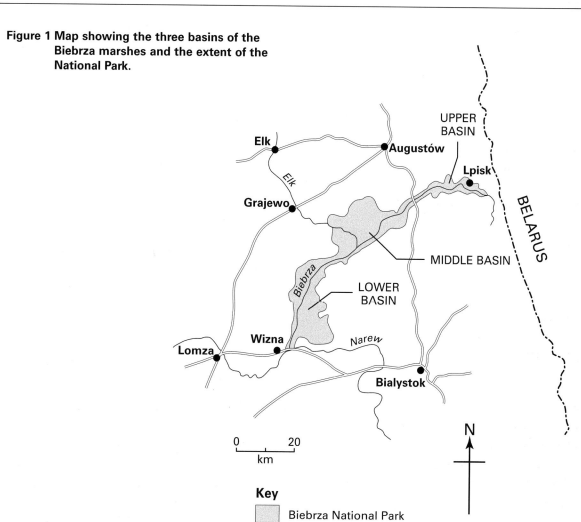

Figure 2 Percentage mean annual hydrograph for
the Biebrza River (after Byczkowski
and Kicinski 1984).

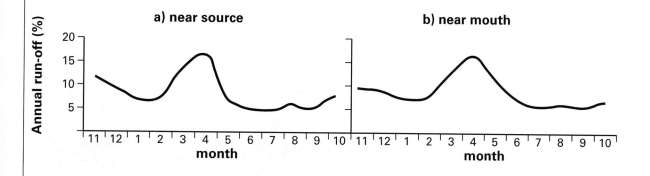

Climate

The climate has a marked continental and a lesser boreal influence.

Mean annual precipitation (Bialystok): 556 mm
Average daily air temperature (Bialystok):
Winter (February) –4.9°C
Summer (July) 18.1°C.
Annual snow cover: 110–140 days.

Designations

National Park (IUCN category V) established in 1993. The Biebrza valley includes three IBAs (Polish IBA Nos 100–102), two of which are included within the National Park.

Tenure/Ownership

Half the National Park (mostly wooded) is state-owned, the remaining largely agricultural biotopes are privately owned.

Mechanisms

There are currently no mechanisms in place to promote and ensure the continuation of environmentally friendly farming practices.

Background

The Biebrza wetlands occupy a valley about 100 km in length and 10–30 km wide which is separated into three distinct basins (Figure 1). The natural fens contained within these three basins are one of the largest expanses of their type in Europe (see also Case Study 2).

The National Park has a high degree of naturalness and includes the best-preserved and most naturally valuable areas of the middle and lower basins of the Biebrza valley (Plate 2). It lies across the boundary of two major geo-botanical zones: those of central Europe and those of boreal eastern Europe. This adds further to the high community diversity found within the park. The park contains Poland's largest peatland complex.

Open areas have been mown for centuries for low-quality hay. As late as the 1950s vast areas were mown, but since then many farmers have migrated to the cities and agricultural intensification has allowed grass crops to be grown in less marginal areas. Many former meadows have, as a result, suffered from neglect and have become overgrown by *Salix* scrub and *Betula* trees. The degree of agricultural intensification (mechanisation, addition of pesticides and fertilisers) is low and comparable to the level found in most western European countries before the Second World War.

The fauna of the national park is diverse, with 178 breeding bird species, mammals such as *Alces alces*, *Lupus lupus* and *Castor fiber*, 36 freshwater fish species and a rich invertebrate fauna. The diversity of the area prompted the designation of part of it as a landscape park in 1989. Within five years the National Foundation for Environmental Protection and the Worldwide Fund for Nature had developed the plans for the future National Park and the present area was designated in September 1993.

Paul José

Plate 2 The floodplain topography of the Biebrza is still largely intact.

Natural processes

- The Biebrza valley still has a classic, well preserved and intact longitudinal and lateral zonation of floodplain habitats, which is extremely rare in Europe. Maintaining natural processes, especially hydrological conditions, is important for sustaining the ecological integrity of the area. Preservation of an unregulated flow and good water quality within the Biebrza River is essential for maintaining the current biodiversity interest.

- Tranverse zones are most clearly developed in the southern basin of the valley. Along a cross-section from the river bank to the valley borders the following zones occur:

  - the flood zone, with the associations of the alliance *Phragmition* (C53.1) close to the riverbanks and associations of the alliance *Magnocaricion* (C53.21) farther away in shallow floodwater
  - the sporadically flooded zone, which has tussocky associations of the mire community *Calamogrostion neglectae* (C54.5E)
  - the flood-free zone with associations of the alliance *Caricion diandrae*

- the valley border zone subject to run-off and spring water, where *Alnus* forest with *Carex elongata* tends to dominate.

- Longitudinal zones are different in that the flood zones and the border zones of *Alnus* forest shrink and gradually recede upstream, giving way to an expanded area of flood-free vegetation dominated by the *Caricion diandrae* alliance.

Low-intensity management

- Agriculture within the National Park is predominantly based upon cattle grazing and mowing of meadows. Mowing has been a traditional land use for centuries and is important for preventing areas from becoming overgrown.

- The main problem currently being addressed is the invasion of scrub into open fen mires in the non-flooded zone caused by the decline in agricultural activities. This problem is being exacerbated by a decline in water table levels in some areas. Experimental scrub removal has been undertaken and the scrub invasion problem is the subject of a great deal of discussion.

- Burning is not usually a management option on peat sites, especially in spring, as it can result in subterranean fires which can burn for many years. Controlled burning in late autumn/winter is being considered to keep small areas clear.

- It is hoped that private farms within the National Park and its buffer zone will gradually adopt environmentally friendly methods of management. A pilot agri-environment scheme (funded by the Dutch Ministry of Agriculture, Nature Management and Fisheries) is currently being developed for the National Park with prescriptions relating to mowing, grazing and the application of agro-chemicals.

- Currently farmers are encouraged not to use pesticides, to mow in late summer and, by cutting from the centre of fields outwards, to protect nesting birds and other wildlife (see Case Study 4). Fertiliser use is minimal and involves low rates of application (15–25 kg N ha^{-1}).

Benefits

- The Biebrza valley provides natural capacity for storage of floodwater in winter, spring and summer. Extensive peat deposits gradually release this water back into the Biebrza River ensuring maintenance of downstream flows in the Narew River throughout dry periods.

- The Biebrza valley provides a significant nutrient storage function – peat accumulation forms the main nutrient sink and relies on water retention.

- The Biebrza National Park supports a number of nationally rare plant species (many of them boreal/glacial relicts) including: *Pedicularis sceptrum-carolinum, Saxifraga hirculus, Polemonium coeruleum, Eriophorum gracile, Carex buxbaumii, Trichophorum alpinum, Scolochloa festucacea* and *Senecio paludosus*. Uncommon species include; *Sweertia perennis, Dactylorhiza incarnata, Viola stagnina, Potentilla norvegica, Carex chordorrhiza* and *Carex dioica*.

- The National Park is exceptionally important for birds, supporting populations of: *Podiceps grisegena, Ciconia nigra* (c 25 pairs), *Anas penelope* (5–10 pairs), *Anas acuta* (<10 pairs), *Anas clypeata* (100–300 pairs), *Circus cyaneus* (15–20 females), *Circus pygargus* (60–80 females), *Crex crex* (800 singing males), *Porzana porzana* (800–1600 singing males), *Porzana parva* (30–50 singing males), *Grus grus* (250 pairs), *Vanellus vanellus, Calidris alpina* (5–10 pairs), *Philomachus pugnax* (5 females), *Gallinago gallinago, Gallinago media* (300–400 displaying males), *Lymnocryptes minimus* (<20 displaying males), *Limosa limosa* (992 pairs), *Numenius arquata* (50–80 pairs), *Tringa totanus* (195 pairs), *Tringa ochropus, Larus minutus* (occasional, 16–55 pairs), *Chlidonias niger, Chlidonias leucopterus* (475–1000 pairs), *Acrocephalus paludicola* (2041–2082 singing males) and *Remiz pendulinus*. Breeding populations of many species fluctuate according to the degree of flooding in any one year. The following birds of prey also hunt over wet grassland and nest in nearby woodland: *Haliaeetus albicilla* (3–4 pairs), *Hieraaetus pennatus* (1–3 pairs), *Aquila clanga* (10–13 pairs) and *Aquila pomarina* (40–55 pairs).

- Bird densities are much higher in 'natural' grassland areas than in those that have been partly drained (Table 1).

- Predation rates on the nests of breeding waders are appreciably higher in partly drained areas than in natural areas (Table 2).

- Mammals are also well represented with *Lutra lutra* (common), *Alces alces* (200–300), *Canis lupus* (4–6 packs) and *Castor fiber* (250 groups, up to 1000 animals).

Table 1 Comparison of breeding populations of birds occurring on open natural fen-grassland and partly drained fen-grassland in Biebrza valley (after Dyrcz *et al* 1985b). + = occurred near transect.

| | Number of pairs per 10 ha | | | |
| | Open natural areas | | Partly drained areas | |
Species	1977	1978	1977	1978
Anas platyrhynchos	2.5	2.7	+	
Anas querquedula	3.6	1.8	+	
Anas clypeata	0.7	0.7		
Crex crex	+	0.2	+	0.5
Porzana porzana	0.9	0.7		
Vanellus vanellus	4.3	3.0	6.0	2.0
Philomachus pugnax	2.3	4.3	2.0	
Gallinago gallinago	8.0	5.9	2.0	
Lymnocryptes minimus	0.5	+		
Limosa limosa	10.5	16.1	4.0	1.0
Tringa totanus	0.5	1.1	0.5	
Alauda arvensis			2.5	4.0
Anthus pratensis	3.6	5.9	4.0	0.5
Motacilla flava			1.5	1.0
Saxicola rubetra	0.2	+		1.0
Acrocephalus paludicola	5.8	4.7	+	
Acrocephalus schoenobaenus	0.2	0.6		
Emberiza schoeniclus	5.2	4.2		
Density of pairs (per 10 ha)	48.8	51.9	22.5	10.0

Table 2 Total density and predation rates of breeding populations of *Limosa limosa* and *Vanellus vanellus* occurring on open natural fen-grassland and partly drained wet meadows in Biebrza valley (after Dyrcz *et al* 1985b).

Biotope	Density of Breeding pairs/10 ha	No. of successful broods	No. of destroyed	% of broods destroyed
Open natural areas	16.1	76	14	15.6
Drained wet meadows	5.8	1	11	91.7

References and further reading

Byczkowski, A and Kicinski, T (1984) Surface water in the Biebrza river drainage basin. *Polish Ecological Studies* 10 (3–4): 271–299.

Dyrcz, A, Kozikowska, Z, Palczynski, A, Raczynski, J and Witkowski, J (1985a) The problems of nature protection and peatland management in the valley of the Biebrza river. *Polish Ecological Studies* 11 (1): 107–121.

Dyrcz, A, Okulewicz, J and Witkowski, J (1984) Bird communities of the Biebrza valley. *Polish Ecological Studies* 10 (3–4): 403–423.

Dyrcz, A, Okulewicz, J and Witkowski, J (1985b) Changes in bird communities as the effect of peatland management. *Polish Ecological Studies* 11 (1): 79–85.

Palczynski, A (1984) Natural differentiation of plant communities in relation to hydrological conditions of the Biebrza valley. *Polish Ecological Studies* 10 (3–4): 347–385.

Case Study Authors/Consultants: Andrzej Dyrcz (Wroclaw University) and Piotr Banaszuk (National Foundation for Environmental Protection).

Srednyaya Pripyat

(Floodplain of Mid Pripyat River), Belarus

Case Study 2

Techniques

Natural processes
Site designation and protection

Main management objective

- To preserve a unique floodplain ecosystem with numerous undisturbed biotopes that are endangered throughout Europe, eg open lowland *Carex* mires, floodplain ox-bow and pool complexes, floodplain meadows and *Quercus* forests. This is to be achieved by:

  - creation of a united protected area that will prevent damaging drainage and dam developments in the Pripyat floodplain
  - maintenance of extensive cattle grazing in wet grasslands
  - reinstatement of hay-making in some wet grasslands to prevent scrub invasion
  - cessation of spring burning within the floodplain.

Location

South-east of Pinsk, Stolin Luninets and Pinsk district of Brest region and Zhitkavichi District of Gomel region, Belarus. 52°10'N, 28°30'E.

Area

Total Mid Pripyat floodplain area: 950 km² (Figure 1).

Wet grassland type

Eutrophic mire and swamp communities and acidic mire communities dominate the floodplain (Figure 1, Plate 1). Currently swamp vegetation (a fifth of which is dominated by scrub) occupies approximately 10% of the floodplain, whilst the remainder is made up of lowland mire. Meadows occupy approximately 420 km² (or 44% of the area), and a wide variety of different meadow communities occurs, from xeric grassland to wet *Carex* beds.

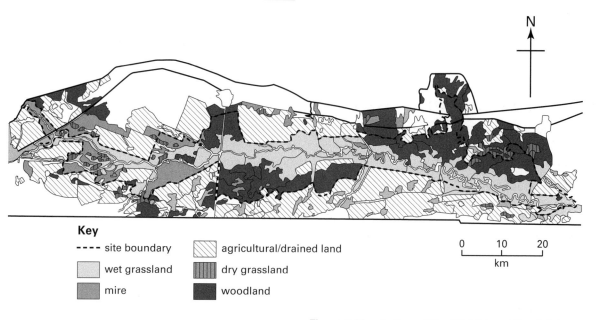

Key

- - - - site boundary
▨ agricultural/drained land
▢ wet grassland
▥ dry grassland
▤ mire
■ woodland

0   10   20
km

Figure 1 Vegetation of the Mid Pripyat floodplain.

Norbert Schäffer

Plate 1 Natural floodplains are a mosaic of biotope types and support high plant and animal diversity.

C53.1, C53.21 and C54 communities are the most widespread (eg *Caricetum ripariae, Caricetum distichae, Phalaridetum arundinaceae, Calamagrostidetum canescentis, Phragmitetum australis,* and *Caricetum gracilis*). These communities occur in large areas across the floodplain from river bed to floodplain terraces. They form 50–60% (sometimes over 75%) of vegetation communities. Species diversity is relatively low in *Phragmitetum australis* communities (7–18 species ha^{-1}) but higher in mire communities (24–35 species ha^{-1}), eg *Caricetum distichae* and *Caricetum ripariae* associations.

Soil

Soil cover is diverse and patchy: sands, sandy loams, and loams dominate among alluvial sediments. About half of the area has floodplain peat-swamp soils, many of these are acid or moderately acid.

Hydrology

The River Pripyat, 761 km in length, is the largest tributary of the River Dnieper and has a catchment of 121 969 km^2, most of which falls inside Belarus. Drainage has taken place on about 20% of the catchment area. The spring flooding regime is variable and flooding does not occur every year. Normally the duration of flooding in spring varies from 40–45 days along small tributaries to 105–120 days along the River Pripyat. The peak of spring flood during mid-March–early April. High rainfall causes summer and autumn floods almost every year. The highest and longest floods can occur in autumn, whilst snow melt during winter thaws also causes flooding. The average annual flow of the River Pripyat is 14.5 km^3, with 60% of this occurring during the main flooding period (March–May).

Climate

Moderately continental, with rather warm summers and moderate winters. Permanent snow cover is usual between late December and early March.

Mean annual precipitation (Pinsk): 690 mm
Average air temperature (Pinsk):
Winter (January) –5.3°C
Summer (July) 18.6°C.

Designations

Currently four nature reserves (zakazniks, IUCN category V) already exist occupying 11 800 ha (12% of the floodplain area). The area forms part of the Pripyat IBA (No. 030 of the former USSR) which covers 62 213 ha.

Tenure/ownership

All lands within and around the area are owned by the State. Some of the agricultural land and meadows are managed by co-operative collective farms (kolhozs). A very small proportion of the land, mainly within the villages, is in private ownership.

Background

The Pripyat valley is situated in the central part of Polessie Lowland. It has three consecutive floodplain terraces from 0.5–1.0 m to 11–20 m above the river level. The average floodplain width is 8–9 km, exceptionally up to 18 km. The generally flat landscape is relieved by numerous ponds, pools and ox-bows and scattered low depressions (0.5–1.0 m). The river meanders considerably, its inclination (gradient approximately 0.0004) reflects the flat topography, and the width in the lowest part of the watercourse is 100–175 m. Water depth generally ranges between 1.0 and 3.0 m, but can reach 6.0 m.

Land use in the floodplain centres around hay-making, cattle grazing, crop growing, fishing, forestry and hunting. The main threat to the wetland during the last 20–30 years has been drainage activity. About a quarter of the floodplain has been drained (mainly lowland *Carex* mires). This has resulted in an increase in the flow of nutrients from the agricultural lands and subsequent increase in eutrophication. Changes of flooding depth and duration are also connected with past and recent drainage activities. Additional threats include water pollution downstream of Pinsk (the largest city on the River Pripyat) and an increase in scrub on open mires and meadows as a result of the decline in hay-cutting. Spring burning to remove old growth can also be a problem in dry seasons as it seriously damages the upper soil layer as well as plant and invertebrate communities.

The Pripyat floodplain supports 155 breeding bird species, mostly associated with wetland biotopes, and attracts large numbers of migrating wildfowl during the spring and autumn. The main factor determining the number of waterbirds breeding in the Pripyat floodplain is the occurrence, depth and duration of spring flooding. The number of breeding waterbirds usually decreases during dry springs.

Natural processes

- Intensive management is not necessary to maintain biodiversity in the Pripyat floodplain since floodplain wet grasslands are under near-natural conditions (Plates 1 & 2). The naturally variable occurrence, depth and duration of floods is the main factor determining conditions. Studies are underway to investigate the influence of spring flooding and its duration on plant and animal communities.

Site designation and protection

- Conservation efforts are currently concentrated on the creation of a new protected area in the Pripyat floodplain (Figure 1). The proposed new zakaznik will restrict activities over a large part of the floodplain. Designation would result in restrictions on:

  - drainage or any other work altering the existing hydrological regime
  - ploughing
  - re-seeding or agricultural improvement of hay meadows
  - use of herbicides and insecticides
  - spring burning
  - discharge of untreated waste
  - unregulated tourist activities.

- There is a proposal for land use within the proposed protected area to be zoned with respect to agricultural activities with:

  - a complete ban on hay-making and cattle grazing in areas close to the river
  - low-intensity hay-making and cattle grazing in areas where agriculture is a traditional activity, ie the edges of floodplain.

Benefits

- The Pripyat floodplain is considered to be of international importance because of its relatively contiguous wetland biotopes and intact natural ecological and hydrological functions. Maintenance of the natural hydrology sustains the status of the dependent hydrological regime of the entire region of Polessia, functioning to regulate flow, supply groundwater, transport water, remove nutrients and retain sediments and toxic materials. Additionally the area acts as a carbon sink.

- The floodplain supports important breeding populations of the following globally threatened species; *Aythya nyroca* (sporadic breeder), *Aquila clanga* (2 pairs), *Crex crex* (250 singing males), *Gallinago media* (50 displaying males), *Acrocephalus paludicola* (50–300 singing males). Additionally, small numbers of *Anser erythropus* (50–150) use the site on migration.

- Considerable proportions of the Belarusian populations of the following bird species of national conservation concern inhabit the area: *Ciconia nigra* (50–70 pairs), *Anas acuta* (20–60 pairs), *Anas querquedula* (10 000 pairs), *Porzana parva* (300 singing males), *Xenus cinereus* (20–50 pairs), *Larus minutus* (50–100 pairs), *Luscinia svecica* (300 pairs), *Remiz pendulinus* (200 pairs) and *Parus cyanus* (50–100 pairs).

Plate 2
Much of the Pripyat floodplain remains under natural conditions.

Paul José

- The area is an exceptionally important stop-over site for migrating wildfowl being used annually by more than 50 000 geese and 30 000 ducks, including *Anser fabalis* (10 000), *Anser albifrons* (30 000), and *Anas penelope* (20 000). Additionally some 15 000 *Philomachus pugnax* use the site on passage.

- Good populations of *Lutra lutra* (40 individuals), *Castor fiber* and *Alces alces* occur in the Pripyat floodplain. *Canis lupus* also occurs, but is very rare.

- The intact floodplain ecosystem provides conditions that allow the survival of numerous rare, relict and endangered vegetation types, including those of dry, sandy situations (eg *Festucetum polesicae, Corynephoretum canescentis* and *Koelerietum delavignei*) and wetter conditions (*Caricetum omskianae and Hierochloetosum odoratae*). Additionally populations of some nationally rare plant species occur eg *Nymphaea alba, Petasites spurius, Carex hartmanii* and *Carex contigua*.

References and further reading

Kovalenko, E P and Taskaev, V I (1987) Water resource use in the Pripyat River basin. *Problemy Polessia* 11: 168–170. [In Russian]

Kozulin, A V, Nikiforov, M E and Pareiko, O A (1995) Goose migration in Belarus. *IWRB Goose Research Group Bulletin* 6: 20–24.

Kozulin, A V, Nikiforov, M E Mongin, E A, Pareiko, O A, Samusenko, I E, Cherkas, N D, Shokalo, S I and Byshnev, I I (1997) Waterfowl migration in Belarus. *Belovezhskaya pushcha Forest Biodiversity Conservation*: 262–280.

Voznyachuk, L N, Kopisov, Y G, Kononov, A N and Mahnach, A S (1972) Geological structure, relief and climate of Polessie region. *Problemy Polessia* 1: 38–108. [In Russian]

Yurkevich, I D, Kruganova, E A, Burtis, N A and Petrucguk, N I (1975) Pripyat floodplain meadows. *Problemy Polessia* 4: 3–28. [In Russian]

Case Study Authors/Consultants: A Kozulin (Institute of Zoology of National Academy of Science Belarus) and. I Stepanovich (Institute of Experimental Botany of National Academy of Science Belarus).

Pulborough Brooks

United Kingdom

Technique

Management planning

Main management objectives

- To manage the site for the benefit of nationally important assemblages of wintering and breeding waterfowl.

- To enhance the wildlife value by manipulation of water levels and grazing and mowing regimes.

Location

2 km south of Pulborough in the Arun floodplain, West Sussex, UK. 50°56'N, 00°31'W.

Area

Total area: 171 ha
Wet grassland covers 121 ha.

Wet grassland type

- Eutrophic humid *Holcus lanatus – Deschampsia cespitosa* grassland (C37.213)

- *Agrostis stolonifera – Alopecurus geniculatus* flood-swards and related communities (C37.242)

Soil

Mainly silts and clays.

Hydrology

Pulborough Brooks is situated on a tidal floodplain at the confluence of the Rivers Arun and Stor (Figure 1).

Embankment of the River Arun in the mid-1960s resulted in the loss of natural riverine flooding on the site. However, large-bore sluices originally installed to improve gravity flow to the River Arun are now used to inundate the site.

Climate

Sub-Atlantic, wet and cool.
Mean annual precipitation: 873 mm
Average maximum air temperature:
Winter (February) 8.8°C
Summer (July) 18.2°C.

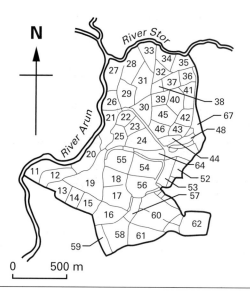

Figure 1
Location of the RSPB Pulborough Brooks Reserve, showing the compartments of the reserve. Numbering compartments aids administration of management practices on different areas of the reserve, thus enabling resources to be more effectively targeted and prioritised.

Designations

A nature reserve (IUCN category IV). Following restoration notified as a Site of Special Scientific Interest. Also part of UK IBA No 201.

Tenure/ownership

The majority of the site is owned by the Royal Society for the Protection of Birds (RSPB).

Mechanisms

The reserve is registered under a Ministry of Agriculture, Fisheries and Food agri-environment scheme called the Countryside Stewardship Scheme.

Background

The Pulborough Brooks are part (8%) of the River Arun floodplain, which were managed for centuries as water meadows (Figure 1). Drainage improvements, including canalisation and embankment of the River Arun, and intensive farming practices, have had a detrimental effect on the wildlife of Pulborough Brooks and the rest of the valley. Additionally this area of the Brooks fell into dereliction during the mid to late 1980s when farming ceased. The grassland is currently rather species-poor, and aquatic plants in the drainage channels continue to hold the main botanical interest. The reserve supports a diverse fauna with important populations of birds and mammals of conservation significance and eight Red Data Book invertebrates and a further 36 nationally scarce invertebrates.

The RSPB purchased 121 ha of floodplain grassland in 1989 and began restoring the wet grassland and its associated drainage system. The restoration approach centred on the concept of the use of existing drainage infrastructure to control and manipulate water levels rather than the complete removal of flood defence structures. In order to improve hydrological control within the site dropboard sluices, flexi-pipe sluices and earth bunds were installed, dividing the reserve into three hydrological units. These improvements allowed the creation of shallow temporary flooding, which is very important for birds on clay sites.

The RSPB has also re-established traditional mowing and grazing regimes to improve the botanical interest of the grassland sward and to benefit breeding and wintering birds. Twenty-three ha is cut for hay between mid-June and late July. One hundred and twenty-five ha is summer grazed, with the RSPB offering a full shepherding service to graziers for their stock. Drainage channels have been restored to management, after years of neglect, to increase both their wildlife value and effectiveness.

Management planning

- The nature reserve has a written Management Plan which describes in detail how the site is to be managed and the rationale for these actions.

- The first step in the management planning process was the preliminary Pathfinder meeting (Plate 1), essentially a scoping exercise, which:

  - involved all stakeholders including relevant statutory government agencies, neighbours and farmers
  - reviewed achievements against objectives/targets in the previous plan
  - translated the organisational objectives of the RSPB into the site management plan
  - agreed policies, objectives and species targets for the site
  - set the timetable for production of the management plan.

- Representations and presentations were made to relevant local community bodies.

- The management planning process followed the format below:

  Information gathering
  - general information; site status, tenure, legal constraints and permissions, fixed assets
  - an audit of the site including information on: climate, hydrology, geology, soils, biotopes, flora and fauna, commercial use, recreational use, research, survey and monitoring, conservation management achieved.

Andrew Hay (RSPB Images)

Plate 1 Pathfinder meetings allow the different stakeholders both within and outside the managing organisation to influence site management policy and practice.

Site evaluation

- criteria used were size, diversity, naturalness, rarity, fragility and replaceability, typicalness, recorded history, position in ecological/geographical unit, potential value, intrinsic appeal, identification/confirmation of important features, operations likely to damage the special interest, land of conservation or strategic importance in the vicinity of the reserve.

Intention

- management rationale, aims and policies.

Action

- operational objectives, outline prescriptions and projects
- five-year work programme.

- The aims of management at Pulborough Brooks are clearly stated in the current Management Plan:

  - To maintain the site as an integral part of the candidate Arun Valley Special Protection Area (SPA)/Ramsar site, principally for the benefit of its nationally important communities of wintering waterfowl, ditch flora, breeding waterfowl and aquatic and terrestrial invertebrates.
  - To continue to develop appropriate facilities to deliver the outstanding visitor and educational potential of the reserve.

- The management policies that will ensure that these aims are met are also stated:

  - To manage the site as an area of lowland wet grassland, principally for the benefit of nationally important assemblages of wintering wildfowl and waders and potentially breeding wildfowl and waders.
  - To maximise the conservation value of the reserve's lowland wet grassland by manipulation of water levels and grazing regimes in three hydrological units.
  - To preserve and enhance the high quality of the local landscape.
  - To manage and develop appropriate facilities to continue to enable the outstanding visitor and educational potential of the reserve to be delivered.
  - To carry out and foster research, survey and monitoring programmes by standard methods to assess the response of key bird species, vegetation and RDB invertebrates to management.
  - To develop and promote the use of the reserve for demonstration and advisory purposes and for lobbying land managers and decision makers.

- The part of the plan dealing with management actions states the operational objectives (always linked to one or more of the management policies – see above), followed by a number of outline prescriptions. For example:

Operational Objective 5.1
To enhance the lowland wet grassland for its nationally important numbers of wintering wildfowl and create suitable habitat for breeding waterfowl.

One of the outline prescriptions under this operational objective is:
5.1.1 Summer grazing by cattle and/or sheep

Under 5.1.1 individual projects relating to summer grazing were described (note: the reserve is divided into numbered compartments to aid management, Figure 1), eg:

MH10.01 Manage habitat, grassland, by controlled grazing
Light summer grazing
Compartments: 24, 30, 38, 39
To graze c 10 ha (10%) lightly, 100 livestock unit days ha^{-1}, from July to October to promote a very varied vegetation structure for wintering and breeding *Gallinago gallinago* and for breeding wildfowl.

MH10.02 Manage habitat, grassland, by controlled grazing
Moderate summer grazing
Compartments: 11, 12, 19, 20, 22, 23, 40, 41, 44–46
To graze 30 ha (25%) moderately, 100–250 livestock unit days ha^{-1}, to promote a varied vegetation structure, principally for the benefit of breeding waterfowl, especially *Gallinago gallinago*, *Tringa totanus*, *Anas clypeata* and *Anas crecca*.

MH10.03 Manage habitat, grassland, by

```
            controlled grazing
            Heavy summer grazing
            Compartments: 16-18, 21, 25,
            42, 43
            To graze c 24 ha (20%)
            heavily, 250 livestock unit
            days ha⁻¹ to produce short
            swards with some structural
            diversity, principally for
            winter wildfowl, but also for
            breeding waders. Grazing by
            cattle/sheep controlled to
            limit nest trampling in
            April/May. Some topping of
            over mature tussocks from
            late July.

  MH10.04 Manage habitat, grassland, by
            controlled grazing
            Grazing followed by topping
            Compartments: 11, 19, 22, 23,
            42-46 Mechanically top, after
            grazing, at 5-10 cm, to
            ensure a short sward around
            pools for wintering Anas
            penelope and Cygnus
            columbianus.
```

- Monitoring mechanisms by which the effectiveness of the work programme is assessed include:

```
Operational Objective 5.7
To carry out and encourage research,
survey and monitoring of response of
key flora and fauna to habitat
management.
```

This operational objective has a number of outline prescriptions (all with associated projects) including:

```
5.7.1 Water level monitoring/control
5.7.2 Monitor flora
5.7.3 Monitor invertebrates
5.7.4 Monitor breeding and wintering
      birds
```

By way of an example, the following invertebrate monitoring project is included:

```
RA82.02 Collect data, molluscs
         Instigate survey of Mollusca
         Survey Mollusca on the
         brooks, recording
         distribution, abundance, etc
         by recognised authority. Data
         to be collected in July and
         August. Other aquatic
         invertebrates will be
         recorded.
```

- A five-year work programme (Table 1) prioritises work and indicates in which years it will be carried out. Priority codes are: 1 = essential, action essential to safeguard species or biotopes; 2 = important task for the routine management of the reserve, missing task for one year will not immediately affect species or biotopes; 3 = desirable task if time and/or resources permit.

Benefits

- The consultation and Pathfinder process involves all stakeholders, including local community groups, ensuring that the views of all bodies concerned with the site are considered.

- Management plans provide a clear framework for all actions taken on a site and ensure that:

  - a physical and biological audit of the site is undertaken
  - clear aims, policies and management objectives are laid out
  - any conflicts between, and problems achieving, the site objectives are anticipated, allowing action to be taken to resolve them
  - relevant management to achieve these objectives is planned and carried out
  - monitoring systems are installed to ensure that projects are achieving objectives and allowing a feedback mechanism whereby management can be altered according to results

Table 1 Five-year work programme for selected projects at Pulborough Brooks

	Years active				
	97/98	98/99	99/00	00/01	01/02
MH10.01 Light summer grazing	2	2	2	2	2
MH10.02 Moderate summer grazing	2	2	2	2	2
MH10.03 Heavy summer grazing	2	2	2	2	2
MH10.04 Grazing followed by topping etc	1	1	1	1	1
RA82.02 Collect data, molluscs	2	2			

- project results are systematically recorded (allowing the effectiveness of management to be demonstrated)
- staff and funding are organised
- there is continuity of management in the event of staff changes.

- The use of a management plan containing clear prescriptive guidelines on the Pulborough Brooks reserve has enabled the following to be achieved during the first five-year reporting period (1992–97):

  - the re-establishment of traditional grazing which has resulted in an increase in botanical diversity and an increase in use by key wet grassland bird species
  - the re-establishment of regular flooding and raised water levels has benefited breeding waders and increased the total wintering waterfowl five-year mean maxima from 680 (1985–90) to 19 500 (1992–96).
  - the clearing of 6.8 km of drainage channels to benefit aquatic plants and invertebrates
  - the installation of visitor infrastructure that attracts in excess of 100 000 visitors per year.

References and further reading

Benstead, P, Drake, M, José, P, Mountford, O, Newbold, C and Treweek, J (1997) *The wet grassland guide. Managing floodplain and coastal wet grasslands for wildlife.* RSPB, Sandy.

Callaway, T and Glover, J (1993) *Management plan – Pulborough Brooks RSPB reserve.* Unpublished report. RSPB, Sandy.

Callaway, T and Glover, J (1998) *Management plan – Pulborough Brooks RSPB reserve.* Unpublished report. RSPB, Sandy.

Callaway, T (1998) Restoration of lowland wet grassland at Pulborough Brooks RSPB Nature Reserve. In R G Bailey, P V José and B R Sherwood (Eds) *United Kingdom floodplains*, pp 459–63. Westbury, West Yorkshire.

NCC (1988) *Site management plans for nature conservation – a working guide.* Nature Conservancy Council, Peterborough.

Case Study Author/Consultant: Tim Callaway (RSPB).

The Shannon Callows

Case Study 4

Republic of Ireland

Technique

Targeted species conservation mechanisms – incentive schemes for *Crex crex*

Main management objectives

- To encourage traditional management that benefits both breeding and wintering birds and grassland botanical interest.

- To increase the reproductive success of *Crex crex* breeding in the area by influencing land management practices.

Location

Between Athlone and Portumna, Republic of Ireland (Figure 1). 53°07' to 53°09'N, 07°56' to 08°06'W.

Area

Total wet grassland area approximately 2500 ha. In 1987, a total of 23% of the area was cut for hay, with the remainder being grazed, mainly by cattle (Nairn *et al* 1988).

Wet grassland types

The major types according to Nairn *et al* (1988) are:

- wet alluvial grasslands characterised by *Glyceria fluitans*, *Agrostis stolonifera* and *Alopecurus geniculatus* (C37.242)

- tall grass washlands with *Phalaris arundinacea* (C53.16)

- tall grass washlands with *Glyceria maxima* (C53.15)

- base-rich marshes with *Caltha palustris*, *Carex disticha*, *Hydrocotyle vulgaris*, *Mentha aquatica* and *Galium palustre* (C54.2) and sedge-rich grasslands with *Carex panicea*, *Carex flacca*, *Carex flava* agg., *Carex pulicaris*, *Carex hostiana*, *Briza media*, *Danthonia decumbens*, *Anthoxanthum odoratum*, *Potentilla erecta* and *Cirsium dissectum* (C54.25).

Soil

Grey-brown podzolic soil, found on calcareous parent materials such as gravel and till. Associated with this are brown earths (on lime-deficient soils) and basin peats (in depressions). Organic soils, ranging from

peaty gleys and podzols through fen peat to bog peat are also found throughout the area (Hooijer 1996).

Hydrology

The Shannon is the longest river in Ireland (359 km), with a catchment of 14 100 km², over 20% of the Republic of Ireland (Hooijer 1996). The river has the shallowest gradient of any in Europe. Between Lough Allen and Lough Derg (205 km) it drops just 12 m (Heery 1993). This shallow gradient leads to extensive winter flooding, which can last for 1–6 months. The width of the flooded area is generally 0.5–1.5 km (Heery 1991).

In contrast to most major Irish rivers, the Shannon has not been subjected to comprehensive arterial drainage work. However, the removal of shallows and the construction of locks and weirs at Athlone and Meelick around 1840 has lowered the average river level by approximately 30 cm at Clonmacnois (Tubridy 1987). Additionally, the west bank of the river between Meelick and Portumna was embanked in the 1920s. These developments resulted in a decrease in flooding frequency and reduced the area frequently or periodically flooded from almost 6000 ha in the 1830s to 3500 ha in the 1980s (Nairn *et al* 1988).

While no large-scale land drainage has been carried out, drainage channels have been dug by individual farmers, probably resulting locally in lower water tables and interception of groundwater flows (Hooijer 1996).

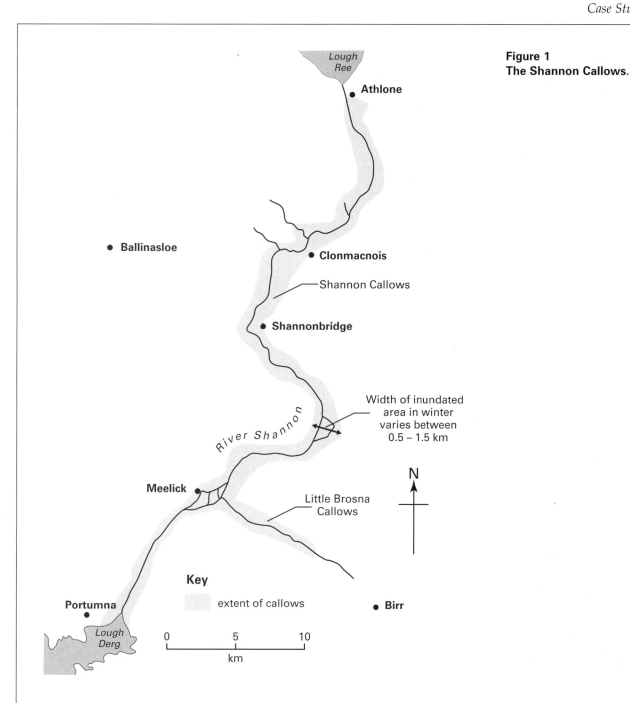

**Figure 1
The Shannon Callows.**

Lough Ree

● Athlone

● Ballinasloe

● Clonmacnois

Shannon Callows

● Shannonbridge

River Shannon

Width of inundated area in winter varies between 0.5 – 1.5 km

N

Meelick ●

Little Brosna Callows

Key

extent of callows

● Birr

Portumna ●

Lough Derg

0   5   10

km

Climate

Mild, wet and equable climate.
Mean annual precipitation: 800–950 mm.
Average air temperature:
Winter (October–March) 6.3°C
Summer (April–September) 11.1°C.

Designations

Designated SPA and Natural Heritage Area. The site falls within the Republic of Ireland's River Shannon Callows IBA No 097 and the adjacent River Little Brosna IBA No 098.

Ownership

The ownership pattern on the callows is very complex.

Most farmers have a farm some distance away, and own just a small area of meadow or pasture on the callows. The average meadow holding for farmers in the Corncrake Grant Scheme (see below) is 2.9 ha. Callow fields, and in particular meadows, can appear to be very large, as most field boundaries are not fenced. This obscures the fact that in each meadow many farmers may own one or more narrow strips, delineated by marker stones at their four corners. For example, Mather's Callow, north of Shannonbridge in County Roscommon contains 47 ha of meadow owned by more than 40 farmers. This complex ownership pattern has been to the benefit of the wildlife in the past, as even the more 'progressive' farmers have not been able to intensify farming practices on the callows.

Part of the area is owned and managed for nature conservation by NGOs (BirdWatch Ireland owns

21.3 ha; the Irish Wildlife Trust approximately 5 ha). The Irish Government, through the National Parks and Wildlife Service is currently in the process of acquiring land in the Callows to be managed for *Crex crex*, breeding waders and botanical interest.

Mechanisms

- **Agri-environment measures**
  Farmers with land in the Shannon Callows Natural Heritage Area (NHA) who join the Irish agri-environment scheme, called the Rural Environmental Protection Scheme (REPS), are required to fulfil certain extra conditions in the NHA, for which they receive a payment of €294 ha⁻¹ (substantially more than the basic REPS payment of €182 ha⁻¹). To date, about 30% of the farmers in the Shannon Callows NHA have joined REPS since its launch in 1994.

- **NGO grant scheme**
  Since 1993, BirdWatch Ireland has operated a Corncrake Grant Scheme in the Shannon Callows, with funding from the RSPB and the Irish National Parks and Wildlife Service. This scheme, which has had an 80% uptake rate since 1994, uses grant payments to encourage farmers to delay mowing in areas where singing *Crex crex* males have been recorded each year. Farmers are also paid to undertake centre-out mowing, and habitat management. Such schemes are very much interim emergency measures put into place pending the introduction of more effective government agri-environment measures.

- **Management on SPAs/Special Areas of Conservation (SACs)**
  Following the Irish Government's adoption of the Habitats Directive in 1997, a system of compulsory management on SACs, with attendant compensation, is currently being introduced. This scheme will now also apply to SPAs, and farmers on the Shannon Callows will be required to implement specific management prescriptions designed to benefit *Crex crex*, for which they will be compensated. However, this scheme is now at the public consultation stage, and was not in place in time for the 1998 *Crex crex* breeding season. BirdWatch Ireland's Corncrake Grant Scheme will therefore continue until this scheme is finalised.

Background

The Shannon Callows are flooded fields on either side of the River Shannon between Lough Ree (Athlone) and Lough Derg (Portumna) (Figure 1). Regular flooding and low-intensity farming contribute to the unique character of the area and its importance for bird communities.

In winter, when the callows are extensively flooded, they support internationally important numbers of wildfowl and waders, including *Cygnus cygnus, Cygnus columbianus, Anser albifrons flavirostris, Anas penelope, Limosa limosa* and *Pluvialis apricaria*. In summer, the callows support a range of breeding birds, including *Crex crex, Coturnix coturnix* and waders (*Vanellus vanellus, Tringa totanus, Gallinago gallinago* and *Numenius arquata*). Seventeen plant species which are classified as rare in Ireland, including *Groenlandia densa*, are found on the callows (Heery 1993).

One of the most important birds found on the Shannon Callows is *Crex crex*, a globally threatened species (Collar *et al* 1994). This species has been in decline throughout Europe, including the Republic of Ireland, during the 20th century. The rate of decline in the Republic of Ireland has increased in the last two decades. A national census in 1993 recorded a decrease of over 80% in the five years since the previous census, to a minimum of only 174 singing males (Sheppard and Green 1994). In 1993, *Crex crex* was almost totally restricted to just three core areas in Ireland; one of which was the Shannon Callows.

The vegetation on the callows is semi-natural wet grasslands and marshes, and would probably revert to fen woodland if farming activity ceased. The wildlife of the callows therefore depends on maintenance of the existing farming system of low-intensity hay-cropping (Plate 1). Regular flooding is also critical to the ecology of the area, both for the direct physical impact of inundation and for its consequent effect on farming practices. No ploughing or re-seeding and little fertiliser or herbicide use takes place on the callows.

Catherine Casey

Plate 1 The agricultural system in the Shannon Callows has created a herb-rich wet grassland and a diverse associated fauna.

Targeted species conservation mechanisms – incentive schemes for *Crex crex*

Increasing *Crex crex* productivity is achieved primarily through the operation of the Corncrake Grant Scheme, which has the following measures:

- the delay of mowing of meadows until 1 August, allowing the species to hatch two broods

- the adoption of Corncrake-friendly mowing techniques (Figure 2)

- the provision of vegetation cover for *Crex crex* both early and late in the season.

Delayed mowing

- This grant is available to farmers with a singing male *Crex crex* on or within 250 m of suitable habitat (ie a hay or silage meadow), where the bird remains in the area for at least three days. Farmers who are participating in the Rural Environment Protection Scheme (REPS) and have received the premium payment for their land contained within the NHA are not eligible for entry to the Corncrake Grant Scheme.

- Farmers are obliged to delay mowing of hay or silage in areas likely to contain *Crex crex* nests until after 1 August, by which time most birds should have hatched two broods. For this, they receive a payment of €133 ha⁻¹.

Mowing for *Crex crex*

- Farmers usually mow meadows in a clockwise spiral from the edges of the field towards the centre. This method has the effect of herding *Crex crex* (especially unfledged young) into an ever-decreasing island of grass at the centre of the field, separated from safety by a broad expanse of cut grass. Consequently mortality is high. BirdWatch Ireland grant schemes encourage farmers to mow grass in the opposite direction, from the centre of the field outwards, which will drive the birds under cover towards the edges of the fields and safety (Figure 2). The payment for safe mowing is €30 ha⁻¹, with a minimum total payment of €22.

- There are two main mowing options:

  - cutting centre-out strips (Figure 2), which is most effective in long, narrow plots such as those found on the Shannon Callows
  - cutting out from the centre in a spiral, which reduces the dead-time (time spent travelling over areas that have already been mown) in squarer fields.

- Neither mowing method can prevent the destruction of nests, and these techniques are most effective when used to complement the delayed mowing option. However, as there are likely to be flightless young in the meadows from mid-June onwards, the adoption of safer mowing methods alone can still prevent the loss of large numbers of *Crex crex*. A detailed study in Ireland and Scotland (Green *et al* 1997) found that only 17% of chicks were killed during centre-out mowing, compared to 57% during outside-in mowing.

- An important limitation of centre-out mowing is

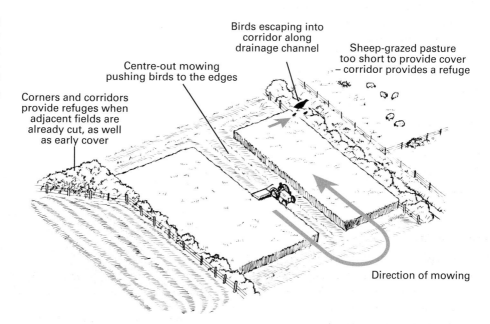

**Figure 2
The mowing technique that limits the destruction of unfledged *Crex crex* broods.**

Birds escaping into corridor along drainage channel

Sheep-grazed pasture too short to provide cover – corridor provides a refuge

Centre-out mowing pushing birds to the edges

Corners and corridors provide refuges when adjacent fields are already cut, as well as early cover

Direction of mowing

particularly evident on the Shannon Callows, where most plots are not fenced, but are marked at the corners with marker stones. If the plots on either side of a particular plot have been mown recently, there may be no cover for chicks to escape to at the edges, even if a farmer mows centre-out. In this case, centre-out mowing may be less likely to be successful, but it appears that it is still safer than outside-in mowing, as the tractor is driving the chicks in one direction all the time, ie towards the edges of the plot.

The results of vegetation surveys carried out in conjunction with the *Crex crex* census in 1993, and the continued dramatic declines of breeding *Crex crex* in 1994, highlighted problems related to the provision of vegetation cover.

Providing early cover

- In 1993, the distribution of singing male *Crex crex* was closely related to the occurrence of vegetation which provided cover early in the season. In some areas otherwise suitable for the species, the amount of cover available early in the season may be limiting. This shortage of cover can increase mortality by exposing birds to predators as they move between the patches of cover to feed, and may also reduce breeding success, as males delay the setting up of territories. Good early cover species include *Phalaris arundinacea, Glyceria maxima* and *Iris pseudacorus* which start growing before meadow grasses and provide the beneficial structure of dense vegetative cover overhead while still being easily penetrated by the birds at ground level (Plate 2).

- Early cover vegetation can be encouraged to spread from drains and field margins by leaving a 4 m headland unmown and ungrazed at the end of the season. The vegetation should then be available for *Crex crex* to use the following April. This vegetation will need to be mown or grazed on a regular basis

(at least every two years in late autumn/winter) to prevent it from becoming too rank to be used by *Crex crex* the following year.

- Under the Corncrake Grant Scheme an early cover option (€222 ha⁻¹) is offered to selected farmers on a limited basis, depending on where appropriate species are present, where late-cut meadow can be assured and where early cover is lacking. As the areas involved in early cover creation are generally small, there is a minimum payment of €45.

Providing late cover

- Cover may also be in short supply late in the season when mowing and aftermath grazing remove all suitable tall vegetation. This is a particular problem on the Shannon Callows, where *Crex crex* nest in large expanses of meadow, with few other types of land use present. In nearby Donegal, meadows occur alongside fields of corn, rough pasture and vegetables which can provide cover after hay has been cut.

- Before mechanisation became common and sophisticated, the period of time between the start and end of mowing was measured in weeks, so that by the time the last of the grass was cut there was substantial re-growth on the early-cut fields. Until fairly recently, this was the dominant pattern on the Shannon Callows. Currently, and to some extent as a result of the uptake of the Corncrake Grant Scheme, mowing on the callows may be completed within two weeks. During this very short period, all suitable cover is removed, leaving *Crex crex* to shelter in drainage channels, where they are particularly vulnerable to mammalian predators. This can be a dangerous time for unfledged *Crex crex*, and also for moulting adults, which are temporarily flightless.

- In an attempt to address the problem, BirdWatch

**Plate 2
Vegetation cover available in the early part of the season, such as this *Urtica dioica* bed, is vitally important for the newly arrived *Crex crex*.**

Catherine Casey

Ireland introduced a Late Cover Grant Scheme in the Shannon Callows in 1995. Selected farmers were offered a higher rate of grant payment (€222 ha⁻¹) to delay mowing until 1 September. In 1996, a further tier was added to the scheme, with some farmers offered €170 ha⁻¹ to delay mowing to 15 August. This new tier, and poor hay-making weather in early August, combined to shift the peak mowing date in 1996 towards the middle of August, and to reduce the severity of the peak, staggering mowing over the whole month (Figure 3). This scheme was continued in 1997 and 1998.

- In the future, it is hoped to increase the amount of habitat management carried out and also to incorporate provisions for the delay of grazing in order to provide tall vegetation throughout the summer in areas where hay-cutting is not feasible. This option, which has been used very successfully by the RSPB on their reserve in Coll, Scotland (Niemann 1995), would be aimed particularly at areas where there is already adequate early cover. A scheme encouraging hay-making could also be used to increase the area of hay meadow available to *Crex crex*.

Benefits

- There was an increase in the number of *Crex crex* in Ireland in 1995, for the first time since recording began in 1991. Numbers rose by 35% on the 1994 figure, to 174 singing males. This upward trend continued in 1996, when *Crex crex* numbers rose to 186 males, a 6% increase. This positive result can be related to the successful operation of the Corncrake

Grant Scheme which has been honed over the four years of its operation in the Shannon Callows.

- *Crex crex* numbers in the Shannon Callows, however, continued to fall until 1996, despite good uptake of the grant scheme. Attempts were made in 1995 and 1996 to address this situation (see above), and stability in *Crex crex* numbers was seen in the callows in 1997 for the first time since recording began. In 1998, the population rose by over 25% (to 70 singing males), the first increase since the project began. This is likely to be linked to the extra delay in mowing from 1996, caused by a combination of the successful operation of the late cover scheme and poor hay-making weather in the first two weeks in August in subsequent years.

- BirdWatch Ireland's Corncrake Grant Scheme, while targeted solely at *Crex crex* will benefit other ground-nesting birds in the meadows, such as *Alauda arvensis* and *Anthus pratensis*. The scheme is also likely to benefit the botanical diversity of the area, as fertiliser use is discouraged, retention of hay meadow is encouraged and mowing is delayed until many flowering plants and grasses have set seed.

- At present, the bulk of the funding spent on the Corncrake Grant Scheme is on grants for delayed and centre-out mowing. It is now apparent, however, that in the absence of adequate supporting habitat management, these measures alone are unlikely to deliver increases in *Crex crex* numbers. Owing to inadequate funding, only a limited amount of habitat management to provide early or late cover has been undertaken, and this has almost certainly reduced the success of the project, especially in the Shannon Callows.

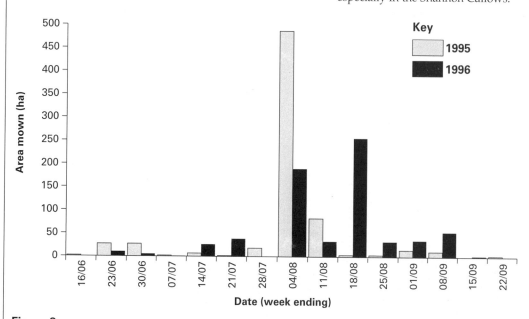

Figure 3
Comparison of peak mowing on the Shannon Callows in 1995 and 1996. The two-tier late cover grant scheme was introduced in 1996, and this graph shows the difference in the timing of mowing that this has encouraged.

References and further reading

Collar, N J, Crosby, M J and Stattersfield, A J (1994) *Birds to watch 2: the world list of threatened birds.* BirdLife International, Cambridge.

Green, R E, Tyler, G A, Stowe, T J and Newton, A V A (1997) A simulation model of the effect of mowing of agricultural grassland on the breeding success of the corncrake (*Crex crex*). *J. Zool.* 243: 81–115.

Heery, S (1991) The plant communities of the grazed and mown grassland of the River Shannon Callows. *Proceedings of the Royal Irish Academy* 91B: 1–19.

Heery, S (1993) *The Shannon Floodlands: a natural history of the Shannon Callows.* Tir Eolas, Kinvara.

Hooijer, A (1996) *Floodplain hydrology: an ecologically oriented study of the Shannon Callows, Ireland.* PhD thesis. Vrije Universitiet, Amsterdam, Netherlands.

Nairn, R G W, Herbert, I J and Heery, S (1988) Breeding waders and other wet grassland birds of the River Shannon Callows. *Irish Birds* 3: 521–537.

Niemann, S (1995) *Habitat management for corncrakes.* Unpublished report. RSPB, Sandy.

Sheppard, R and Green, R E (1994) Status of the Corncrake in Ireland in 1993. *Irish Birds* 5 (2): 125–138.

Tubridy, M (1987) *The Heritage of Clonmacnois.* Unpublished report. Environmental Sciences Unit, Trinity College, Dublin.

Case Study Author/Consultant: Catherine Casey (BirdWatch Ireland).

The Broads Grazing Marshes

Case Study 5

United Kingdom

Techniques

Establishment of an agri-environment scheme
Ecological monitoring

Main management objectives

- To conserve landscape, wildlife and historic features, especially those contributing to the character of traditional grassland areas

- To extend area of wet grassland

- To maintain traditional livestock farming on permanent grassland.

Location

The floodplains of the Rivers Thurne, Ant, Bure, Yare and Waveney in Norfolk and Suffolk, East Anglia, UK (Figure 1).
Upper Thurne Broads and Marshes 52°44'N, 01°35'E
Ant Broads and Marshes 52°43'N, 01°31'E
Bure Broads and Marshes 52°41'N, 01°28'E
Yare Broads and Marshes 52°35'N, 01°27'E
Halvergate Marshes 52°35'N, 01°38'E

Area

Total area approximately 56 000 ha, of which 16 300 ha is wet grassland.

Wet grassland type

Several grassland associations are represented (ADAS 1996a):

- two species-poor, agriculturally improved or semi-improved communities are most frequently encountered; *Lolium perenne* leys (C81.2) and *Lolium perenne–Cynosurus cristatus* grassland (C38.12).

- a species-poor semi-natural grassland, *Festuca rubra–Agrostis stolonifera–Potentilla anserina* community (C37.242).

- high-diversity fen communities; notably *Juncus subnodulosus–Cirsium palustre* fen-meadow (C37.218) and a small quantity of *Molinia caerulea–Cirsium dissectum* fen-meadow (C37.312), a scarce community in the UK.

Soil

Seaward ends of valleys are typified by marine clays and silts. Peat occurs farther inland and along valley margins. Soil pattern can, however, be complex, and interlayers of peat, sand and clay occur (George 1992).

Hydrology

The Broads rivers have a relatively large total catchment by UK standards, totalling 318 100 ha (NRA 1995). They have low gradients as they flow through the Broads (3 cm km^{-1}). Their water regimes are complicated by tidal influences and the difference in run-off rates between catchments (George 1992).

Climate

Sub-Atlantic, wet and cool.
Mean annual precipitation: 644 mm
Average air temperature:
Winter (December–February) 6.1°C
Summer (June–August) 19.4°C.

Designations

The Broads includes Sites of Special Scientific Interest and eight National Nature Reserves, covering approximately a third of the area. The majority of this designated series of sites is also recognised within the Broadland SPA, Broadland Ramsar site and Broads candidate SAC. The attractiveness of the landscape

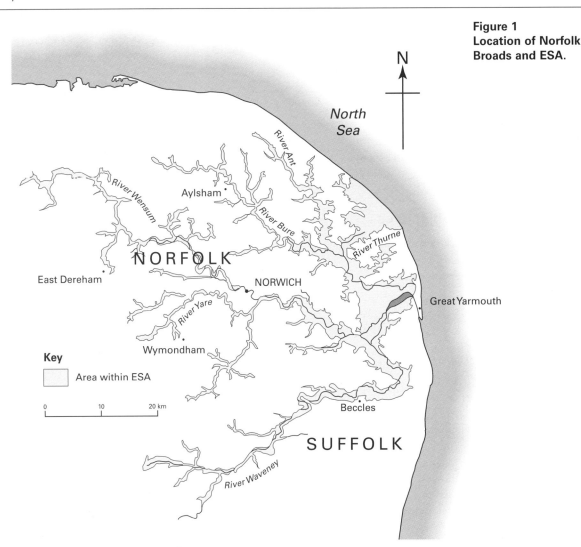

Figure 1
Location of Norfolk
Broads and ESA.

was recognised in 1988 when legislation was passed which afforded it a status equivalent to a National Park (IUCN category V). The following four UK IBAs fall within the Broads area: No 166 Upper Thurne Broads and Marshes, No 167 Ant Broads and Marshes, No 168 Bure Broads and Marshes and No 169 Yare Broads and Marshes.

Tenure/ownership

Largely private; approximately 3750 ha of the total area is owned and/or managed by nature conservation bodies.

Mechanisms

Most of the wet grassland falls within the Broads Environmentally Sensitive Area (ESA) scheme (Figure 1). The ESA scheme is one of the mechanisms promoted by the UK government in response to the EU Agri-Environment Regulation 2078/92. The ESA scheme supports those farmers who undertake traditional management in areas of landscape and wildlife importance. All ESAs offer:

- voluntary entry

- annual payment based on the amount of land under agreement

- several farm management options

- payments reviewed every two years

- a ten-year agreement with an option to opt-out after five years

- possibility of grants for capital work.

Background

The area known as the Broads takes its name from a series of shallow flooded medieval peat workings. These are mostly located alongside the middle reaches of the three largest rivers in the area; the Waveney, Yare and Bure. These rivers and the associated broads are bordered by areas of drained grazing marsh and unreclaimed fen. This mixture of open water and semi-natural biotopes creates a unique landscape and the whole area has a very high nature conservation value.

The grazing marshes of the Broads constitute one of the largest areas of floodplain and coastal wet grassland in the UK. The grassland itself can have a rich flora, while the associated drainage channels contain many rare species of plants and animals. Over 80% of the grazing marshes support drainage channel communities which are at least of national importance, including 108 species of submerged, floating-leaved or emergent plants and approximately 180 nationally important invertebrate species (Holve 1996). Rare invertebrates in the UK context include: the Mollusca *Segmentina nitida* and *Anisus vorticulus*, and the Odonata *Aeshna isosceles* and *Libellula fulva*. Rare aquatic plants include *Luronium natans, Potamogeton compressus* and *Potamogeton acutifolius*.

Four species of wading bird, *Tringa totanus, Gallinago gallinago, Vanellus vanellus* and *Haematopus ostralegus*, are characteristic breeding species in the area. The area is an important site for overwintering waterfowl, eg internationally important numbers of *Anas strepera* and *Anas clypeata*. There is a nationally important breeding population of *Anas querquedula*, which is dependent on the grazing marshes of the Broads.

Unfortunately, the nature conservation interest of the Broads area has declined since the 1940s because:

- water quality has suffered from inputs of phosphorus and nitrates from sewage and agricultural run-off respectively, leading to major losses of botanical and invertebrate interest and affecting breeding birds

- grazing marsh has been converted to arable or intensively managed for grass with improved drainage.

Many of the biotopes of the Broads depend on traditional management. Grassland areas are mostly managed by summer grazing (Plate 1). Maintenance of traditional management is one of the main objectives of the agri-environment mechanism operating in the area. The Broads ESA (the first of its kind) was established in 1987 following a trial scheme in part of the area and has been extended subsequently. It now covers over 36 000 ha of river valley wetlands in east Norfolk and Suffolk (Figure 1). Large-scale conservation and restoration projects are underway and there are encouraging results for wildlife in the area.

The Broads Environmentally Sensitive Area Scheme

- The ESA currently offers grassland management agreements to farmers under four tiers (Figure 2):

  - Tier 1 (€215 ha^{-1}) specifies a grazing regime with restrictions on mowing and fertiliser use, and prohibition in the applications of agro-chemicals.

  - Tier 2 (€333 ha^{-1}) imposes further restrictions on winter grazing, mowing dates and fertiliser use. A key requirement is the maintenance of summer drainage channel levels to within 45 cm of marsh level.

  - Tier 3 (€445 ha^{-1}), in addition to the requirements of the lower tiers, restricts spring grazing and stocking rates, and requires maintenance of the water table at marsh level during the winter and early spring so as to create shallow pools for wintering wildfowl and breeding waders.

  - Tier 4a (€385 ha^{-1}) subsidises farmers for the reversion of arable land to permanent

**Plate 1
Summer grazing by cattle has maintained the wet grasslands of the Broads for centuries.**

C H Gomersall (RSPB Images)

83

Figure 2 Broads ESA management prescriptions under the three grassland management tiers.

Tier 1

	J	F	M	A	M	J	J	A	S	O	N	D
Drainage channel water levels	>31 cm		High enough to allow grazing								>31 cm	
Grazing	Grazing allowed (no pigs or poultry)											
Grassland management	Maintain grassland. If grass is cut the aftermath must be grazed											

Pesticide use — No use of fungicides or insecticides. Herbicides to be applied using weedwiper or by spot treatment.

Fertiliser use — Existing level of fertiliser use must not be exceeded. Do not exceed 125 kg of nitrogen, 75 kg of phosphate and 75 kg of potash ha^{-1}year^{-1}. Use no more than 94 kg of nitrogen ha^{-1} in any single application. Do not apply more than 30 tonnes ha^{-1} of home-produced manure in any one year .

Tier 2

	J	F	M	A	M	J	J	A	S	O	N	D
Drainage channel water levels	>60cm		<45 cm below marsh level								>60 cm	
Water level supplement*			<30 cm below marsh level									
Grazing			Grazing allowed									
Grassland management			No management **									
Drainage channel management				No management								

Fertiliser use — Do not exceed existing level of nitrogen and in any case do not exceed 44 kg of nitrogen ha^{-1}year^{-1}. Do not apply phosphate or potash or any organic manure.

Tier 3

	J	F	M	A	M	J	J	A	S	O	N	D
Drainage channel water levels	At marsh level			<45 cm below marsh level							>60 cm	
Water level supplement*			<30 cm below marsh level									
Grazing				Grazing allowed ***								
Grassland management			No management **									
Drainage channel management				No management								

Fertiliser use — Do not apply any inorganic or organic fertiliser .

*Additional payments (€ 52 ha^{-1}) are made for high level water management. Additional prescriptions for these additional payments include:
• no application of inorganic or organic fertiliser or manure
• from 1 April to 31 May grazing density must not exceed one bovine animal per 0.75 ha
• sheep grazing only after 1 June.

** Do not apply lime, or any other substance to reduce soil acidity.

***Before 30 June do not exceed a grazing density of one bovine animal per 0.75 ha.

grassland, while 4b (€489 ha[-1]) encourages the creation of grassland margins in arable fields alongside drainage channels.

- Additionally, agreed capital works are eligible for part-funding under the scheme and include the creation/reinstatement of scrapes and drainage channels for the benefit of wildlife, the construction of bunds, sluices, culverts and other works to control water levels and the re-creation of herb-rich meadows.

- **Compliance monitoring**
  In order to ensure that participants in the scheme adhere to the prescriptions, the Farming and Rural Conservation Agency (the government agency responsible for managing ESA schemes in England and Wales) has a compliance monitoring system. Scheme entrants are monitored by employing aerial photography and random ground checks.

Review and monitoring

- The ESA prescriptions are subject to a review every five years. The prescriptions were reviewed in 1996 and both government agencies and NGOs made recommendations for improvement.

- Regular monitoring of Tiers 1, 2 and 3 areas is necessary to check whether any adjustments need to be made to the prescriptions when they are reviewed every five years.

  - grassland botanical composition and drainage channel flora have been routinely monitored at a number of sample sites as part of the ESA monitoring process. In addition, English Nature, with assistance from the Broads Authority and the Environment Agency (government agencies), has undertaken a Broads-wide monitoring exercise of drainage channel flora
  - the RSPB, with the support of the government agencies, has undertaken monitoring of both breeding waders and wintering waterfowl in the Broads in order to evaluate the success of the ESA scheme and provide data for Water Level Management Plans (which attempt to accommodate all user interests within a defined

hydrological unit thereby giving some surety of supply to sites of acknowledged wildlife interest).

- The results of the breeding wader survey of 1995 (Weaver 1995 – summarised in Table 1) indicate that:

  - Tier 1 management was the poorest for breeding waders, worse than the average for the ESA as a whole and lower than non-tier land.
  - Tier 2 had the largest proportions of each of the four wader species populations. Densities were above the overall ESA average. Densities were variable and many traditional wader breeding strongholds are included within this tier.
  - in Tier 3 only 50 ha existed outside reserves, mainly in small, already wet, peaty valley edge sites. These areas held locally important *Gallinago gallinago* populations.
  - comparison with 1988 baseline data revealed that: *Gallinago gallinago* had declined by 40% (mirroring the national trend), *Vanellus vanellus* had decreased by 14% (largely due to decreases in Tier 1 and non-tier land), *Tringa totanus* had remained stable (but declines were evident on privately owned land in Tiers 1 and 2). Only *Haematopus ostralegus* had increased, by 37%, in line with the current national trend on inland habitats.
  - All increasing or stable populations were either on reserves or on privately owned Tier 2 areas under agreement since 1988 with traditionally good populations.
  - the survey showed that breeding densities were very variable on Tiers 1 and 2, reflecting the wide variation in soil type and location. The survey indicated that summer drainage channel water levels could be too low under Tier 2, particularly on clay soils. The presence of footdrains was also perceived to be important in providing edge habitat for breeding waders. Tiers 1 and 2 were shown to be most effective when enhanced by planned water control measures for entire or substantial areas of catchment.

Table 1 Breeding densities (pairs km[-2]) for wader species on grassland within the ESA boundary in 1995 (after Weaver 1995).

Species	Non-tier	Tier 1	Tier 2	Tier 3	Reserves	Overall
Gallinago gallinago	0.9	0.2	0.6	17.6	2.4	0.6
Tringa totanus	0.4	0.4	2.2	0	7.2	1.5
Vanellus vanellus	3.6	1.9	4.7	7.8	11.3	3.6
Haematopus ostralegus	0.8	0.5	1.5	0	2.0	1.0

- The wintering waterfowl survey of 1996/97 (Babbs *et al* 1997) was the first full survey of the Broads ESA. Two hundred and eleven sites were surveyed and information was also collected on vegetation, land use and surface flooding. The survey revealed that the Broadland ESA:

    - supported internationally important wintering populations of *Cygnus columbianus*, *Anser brachyrhynchus*, *Anas penelope*, *Anas strepera*, *Anas clypeata* and *Vanellus vanellus*.
    - supported nationally important wintering populations of *Cygnus olor*, *Cygnus cygnus*, *Anser fabalis*, *Anser albifrons*, *Aythya fuligula*, *Fulica atra* and *Pluvialis apricaria*.
    - Tier 3 areas were consistently good for wintering waterfowl.

Benefits

- Uptake in the Broadland ESA has been high (43% of eligible land is under agreement), with 54.2% of ESA land in Tier 1, 41.3% in Tier 2 and 2.4% in Tier 3.

- In the first three years of the scheme, land-use changes were reversed and there was a 5.6% increase in grassland cover. This has enhanced the landscape character by consolidating areas of grassland previously fragmented by intrusive arable areas. Additionally there have been some localised qualitative changes in wet grassland towards botanically species-rich communities (ADAS 1996b).

- The ESA has slowed, but not reversed, the trend of deteriorating wildlife assets.

- Within the ESA there has been a considerable expansion of nature reserves in recent years, with government agencies and NGOs all extending existing holdings. Most of these reserves are now being managed with high drainage channel levels and traditional grazing, making optimum use of Tier 2 and Tier 3 agreements (Plate 2).

- During the review of prescriptions, many of the amendments suggested by the conservation organisations were taken up including:

    - the introduction of a fen tier to conserve and enhance reedbeds and species-rich litter marshes by encouraging management
    - extension of the grazing period for Tier 2 from the end of October to the end of December
    - introduction of a water level supplement for Tiers 1 and 2 to encourage maintenance of higher summer drainage channel levels than otherwise required by these tiers and low grazing densities at the start of the season, and a delayed start to sheep grazing
    - flexibility to alter individual agreements according to specific biodiversity requirements on sites.

- Monitoring of the wader population after the first five years of the scheme showed that the ESA scheme was failing to deliver for this group. Tier 3 prescriptions and improved water management prescriptions were introduced in 1992 targeted at breeding waders and wintering wildfowl.

- Steps to reconcile conflicts between drainage needs and the need to re-wet grassland for conservation reasons are being identified and, where possible, conservation enhancement works are being implemented through Water Level Management Plans. These include realistic targets for drainage channel flora and breeding and wintering birds based on surveys recently undertaken.

Plate 2
Existing nature reserves, such as RSPB Berney Marshes, have expanded during the lifetime of the Broads ESA scheme and many are managed successfully under Tier 2 and Tier 3 high water level management agreements.

C H Gomersall (RSPB Images)

References and further reading

ADAS (1996a) *Botanical monitoring of grassland in the Broads ESA, 1987– 1994*. Report to Ministry of Agriculture, Fisheries and Food. HMSO, London.

ADAS (1996b) *Environmental monitoring in the Broads ESA, 1987–1995*. Report to Ministry of Agriculture, Fisheries and Food. HMSO, London.

Babbs, S, Cook, A S and Durdin, C (1997) *Broads ESA Wintering Waterfowl Survey 1996/1997*. Unpublished report. RSPB, Norwich.

George, M (1992) *The Land Use, Ecology and Conservation of Broadland*. Packard Publishing, Chichester.

Holve, H (1996) *The Broads Natural Area Profile*. English Nature and the Broads Authority, Norwich.

NRA (1995) *Yare Catchment Management Plan*. National Rivers Authority, Norwich.

Parmenter, J (1995) *The Broadland Fen Resource Survey*. Volumes 1– 5. BARS 13a– f. Broads Authority and English Nature, Norwich.

Tallowin, J R B and Mountford, J O (1997) Lowland wet grasslands in ESAs. In R D Sheldrick (Ed) *Grassland management in the 'Environmentally Sensitive Areas'*. Proceedings of the BGS Conference held at University of Lancaster, 23– 25 September 1997. Occasional Symposium No. 32, British Grassland Society.

Weaver, D J (1995) *Broads ESA Breeding Wader Survey 1995*: *Report of Results*. Unpublished report. RSPB, Norwich.

Case Study Authors/Consultants: Jane Madgwick and Sandie Tolhurst (Broads Authority).

Eilandspolder and Polder Mijzen Case Study 6

Netherlands

Technique

Grassland management for breeding wading birds

Main management objectives

- To promote and maintain breeding and wintering bird populations

- To conserve landscape and wildlife features, especially those contributing to the character of the traditional grassland.

Location

Situated between Ursem and De Rijp, 20 km north of Zaandam, Province of Noord-Holland, Netherlands (Figure 1). 52°35'N, 04°52'E.

Area

Total wetland area 2 050 ha comprising three polders: Eilandspolder-Oost (750 ha), and Eilandspolder-West (700 ha) and Polder Mijzen (600 ha). Total area of wet grassland approximately 1120 ha.

Wet grassland type

Three types of wet grassland are represented:

- *Poo–Lolietum* (C38.12) covers much of the farmland improved for agriculture and is dominated by *Lolium perenne* and *Poa trivialis*.

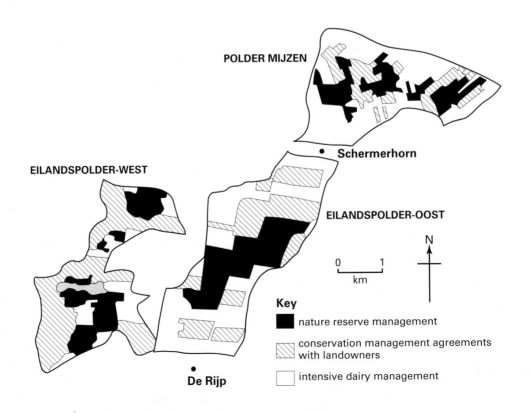

Figure 1 Management regimes at Eilandspolder and Polder Mijzen.

- *Lolio-Potentillion* (C37.242) occurs throughout the reserves and is dominated by *Agrostis stolonifera* and *Alopecurus geniculatus*.

- *Cynosuretum* (C38.12) is present in some fields and is dominated by *Cynosurus cristatus* and *Festuca pratensis*.

These wet grassland types form a matrix with 15 ha of acid swamp vegetation typified by *Phragmites australis* (C53.11) and *Scirpus maritimus* (C53.17) with *Sphagnum* species, *Dryopteris cristata*, *Thelypteris palustris*, *Drosera rotundifolia* and various Orchidaceae.

Soil

Peat and some areas of clay overlying peat.

Hydrology

The whole area is below sea-level and pump-drained. Water levels are 2.3 m below median sea-level in Eilandspolder and 2.4 m below median sea-level in Polder Mijzen. Average soil surface levels in these areas are 1.9–2.2 m below median sea-level.

Climate

Cool, temperate and maritime.
Mean annual precipitation: 700 mm
Average air temperature:
Winter (December–February) 4–6°C
Summer (June–August) 18–20°C.

Designations

Ramsar site and SPA. The area forms part of the Dutch IBA No 038 Zuidelijk Poldergebied, which covers 12 600 ha.

Tenure/ownership

An area of 1208 ha is managed by nature conservation bodies. Staatsbosbeheer (the State Forestry Commission, responsible for conservation) own and manage parts of Polder Mijzen (218 ha) and most of Eilandspolder-Oost (671 ha), while Noordhollands Landschap (a regional landscape conservation NGO) own and manage 323 ha of Eilandspolder-West. The remaining area of the three polders (approximately 820 ha) is scattered and in private, mostly agricultural, ownership (Figure 1).

Mechanisms

The Dutch agri-environment scheme Relatienota was introduced to the area in 1986. Relatienota was conceived in 1975 and allowed the Dutch government to designate 100 000 ha as nature reserves (by purchase of farmland) and a further 100 000 ha as areas where voluntary management agreements would be available to farmers (Reyrink 1988). The initiative provides incentives to farmers for not undertaking intensification works and promotes low-intensity management (eg late summer cutting and low-density grazing). Uptake of management agreements in the Eilandspolder area is currently 65%.

The recently introduced Farming Nature scheme allows the Province of Noord-Holland to compensate farmers for flooding areas of grassland between March and June (providing feeding areas for ducks and waders), protecting nests and for botanical management along drainage channels.

Background

Traditional Dutch polders are flat, open areas reclaimed from saltmarshes or the sea and drained by a network of artificial drainage channels and canals, enabling water-table management. Seasonal water-table regimes are unnatural, being higher in the summer and lower in the winter. Winter inundation still occurs but is rare. In the past, the combination of soil, climate, hydrology and management has created unique conditions for a number of wading birds to breed at high densities on the polders. Typical species are *Tringa totanus*, *Limosa limosa*, *Vanellus vanellus* and recently *Haematopus ostralegus*. *Philomachus pugnax* ceased to breed on Eilandspolder and Polder Mijzen in 1984, probably as a result of agricultural intensification. The importance of these areas is highlighted by the fact that the polders of the Netherlands support approximately half of the European population of *Limosa limosa* (Tucker and Heath 1994).

Agricultural practices in the polders have intensified in recent decades (ie improved drainage, increased fertiliser inputs, earlier mowing and higher stock densities) and have resulted in declining numbers of breeding waders. Conservation of breeding waders involves low-intensity agricultural management and is used to good effect on nature reserves and areas under the Relatienota management agreement scheme.

Grassland management for breeding waders

- Grassland management techniques are varied, ranging from unrestricted agricultural management to low-intensity conservation management. These different techniques are scattered across the whole polder, creating a mosaic of biotope types (Figure 1).

- Grassland management at Polder Mijzen falls into four main categories (Figure 1):

  - a modern dairy management regime with few if any conservation restrictions (approximately 100 ha). Grazing densities are high and mowing occurs in the last week in May and again in August
  - management agreements with farmers – first mowing after 1 June (approximately 50 ha) or 8 June (approximately 50 ha). These areas are aftermath grazed until July at medium to high density. A second cut is taken in August and grazing again takes place until November
  - management agreements with farmers – mown once after 15 June and then aftermath grazed at low density until November (approximately 100 ha)
  - nature reserve management (approximately 100 ha). The area is mown by contractors after 22 June and aftermath grazed at low stock densities until November.

- Grassland management at Eilandspolder-Oost falls into four similar categories (Figure 1):

  - a modern dairy management regime with few restrictions (approximately 200 ha). Areas mown during the last week in May, with a second cut taken in August. Grazing density is high
  - management agreements with farmers – low-intensity grazing regime beginning 1 June with mowing in August (approximately 50 ha).
  - management agreements with farmers – mowing after 15 June, aftermath grazing until November (approximately 200 ha)
  - nature reserve management by Staatsbosbeheer (approximately 200 ha) partly using their own stock (100 Limousin cattle) and also by renting the grazing to private farmers. All grazing is at low density. Half the area is mown in July for hay.

- Grassland management at Eilandspolder-West falls into three categories (Figure 1):

  - a modern dairy management regime (200 ha). Two hay cuts taken in late May and August, both cuts followed by aftermath grazing at high density
  - management agreements with the Ministry of Agriculture (200 ha). Earliest mowing dates vary (ie 1, 8, 15 June), followed by aftermath grazing until November
  - nature reserve management is contracted out to farmers (323 ha), with mowing after 15 June and/or low-intensity grazing until November.

- Eight small areas (9 ha in total) are artificially flooded using a wind pump to provide roosting areas for ducks and waders (Plate 1).

Benefits

- The study demonstrates that manipulating wet grassland to increase wader breeding success is complex and demanding. The importance of an in-depth knowledge of the wet grassland site is highlighted.

- Figure 2 demonstrates the effectiveness of management agreements and reserve management on breeding wader density on Polder Mijzen and Eilandspolder-Oost.

- At Polder Mijzen (Figure 2) reserve management and management agreements appear to benefit breeding waders but there is a discernible negative

Plate 1
Wind pumps are used to create high water level management areas favoured by breeding waders and wildfowl.

F Steenwinkel

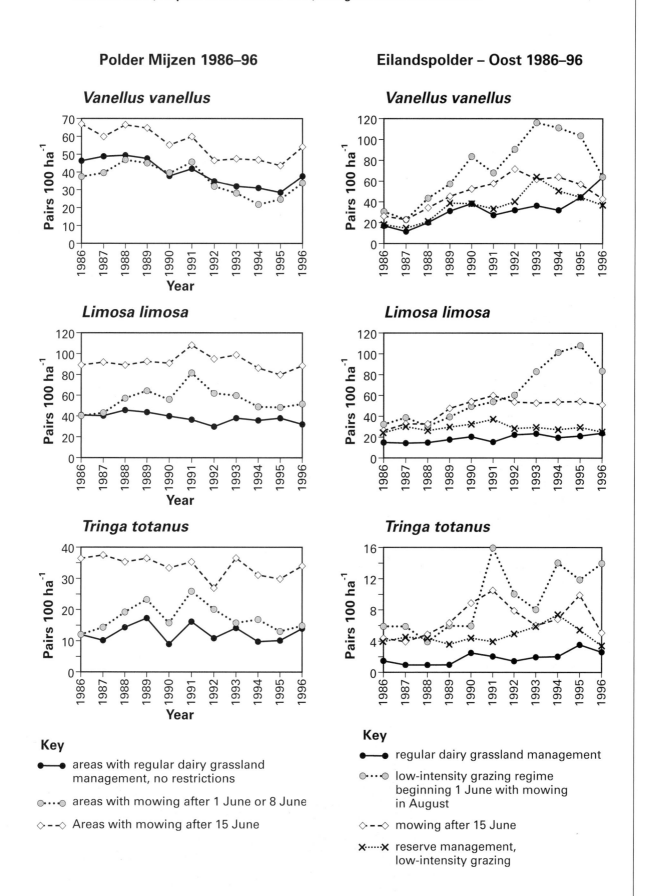

Figure 2 Densities of three breeding wader species at Polder Mijzen and Eilandspolder-Oost between 1986 and 1994 (adapted from Fabritius 1995). Marginal areas are excluded.

H E Fabritius

Plate 2 Low-intensity management coupled with high water levels create ideal conditions for breeding waders such as *Limosa limosa*.

trend in *Vanellus vanellus*. Populations of the two other species, *Tringa totanus* and *Limosa limosa,* appear to be stable, and are currently higher than those found at Eilandspolder-Oost. This is probably due to the greater proportion of land under beneficial management (Plate 2).

■ Overall at Eilandspolder-Oost breeding wader densities seem to be increasing (Figure 2). This is due to beneficial extensive management practices, especially late mowing and the low-intensity grazing regime. Areas managed as nature reserves, unusually, seem to compare poorly with the two

categories of management agreement in this area, most probably due to low fertiliser input and acidification (resulting in a lack of large prey especially worms). *Haematopus ostralegus* density has slowly risen in intensively managed and low-intensity grazed areas. This species has been shown to benefit from increased nutrient inputs. *Vanellus vanellus* is vulnerable to nest trampling as a result of high grazing levels.

■ Wader numbers at Eilandspolder-West on the land managed by Noordhollands Landschap appear to be stable.

References and further reading

Boer, T E den (1995) *Meadowbirds: facts for conservation*. Technical report 16. Vogelbescherming, Zeist. [In Dutch with English summary]

Fabritius, H (1995) Meadow birds in the Mijzenpolder and the Eilandspolder – connections with management, 1986–1993. *Graspieper* 15: 25–32. [In Dutch with English summary]

Reyrink, L A F (1988) Bird Protection in Grassland in the Netherlands. In J R Park (1988) *Environmental Management in Agriculture. European Perspectives*, pp 159–169. Bellhaven Press, London & New York.

Tucker, G M and Heath, M F (1994) *Birds in Europe: their conservation status*. BirdLife International, Cambridge.

Case Study Authors/Consultants: Dr Harry Fabritius (Staatsbosbeheer), Johanna E Winkelman and Eduard Osieck (Vogelbescherming).

Hullo ja Sviby Laht

(Hullo and Sviby Bays), Vormsi, Estonia

Case Study 7

Technique

Low-intensity grassland management for biodiversity

Main management objectives

- To maintain existing biodiversity value and rehabilitate degraded areas

- To sustain a diversity of characteristic plant communities and rare and endangered species, such as orchids (eg *Herminium monorchis*)

- To manage for internationally important migratory and breeding birds

- To monitor in order to guide management.

Location

Along the southern coast of Vormsi island, off the west coast of Estonia. 58°58'N 23°11'E.

Area

Vormsi island (area 93 km²) supports 1 480 ha of natural coastal wet grassland (including coastal reedbeds). Hullo and Sviby Bays include 190 ha of wet grassland and 75 ha of reeds (Figure 1).

Wet grassland type

Three wet grassland associations are well represented:

- *Juncus gerardii* brackish stands (C15.331)

- *Festuca rubra–Agrostis stolonifera* stands (C15.333)

- *Molinia caerulea* stands (C37.312)

Additionally *Carex* swamp (C53.21) vegetation is widespread and occurs in association with the wet grassland types above.

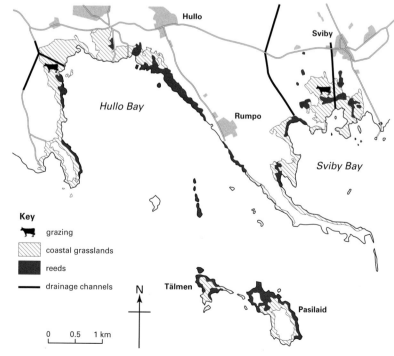

Key

- 🐄 grazing
- ▨ coastal grasslands
- ■ reeds
- — drainage channels

0 0.5 1 km

**Figure 1
Biotopes and management of Hullo and Sviby Bays, Vormsi Island.**

Soil

Saline alluvial soils on marine sand, silt or till.

Hydrology

Seasonal fluctuations in the level of the Baltic Sea are induced by changing meteorological conditions, particularly prevailing wind direction. Low spring and early summer sea-levels are frequently followed by floods in late summer and high autumn and winter levels. Salinity of the water in the Baltic Sea is 6.0–6.5‰ (ie brackish; sea water is approximately 30‰ on average).

Climate

Generally temperate.
Mean annual precipitation: 600 mm
Average air temperature:
Winter (December–February) –1.5° to –5°C
Summer (June–July) 13° to 16.5°C.

Designations

Within the West-Estonia Archipelago Biosphere Reserve (IUCN category IX).

Tenure/ownership

Re-privatisation is in progress, with some land already privately owned. It is planned that the Rumpo peninsula and Hullo Bay islets (Figure 1) will become state-owned in order to ensure that nature conservation objectives are met.

Mechanisms

The Biosphere Reserve administration has produced a conservation strategy for the Vormsi coastal grasslands based on an inventory of the present status, nature conservation value and management of the resource. The strategy is based on large-scale mapping of plant community types and investigations of the past land use utilising archive maps and data. Mechanisms between the Biosphere Reserve administration and local farmers for the conservation management of Hullo and Sviby Bays are being developed based on the strategy. These include recommendations to establish special management areas for which financial incentives are available for farmers to manage the grasslands in a traditional manner, such as by extensive grazing.

Background

Coastal wet grasslands are a characteristic feature of the west Estonian landscape. They have high levels of biodiversity, and support internationally and nationally rare plant communities and species, and migrating and breeding birds. Formerly, coastal grasslands were grazed or cut for hay, but management has declined, resulting in reduction of biodiversity and the extent of characteristic wet grassland communities due to the invasion of *Phragmites australis*, shrubs (eg *Juniperus communis*) or trees (eg *Alnus glutinosa*) (Plate 1).

Coastal wet grasslands are ancient features of Vormsi island that formerly had great local economic value as pasture and hay. However, Soviet collective farming between the 1950s and 1991 often led to over-exploitation of the resource as large herds of young cattle grazed the grasslands. Since independence in 1992, the deterioration in the Estonian agricultural economy has resulted in a considerable decline in grazing, with a consequent reduction in the conservation value of coastal grassland. Currently, land reprivatisation is underway and there is an immediate need to develop and implement appropriate management on remaining grassland areas and to reinstate management on neglected areas in order to recover biodiversity.

Although in recent years management has been very limited, Hullo and Sviby Bays still support well developed pastures with a characteristic natural zonation of lower and upper shore communities (Plate 2). The low-intensity grazing management that persists in these areas needs to be continued in order to maintain their conservation value. In addition, rehabilitation is needed in order to increase the extent of coastal grassland biotope and populations of its characteristic wildlife.

Low-intensity grassland management for biodiversity

- In the past, Hullo and Sviby Bays were extensively grazed by cattle, which created and maintained species and community diversity. Grazing is now limited in extent and consequently species diversity has declined as potentially dominant species, particularly *Phragmites australis* and other tall grasses, have increased (Figure 2). Eutrophication of the Baltic Sea due to sewage discharge has also promoted the expansion of *Phragmites*.

- Under-grazing has also resulted in increasing homogeneity of the vegetation as succession proceeds. Coastal grasslands have become overgrown and unsuitable for migratory geese, which have started feeding and resting in arable fields, resulting in lost and damaged crops.

- Approximately 60 ha of Hullo and Sviby Bays that still support characteristic coastal grassland plant

Chris Joyce

Elle Puurmann

Plate 1 *Phragmites australis* and *Alnus* spp. invade neglected West Estonian coastal grasslands.

Plate 2 Cattle grazing maintains characteristic coastal grassland plant communities, including rare species.

communities and migrating birds are being managed by low-intensity cattle grazing, which is the tradition.

- Cattle grazing maintains an open sward maximising botanical diversity, and provides areas for breeding waders and feeding migrating geese. Grazing also prevents the encroachment of *Phragmites* and woody species. However, intensive grazing may damage the wetter lower shore zone by excessive trampling.

- Grazing in early spring is particularly important because it weakens or kills *Phragmites* in the upper zone of the shore. The recommended grazing intensity is one cow (or horse) and one sheep ha^{-1} on marshy coastal grasslands and 0.7 cows or horses and 1.4 sheep ha^{-1} on drier coastal grasslands with lower productivity. Grazing normally occurs between mid-May and late September, but it may be delayed where ground-nesting birds are present.

- Approximately 70 ha have been identified for rehabilitation. These are areas of former biodiversity value that have deteriorated owing to lack of management and will be restored by grazing with sheep. Hardy breeds of sheep (at high stocking densities) are able to graze coarse grasses and browse shrubs, leaving a relatively open short sward. The resultant sward is attractive to feeding wildfowl and supports an increased botanical diversity.

- If grazing proves impractical to reinstate, alternative forms of vegetation management, particularly cutting by volunteers but also burning when the ground is frozen, will be considered.

- Water quality problems are being considered and a

sewage treatment plant is planned that would reduce eutrophication of the coastal zone in this area by reducing the amount of nutrients entering the sea, thereby slowing the expansion of *Phragmites*.

- Once more typical open swards and plant communities have been re-established, pastures can be managed less intensively using sheep or cattle to maintain their biodiversity value.

- Monitoring is being organised by the Biosphere Reserve authority and consists of regular counts of migrating waterfowl, a repeated census of the breeding bird population of the islets, and repeated mapping and sampling of grassland communities and plant species along fixed transects and in permanent quadrats.

- Monitoring will continue during the implementation of rehabilitation management in order to guide and refine management.

Benefits

- The biotope supports rare and endangered plant species including; *Carex extensa, Salicornia europaea, Selaginella selaginoides* and orchids such as *Herminium monorchis*. Birds that utilise the area include *Anser anser, Branta leucopsis, Cygnus columbianus, Grus grus, Crex crex, Porzana porzana* and *Recurvirostra avosetta*.

- Since grazing declined in 1992, birds characteristic of the open wet grassland biotope have decreased as breeding species in Hullo and Sviby Bays. Table 1 shows the numbers of breeding waterfowl from the early 1960s, when grassland management was regularly practised, to 1997. Four wader

Figure 2 Changes in biotopes at Hullo Bay, Vormsi Island, showing the invasion of *Phragmites australis* after grazing ceased in 1992.

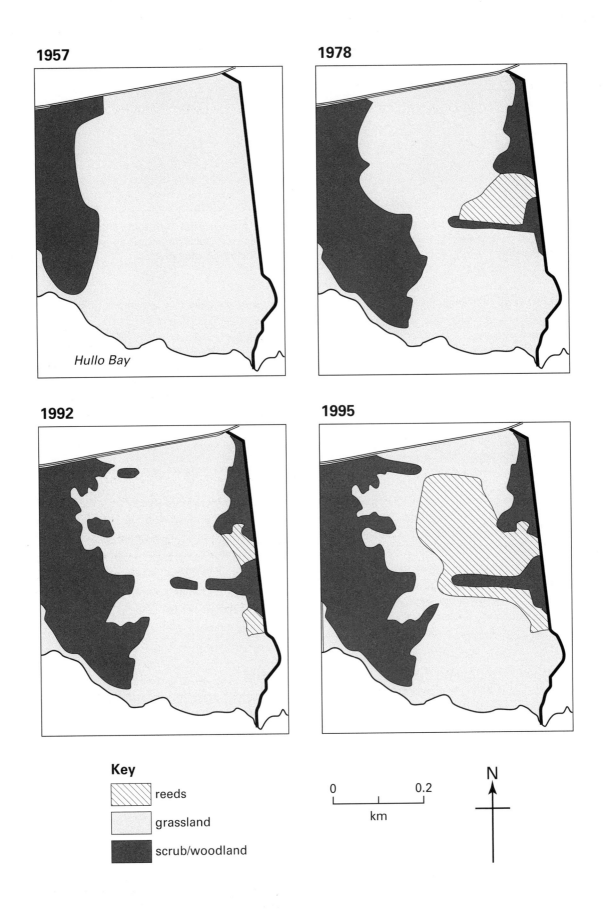

Table 1 Breeding waterfowl of Hullo Bay, Vormsi Island (Ojaste in press).

Species	Number of pairs						
	1962	1969	1972*	1988*	1992	1995*	1997
Cygnus olor		2		32	36	17	29
Anser anser	13	5		18	12	10	10
Anas platyrhynchos	13	4	4	1	5	2	7
Anas clypeata	6	14	10	1	6	2	6
Aythya fuligula	37	1	46	10	15	8	8
Somateria mollissima	4	17	20	23	54	3	81
Haematopus ostralegus	5	6	1	4	5	17	12
Vanellus vanellus	3	23				4	5
Calidris alpina	7	4	3				
Philomachus pugnax		19	4				
Limosa limosa		5	2				
Numenius arquata		3	3				
Tringa totanus	10	28	6	4	32	11	23

*islets were not surveyed in these years

species that formerly bred in Hullo and Sviby Bays have been lost, namely *Limosa limosa, Numenius arquata, Calidris alpina schinzii* and *Philomachus pugnax*. Rehabilitation management aims to restore the numbers and species of such key coastal grassland breeding and migratory birds by increasing the area of open grassland and creating optimal breeding and feeding conditions, such as a short sward with tussocky patches. In doing so, populations of characteristic coastal grassland plant species and areas of typical plant communities will also be increased.

- As well as the nature conservation benefits, it is anticipated that the rehabilitation and conservation management of coastal grasslands at Hullo Bay will provide:

  - a demonstration or reference site, serving as an example of conservation possibilities. This would be used to guide management of other coastal grasslands on Vormsi Island and elsewhere in west Estonia
  - an educational resource, being used to experiment on and monitor the effects of management

  - an eco-tourism attraction.

- Information from the Hullo Bay site will be used to develop an integrated rural development plan for the whole of Vormsi Island which will aim to assimilate conservation, agricultural and tourism objectives in a management plan that protects the coastal grasslands and benefits the local economy and community.

References and further reading

Ojaste, I (in press) Breeding bird fauna of Hullo Bay, Vormsi. *Linnarad* 1998. [In Estonian].

Puurmann, E and Ratas, U (1995) Problems of conservation and management of the west Estonian seashore meadows. In M G Healy and J P Doody (Eds) *Directions in European coastal management*, pp 345–349. Samara Publishing Limited, Cardigan.

Puurmann, E and Ratas, U (1998) The formation, vegetation and management of sea-shore grasslands in west Estonia. In C B Joyce and P M Wade (Eds) *European wet grasslands: biodiversity, management and restoration*, pp 97–110. John Wiley and Sons, Chichester.

Case Study Authors/Consultants: Elle Puurmann and Tiit Randla (West Estonia Archipelago Biosphere Reserve).

Matsalu

Estonia

Techniques

Management planning
Grassland management

Main management objectives

- To maintain breeding and migrating bird populations, including monitoring the effects of management

- To preserve the semi-natural meadow plant communities by traditional management

- To develop facilities and information to promote eco-tourism.

Location

100 km south-west of Tallinn on the west coast of Estonia. 58°40' to 58°50'N, 23°20' to 24°00'E.

Area

Total area of wetland: 48 634 ha, comprising the Matsalu Bay together with the delta of the River Kasari, seashores and over 40 small islets in the bay (Figure 1).

Total area of wet grassland: 7000 ha, comprising coastal grasslands bordering Matsalu Bay in the north and south and occurring on most of the islets (3000 ha), and floodplain grasslands situated in the delta of the River Kasari and associated with other rivers and drainage channels (4000 ha).

Wet grassland type

The coastal grasslands form different zones along the shore according to salinity and soil moisture. The most common community types are:

- *Glauco maritimae – Juncetum gerardii* (C15.331)

- *Festucetum rubrae* (C15.333).

The floodplain grassland communities are determined by flooding regime and the amount of deposited sediments. The most widespread communities are:

- wet floodplain grasslands with tall sedges (ass.

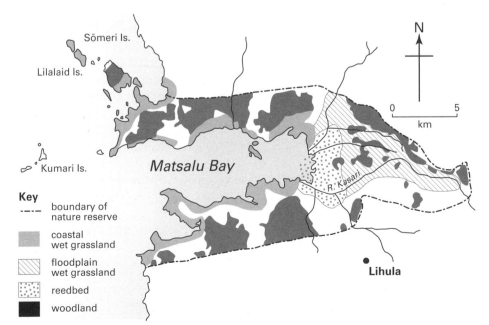

Key

- boundary of nature reserve
- coastal wet grassland
- floodplain wet grassland
- reedbed
- woodland

Sõmeri Is.

Lilalaid Is.

Kumari Is.

Matsalu Bay

R. Kasari

Lihula

N

0 — 5 km

Figure 1
The location of main biotope types at Matsalu Nature Reserve.

Caricetum acutae, Caricetum distichae) and floodplain marshes (ass. *Caricetum elatae*) (C53.21)

- wet floodplain grasslands with tall grasses (ass. *Phalaroidetum*) (C53.16)

- moist floodplain grasslands (ass. *Deschampsieto – Caricetum cespitosae*) (C37.21).

Soil

In the eastern part of Matsalu, soils are rich in clay, moist or wet and alkaline. In coastal areas saline littoral soils and pebble rendzinas are found, and in the river delta alluvial soils occur.

Hydrology

The hydrological network of the Matsalu wetland comprises the shallow water of Matsalu Bay and the lower reaches of drainage channels and rivers which form the River Kasari delta. Although much of the area is drained and water levels are regulated, soils remain predominantly moist or wet and spring floods (in April and May) are common. Additional inundation with seawater can occur during the growing season. Autumn storms raise water levels in the bay and further floods can then occur.

Climate

Generally temperate, characterised by warm summers.

Mean annual precipitation: 600 mm
Average air temperature:
Winter (February) –5.5°C
Summer (July) 17.0°C
Snow cover duration: 100–110 days.

Designations

Ramsar site and National Nature Reserve (generally IUCN category IV but some areas are designated as strict reserves, category I). The area constitutes Matsalu Zaliv, IBA No 005 of the former USSR.

Tenure/ownership

Private and state. During the Soviet period (1944–91) the land was organised into collective farms (from 1948). Since the re-establishment of independence, land reform has been implemented and land is being returned to its former owners.

Mechanisms

A management plan for Matsalu Nature Reserve was developed in 1993 with the support of WWF Sweden.

It serves both as a strategic document and as a detailed action plan for the next few years.

Background

Post-glacial landrise in west Estonia proceeds at a rate of 2–3 mm per year. Consequently, most of the Matsalu wetland is less than 500 years old (although higher parts are up to 2500 years old) and the flat landscape does not generally rise more than 10 m asl. Most grasslands are less than 2 m asl.

The area has been managed by humans since it rose above sea level and most biotopes have been influenced by human activity. Minor drainage activities have long been undertaken, and during the 1920s and 1930s large-scale dredging of the river delta system was carried out and the River Kasari was canalised. Further drainage took place in the 1950s and 1970s. During the last 50 years a gradual abandonment of traditional agricultural practices has occurred. At the same time, increased use of inorganic fertilisers and the concentration of livestock into large farm complexes caused eutrophication. The 1990s have witnessed a dramatic decrease in agricultural production with a consequent acceleration of ecological degradation of semi-natural biotopes. For example, the floristic diversity of the wet grasslands has declined as plant litter accumulated and robust herbaceous and woody species, such as *Deschampsia caespitosa*, *Carex* spp, *Alnus* and *Salix*, invaded (Truus 1998, Truus and Tõnisson 1998).

Matsalu is a wetland of international importance. The flora of the wetland is exceptional with approximately 700 species recorded, many of which are listed in the Red Data Book of the Baltic Region (Kaljuste 1994). Biotope diversity is also high and includes: brackish water; coastal pioneer vegetation; extensive reedbeds; coastal grasslands; alvars; and woodland including wooded pastures and meadows. In addition, Matsalu supports one of the largest complexes of floodplain grassland in Europe.

Matsalu is one of the most important nesting and stop-over sites for migratory birds in northern Europe. Over 260 species nest in the area or use it during their migration, of which approximately 150 species are listed in the Red Data Book of the Baltic Region (Kaljuste 1994). Breeding birds include *Anser anser* (300 pairs), *Botaurus stellaris* (12–15 pairs), *Somateria mollissima* (over 3000 pairs), *Branta leucopsis*, *Haliaeetus albicilla*, *Limosa limosa*, *Philomachus pugnax*, *Calidris alpina* and *Crex crex*. Among the most numerous migratory birds in the spring are 60 000 *Gavia arctica* and *Gavia stellata*, daily counts of up to 9000 *Branta leucopsis*, 14 000 *Anser anser*, *A. fabalis* and *A. albifrons*, 4000 *Cygnus cygnus*, 16 000 *Cygnus columbianus*, 15 000 *Anas platyrhynchos*, 10 000 *Anas acuta*, 9000 *Anas penelope*, 1.6 million *Clangula hyemalis*, 380 000 *Melanitta fusca*, 190 000 *Melanitta nigra*, 11 000 *Aythya marila*, 10 000 *Bucephala clangula*, up to 10 000 *Mergus merganser* and up to 150 *Mergus albellus*. During the autumn migration, 15 000 *Grus grus*, 7000 *Anser anser*, *A. fabalis* and *A. albifrons*, 1000 *Cygnus cygnus*, 1000 *Cygnus columbianus*, up to 300 000 *Clangula hyemalis* and up to 500 *Mergus albellus* pass through during the season.

Over 40 species of mammals have been observed in the wetland, including numerous *Lutra lutra* and five pairs of *Castor fiber*.

Management planning

The Matsalu management plan encourages a strategic approach to conservation:

- The size and diversity of the wetland necessitated zoning the area in order to facilitate and target the reinstatement and continuation of management. These zones are based on natural differences linked to the conservation priorities of each zone. There are three zones within which different management strategies are used:
  - zone 1 (strict reserves) where human intervention is minimised (mostly small islands with high bird value)
  - zone 2 (special management) where specific management is carried out to conserve special communities (eg floodplain meadows, coastal pastures)
  - zone 3 (restricted use) where some limitations are applied, such as road or house construction and wood cutting, that are additional to the general nature conservation rules of the nature reserve.

- In strict reserves (zone 1) human impact is minimised. The main values are breeding birds and the main threats are from disturbance and egg-collecting. Only wardening and bird monitoring are undertaken.

- In the special management zone (zone 2) there are plans for scrub clearance, mowing or grazing, some burning to remove the accumulation of litter in grasslands, marking of tourist trails, building of information boards and birdwatching towers. Most floodplain and coastal grassland fall within this zone.

- Management according to the plan started in 1996. In the first year, scrub removal was a priority while cutting the floodplain grasslands was a focus of the second year. Indeed, in 1997, approximately 3000 ha of floodplain grassland (three-quarters of the total area) was cut. More recently, management

of the meadow communities by supporting appropriate farming practices has become a priority task of the Matsalu Nature Reserve, along with an increase in the area of wet grasslands being managed.

Grassland management

- Management activities have been prioritised for each grassland area, and financial subsidies from the state budget have been calculated for these actions (Table 1). The greatest threat to grassland biotopes is succession owing to neglect so the highest priority actions are aimed at restoring and maintaining conservation value of grasslands that are still being, or were until recently, regularly managed. Actions include scrub clearance and implementing cutting or grazing prescriptions, as these create open conditions suitable for nesting and feeding birds and a diversity of plant species and communities.

- Floodplain meadows are usually cut for hay in July, and grazing of the aftermath sometimes takes place in the autumn. Until the 1970s, the floodplain meadows were regularly cut for hay but since then the cessation of management in some parts has led to a decrease in plant community diversity. The vegetation has became more uniform as robust sedges and grasses, and woody species invade (Truus 1998). A dense litter layer accumulates on the soil surface and the open grassland landscape becomes enclosed by shrubs and trees, both of which reduce feeding and nesting opportunities for wading birds (Mägi *et al* in press). Neglect of floodplain meadows was followed by a decrease in the number of breeding waders, such as *Limosa limosa*, *Philomachus pugnax*, *Vanellus vanellus* and *Tringa totanus*, and an increase in the number of passerines associated with scrub and woodland (Figure 2).

- Neglect of the coastal pastures has led to substantial declines in the numbers of key wader species breeding on the grasslands (Table 2). Traditionally, coastal grasslands have been grazed and therefore maintenance and restoration management for this biotope focuses on this treatment. Grazing typically takes place from mid-May until late September and includes both cattle and sheep (and sometimes horses) grazing the same site at a density of approximately one cow and one sheep ha^{-1} (Table 1). However, grazing may be delayed where ground-nesting birds are present. The management plan for Matsalu prescribes that grassland management should not take place before 15 June or, if spring is late, 5 July, to protect nesting birds. Grazing encourages the

Table 1 Management activities and support costs for a selection of wet grassland sites within the Matsalu Nature Reserve management plan.

Name	Area (ha)	Priority level	Action	€ yr⁻¹ (1998 costings)
Kloostri floodplain meadow	421	Primary	Mowing	1836
			Hay removal	1836
			Burning	1146
		Secondary	Erecting birdwatching tower	1146
			Providing information board	207
Rõude floodplain meadow	362	Primary	Mowing	1446
			Hay removal	1446
			Scrub clearance	918
		Secondary	Erecting birdwatching tower	1146
			Providing information board	207
Põgari-Sassi coastal pasture	219	Primary	Grazing subsidies: 150 cattle and 300 sheep	6701
			Scrub clearance	344
		Secondary	Erecting birdwatching tower	2020
			Providing information board	207
Keemu–Matsalu–Meelva–Metsküla coastal pasture	350	Primary	Grazing subsidies: 350 cattle and 350 sheep	11 016
			Scrub clearance	344
		Secondary	Erecting three birdwatching towers	6059
			Providing information boards	620
Saastna–Teorehe coastal pasture	21	Primary	Grazing subsidies: 20 cattle and 20 sheep	643
		Secondary	Providing information board	207

Table 2 Key wading bird species breeding on coastal grasslands in Matsalu Nature Reserve.

Species	Mean number of pairs yr⁻¹		
	1957–60	1967–71	1992–93
Calidris alpina	315	155	85
Philomachus pugnax	240	115	20
Limosa limosa	220	170	95

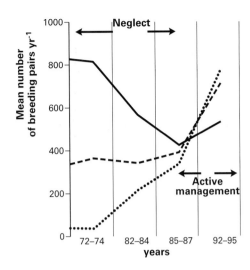

Waders including *Limosa limosa, Philomachus pugnax, Vanellus vanellus* and *Tringa totanus.*

- - - - Passerines of open landscapes including *Motacilla flava, Anthus pratensis* and *Alauda arvensis.*

·········· Passerines of woodland, scrub and reedbeds including *Phylloscopus trochilus, Acrocephalus schoenobaenus, Carpodacus roseus* and *Emberiza schoeniclus.*

Figure 2 Changes in breeding bird numbers using Kasari River floodplain grassland, Matsalu Nature Reserve, 1972–95.

plant species diversity of coastal grasslands by creating and maintaining heterogeneity of vegetation structure and composition.

- Burning neglected grasslands is used in exceptional circumstances in order to remove accumulated litter where no other form of vegetation management is practicable. Burning takes place in early spring, before bird migration has begun, and when the snow has melted but the soil surface is still frozen or wet, so that risks to organisms wintering on the soil surface or in the upper soil horizons are minimised.

- Secondary management activities focus on encouraging and managing tourists, and comprise erection of birdwatching towers and information provision (Table 1, Plate 1). Actions such as wardening, bird monitoring and burning management are undertaken by staff of the nature reserve, whilst landowners are given incentives to undertake scrub control, grazing and mowing of grasslands.

Plate 1
Information provision is a key element of the Matsalu Nature Reserve management plan.

Benefits

- Burning to reduce litter in the mid-1980s and the subsequent reinstatement of the traditional hay meadow management regime has resulted in a recovery of the breeding wader population associated with the open meadows (Figure 2). The open landscape passerines (eg *Motacilla flava, Anthus pratensis* and *Alauda arvensis*) have also benefited. Passerines associated with woodland (eg *Phylloscopus trochilus* and *Carpodacus roseus*) and reed/scrub (eg *Acrocephalus schoenobaenus* and *Emberiza schoeniclus*) have continued to increase, probably because of positive management in these biotopes.

- The preparation of the Matsalu Nature Reserve management plan:

  - enabled management needs to be prioritised and implemented effectively
  - promoted co-operation between nature reserve staff and local people
  - facilitated a system of financial support from the government for farmers and landowners who participate in wetland management as part of the plan, the first such agri-environment scheme in Estonia.

References and further reading

Kaljuste, T (1994) Matsalu – valuable wetland and bird paradise. *WWF Baltic Bulletin* 1: 7–10.

Leibak, E and Lutsar, L (Eds) (1996) *Estonian coastal and floodplain meadows*. Kirjameeste Kirjastus, Tallinn.

Mägi, E, Kastepold, T and Lotman, A (in press) Ornithological monitoring and wetland management in Matsalu. In A Kuresoo (Ed) *Bird numbers 1995. Bird monitoring for conservation*. Proceedings of the 13th International Conference of EBCC, Pärnu.

Pork, K (1985) The flood-plain plant communities of the Kasari River, their utilisation and conservation. In E Kumari (Ed) *Matsalu – a wetland of international importance*, pp 88–112. [In Estonian with English summary]

Rebassoo, H-E (1985) Plant communities of seashore meadows in Matsalu. In E Kumari (Ed) *Matsalu – a wetland of international importance*, pp 77–87. [In Estonian with English summary]

Truus, L (1998) Influence of management cessation on reedbed and floodplain vegetation on the Kloostri floodplain meadow in the delta of the Kasari River, Estonia. *Proceedings of the Estonian Academy of Sciences, Biology and Ecology* 47: 58–72.

Truus, L and Tõnisson, A (1998) The ecology of floodplain grasslands in Estonia. In C B Joyce and P M Wade (Eds) *European wet grasslands: biodiversity, management and restoration*, pp 49–60. John Wiley, Chichester.

Case Study Author/Consultant: Laimi Truus (Institute of Ecology, Tallinn).

De Veenkampen

Netherlands

Technique

Experimental wet grassland restoration

Main management objectives

- To test the usefulness of haying, topsoil stripping and raising the water level for the restoration of botanical diversity to wet grasslands. These measures were expected to reduce the nutrient status of the soil and to increase the botanical diversity of formerly intensively managed grasslands

- To devise prescriptions for the restoration of attractive, flower-rich, moderately productive grasslands and low-productivity vegetation types with a high botanical diversity.

Location

Forms part of the Wageningse Binnenveld in the former floodplain of the River Rhine, near Wageningen, Netherlands. 51°54'N 05°38'E.

Area

Total area of Wageningse Binnenveld: 2100 ha. De Veenkampen experimental area is 13 ha (Plate 1).

Wet grassland type

Before 1945 the Binnenveld was a wetland covered by *Cirsio–Molinietum* (C37.312) grassland. The wet, species-rich community supported nationally rare plant species such as *Gymnadenia conopsea, Dactylorhiza maculata, Gentiana pneumonanthe, Cirsium dissectum, Carex hostiana, Carex flacca, Carex pulicaris* and *Briza media*.

Following agricultural intensification after 1945 the managed grassland that replaced much of this is species-poor, dominated by *Lolium perenne, Poa trivialis, Elymus repens* and *Taraxacum officinale* (C81.2).

P R Stad

Plate 1
Aerial photograph of the De Veenkampen experimental area. Plots of 100 m² are replicated five times. In the foreground is the high water level area, and to the left is the area where water levels remain low. The surrounding grassland is farmed intensively.

Soil

Peaty clay, overlying peat. Soil pH 5.6. Before 1945, soil organic content was 30% but oxidation after drainage has reduced this to 25%.

Hydrology

De Veenkampen lies in the seepage zone between the higher sandy 'Veluwe' infiltration area and the low floodplains of the Rhine. Before drainage, the area was naturally influenced by upwelling calcium-rich groundwater. The groundwater level in summer was 30–40 cm below the soil surface, in winter the area was flooded by groundwater seepage and precipitation. After drainage the seepage water barely reached the rooted zone and flooding no longer occurred in winter.

Climate

Cool, temperate and maritime.
Mean annual precipitation: 770 mm
Average air temperature:
Winter (max and min) 8.4°C and 2.0°C
Summer (max and min) 19.1°C and 8.9°C.

Designations

About 400 ha of the Wageningse Binnenveld is designated to become part of the Relatienota agri-environment scheme (see also Case Study 6).

Tenure/ownership

Currently privately owned by farmers. In the future 400 ha will be bought and restored by the state, under the management of Staatsbosbeheer (the State Forestry Commission, responsible for conservation).

Mechanisms

Experimental and subsequent restoration work funded by the government under the Relatienota agri-environment scheme, which aims to preserve biodiversity in the Netherlands by creating and managing a network of nature conservation sites.

Background

In the Netherlands, drainage and the use of fertilisers have caused a decrease in the extent of low-productivity, species-rich wet grasslands. It is estimated that only 0.7% (7585 ha) of the remaining grassland resource falls into this type of grassland. Maintenance of biodiversity increasingly requires restoration of species-rich grassland, and large-scale measures are being taken to reduce grassland production and raise water levels.

De Veenkampen was established as an experimental grassland in 1978 in order to examine the effect of management regime and raising the water table on nutrient availability, and plant species composition and dynamics. At the beginning of the 20th century the vegetation of the site was a species-rich *Cirsio-Molinietum* mire grassland. Known locally as Blauwgraslanden (blue grassland), this community requires a low nutrient level and a high water table. After 1945, the area was drained, levelled and managed intensively for agriculture. From 1968–78 the average annual applications of nitrogen, phosphorous and potassium fertiliser were 300, 33 and 125 kg ha^{-1} year^{-1} respectively. The grassland was cut several times during the year and/or grazed by cattle. The average yield of this productive, species-poor grassland was 10–11 tonne ha^{-1} year^{-1}. Restoration management started in 1978 when fertiliser application ceased and the above ground biomass was cut and removed twice a year. Restoration experiments continued when the groundwater level was raised in 1985, and topsoil was stripped in 1991.

The research described supports the aims of the Nature Development Plan, a Dutch government policy document aimed at counteracting the national loss of biodiversity. The plan facilitates the creation of an ecologically coherent network of nationally and internationally important ecosystems. To help create this network by 2020, 50 000 ha of intensively used agricultural land is to be set aside. A fifth of this total will be converted to species-rich grassland.

Soil impoverishment

- Lowering grassland production is known to increase species diversity by allowing plants with a lower maximal height, or slower growth, to compete with more vigorous plant species. The optimal grassland production for high botanical diversity is generally lies between 4–6 tonne ha^{-1} year^{-1} (Oomes 1992).

- The effects of three management practices on grassland production and botanical diversity were investigated:

  - cutting and hay removal in June and September
  - topsoil stripping by rotovating to a depth of 5 or 10 cm and removing the loosened material
  - both treatments combined with raising the water table.

- Nine years of cutting and hay removal achieved the desired decrease in grassland productivity to levels of 6–7 tonne ha^{-1} year^{-1}. In the subsequent five years it declined further to 5–6 tonne ha^{-1} year^{-1}.

- As dry matter production declined there was a decrease in the proportion of indicators of high fertility such as *Lolium perenne, Elymus repens, Alopecurus pratensis* and *Taraxacum officinale* and an increase in species such as *Holcus lanatus, Ranunculus repens, Rumex acetosa* and *Juncus* spp.

- The annual dry matter yield on this peaty clay soil mainly decreased due to the restrictions on the availability of potassium. The amount and availability of nitrogen and phosphorous in the soil remained high.

- Under the cutting and hay removal regime, the number of plant species decreased over time (whilst species composition slowly changed) but characteristic species of the Blauwgraslanden did not return.

- In 1991, topsoil stripping to depths of 5 and 10 cm was expected to reduce soil mineral availability to a greater extent than mowing and removal of a grass crop (Plate 2). Although the production of the vegetation that appeared spontaneously was very low, after 4–5 years it produced the same yield as undisturbed grassland. Biomass production was independent of water level. Only the lower nutrient concentrations in the biomass indicated soil impoverishment.

M J M Oomes

Plate 2
The first step in the turf-stripping experiment at De Veenkampen was to rotovate the soil to either 5 or 10 cm, thereafter the loosened soil was removed.

Raising water levels

- Half the study area was restored to high water table management by bunding to retain rainwater and allow infiltration of water through the drainage system in the summer. Water levels were 20–30 cm higher in this section and splash-flooding was maintained during winter and spring.

- The amount of seepage water in the soil is now less and that of rainwater greater, so the current balance between both water types is different from that in the past. Infiltration of seepage water could be stimulated by stopping drainage and enlarging the area under restoration.

- Raising the water level in 1985 lowered the decomposition of organic matter and nitrogen mineralisation in the soil, effectively lowering nutrient availability. In wet fields where cut vegetation was removed, availability of phosphorous and potassium decreased sharply (Oomes 1992, Oomes *et al* 1996).

- Simply raising water levels on clay soils with high organic content does not decrease grassland production. Dry matter production and nutrient uptake barely decreased, as plant species adapted to grow under these wetter conditions became more prevalent, eg *Agrostis stolonifera, Alopecurus geniculatus, Glyceria fluitans* and *Ranunculus repens*.

- Raised water levels resulted in a rapid establishment of species indicative of wet conditions, most of which colonised from nearby drainage channels. The number of species disappearing did not increase (Table 1).

Benefits

- In the first phase of restoration, grassland management must focus on maximising the removal of nutrients, until the production becomes less than 6 tonne ha[-1] year[-1]. Even then aftermath grazing or a second cut is important to create an open sward in autumn and spring which stimulates the germination of seeds and the establishment of seedlings.

- Restoration by hay cutting and removal reduced the dry matter yield to the 1941–46 level. Analysis of amounts of nutrients taken up by vegetation and concentrations in the biomass indicated that phosphorous availability was high and nitrogen was not limited but that potassium levels were very low. This is the opposite situation to that found in 1941–46 when a high potassium concentration and a low phosphorous availability were normal. There is uncertainty about whether the original Blauwgraslanden nutrient target can be attained in the near future or indeed ever.

- Topsoil stripping created a more diverse sward than hay-making alone (Table 1). The bare soil and resulting open sward created favourable

Table 1 Changes in number of plant species at De Veenkampen over time under different management practices.

	Mean number of plant species under different treatments					
	Dry (two cuts)	Wet (two cuts)	Dry (5 cm topsoil stripped)	Wet (5 cm topsoil stripped)	Dry (10 cm topsoil stripped)	Wet (10 cm topsoil stripped)
In 1987	20.4	19.2				
In 1992			24.8	23.8	29.0	39.6
In 1996	15.0	24.4	24.4	27.0	32.2	43.4
New	3.2	14.4	11.8	11.4	15.0	15.8
Constant	11.8	10.0	12.6	15.6	17.2	27.6
Disappeared	8.6	9.2	12.4	7.8	11.6	11.4
% of 1987	42%	48%				
% of 1992			49%	33%	40%	29%

Table 2 Plant species previously common in the Blauwgraslanden and their actual distribution on plots without and with topsoil removal (adapted from Geerts *et al* 1996).

Species previously common in the Blauwgraslanden	Present (1995) in plots without topsoil removal (✳). Additional species recorded between 1985 and 1994 (O).	Present (1995) in plots with topsoil removal in 1985 (✳). Additional species recorded between 1985 and 1994 (O).
Agrostis stolonifera	✳	✳
Holcus lanatus	✳	✳
Juncus conglomeratus	✳	✳
Cardamine pratensis	✳	✳
Carex panicea	✳	✳
Agrostis canina	✳	✳
Ranunculus flammula	✳	✳
Thalictrum flavum	✳	✳
Anthoxanthum odoratum	✳	✳
Galium uliginosum	✳	✳
Ranunculus acris	✳	✳
Vicia cracca	✳	✳
Cirsium palustre	✳	✳
Equisetum palustre	✳	✳
Plantago lanceolata	✳	✳
Lythrum salicaria	O	✳
Potentilla erecta	O	✳
Festuca rubra	O	✳
Leucanthemum vulgare	O	✳
Carex nigra		✳
Viola persicifolia		✳
Galium palustre		✳
Gentiana pneumonanthe		✳
Molinia caerulea		✳
Phragmites australis		✳
Carex hostiana		✳
Lysimachia vulgaris		✳
Prunella vulgaris		O
Viola canina		O
Achillea ptarmica	O	

The following previously common Blauwgraslanden species have not returned to the sward under any of the experimental applications: *Filipendula ulmaria, Centaurea jacea, Danthonia decumbens, Briza media, Festuca ovina, Agrostis capillaris, Eriophorum angustifolium, Luzula campestris, Carex pulicaris, Cirsium dissectum, Succisa pratensis, Rhinanthus angustifolius, Linum catharticum, Valeriana dioica, Gymnadenia conopsea, Leontodon saxatilis* and *Polygala vulgaris*.

germination and establishment conditions for several years. Species that had occurred on the site 50 years ago and which had been absent for many years regenerated from persistent seeds in the seedbank, eg *Carex pallescens, Carex panicea, Carex oederi, Carex hostiana, Gentiana pneumonanthe* and *Viola persicifolia* (Table 2).

■ Topsoil stripping is an effective method of restoring species diversity. In the absence of this technique, recovery would be very lengthy because the soil seedbank is the only source of species that have disappeared from the sward. Stripping to 10 cm depth was found to be most effective. However, the overall potential damage to the soil seedbank must be carefully considered.

■ A combination of a rise in groundwater level and topsoil stripping is optimal for an increase in wet grassland species diversity. However, nutrient removal and raising water levels are only partly successful because not all the desirable species have viable seed remaining in the seedbank. Moreover, the chances of natural colonisation are low due to biotope fragmentation and the lack of seed transport by winter flooding. Active reintroduction is therefore deemed necessary, but may not be feasible until nutrient availability matches the desired restoration target.

References and further reading

Berendse, F, Oomes, M J M, Altena, H J and Elberse, W Th (1992) Experiments on the restoration of species-rich meadows in The Netherlands. *Biological Conservation* 62: 59–65.

Berendse, F, Oomes, M J M, Altena, H J and de Visser, W (1994) A comparative study of nitrogen flows in two similar meadows affected by different groundwater levels. *Journal of Applied Ecology* 31: 40–48.

Geerts, R H E M, Ketelaars, J J M H, Oomes, M J M, Korevaar, H and van der Werf, A K (1996) Reintroduction of grassland species. In *Annual Report 1995 – AB-DLO*, pp 65–68. AB-DLO, Wageningen.

Oomes, M J M (1992) Yield and species density of grasslands during restoration management. *Journal of Vegetation Science* 3: 271–274.

Oomes, M J M (1997) Management of the groundwater-table and changes in grassland production, nutrient availability and biodiversity. In *Management for Grassland Biodiversity*. Proceedings of EGF Occasional Symposium, 1997. Warszawa-Lomza, Poland.

Oomes, M J M, Olff, H and Altena, H J (1996) Effects of vegetation management and raising the water-table on nutrient dynamics and vegetation change in a wet grassland. *Journal of Applied Ecology* 33: 576–588.

Case Study Authors/Consultants: Thies Oomes and Hein Korevaar (AB-DLO, Netherlands).

Vecdaugava

Latvia

Technique

Restoration management for breeding waders

Main management objective

- To restore wet grassland breeding areas for nationally important wader populations

Location

The Vecdaugava peninsula lies in the River Daugava estuary, 0.5–1 km from the Gulf of Riga, in Riga City, Latvia. 57°03'N 24°05'E.

Area

Total area of wetland: 270 ha
Total area of wet grassland: 35 ha.

Wet grassland type

The grassland area includes hydrophytic tall herb communities (C37.1 and C37.21), brackish upper shore communities (C15.331, C15.333 and C15.339) and mesophilic hay meadows (C38.2). Pioneer vegetation of salt muds (C15.12) and open, siliceous grasslands of sandy conditions (C35.22) are also present. The wet grassland is surrounded by reedbeds, scrub and open water.

Soil

Alluvial soils on sand.

Hydrology

Vecdaugava peninsula is surrounded by an ox-bow connected with the Daugava River. The water is slightly brackish (0.5–2.0‰). The water level is dependent on wind conditions, rising when the wind blows water from the Gulf of Riga into the Daugava River estuary. The highest tides occur mainly in autumn; during the summer the tidal range is up to 50 cm.

Climate

Generally temperate, characterised by warm summers.
Mean annual precipitation: 550 mm
Average air temperature:
Winter (January) –4°C
Summer (July) 16°C.

Designations

Nature Reserve or Dabas liegums (IUCN category IV).

Tenure/ownership

The grassland area is state owned and managed by the Riga Environmental Protection Board.

Mechanisms

Management in 1995 was funded by the Swedish Environmental Protection Agency. Other management has been undertaken under agreement between Riga Environmental Protection Board and local farmers and also by using volunteers.

Background

Wet grassland is one of the rarest biotopes in the coastal zone of the Gulf of Riga. There are only six small grassland areas along the coast, mainly situated close to river mouths or breakwaters. These small coastal areas hold assemblages of nationally rare and threatened bird species, and hold a significant part of the total Latvian population for several of these species (Opermanis 1995).

Since 1988, these wet grasslands have deteriorated due to changes in human agricultural activity, notably the cessation of cattle grazing and mowing. This has caused the expansion of both reedbeds and scrub. As a result the sites have partially or totally lost their importance for breeding waders. In the past, Vecdaugava supported populations of the following waders: *Tringa totanus*, *Philomachus pugnax* and *Limosa limosa*, all of which are declining and are included in the Red Data Book of Latvia (Ingelög *et al* 1993). Additionally, *Vanellus vanellus* and *Gallinago gallinago* still occur at Vecdaugava, both species having declined in Latvia over the last 20 years (Strazds *et al* 1994).

The main reason for the decline in breeding wader numbers was a deterioration in the structure of the breeding habitat, ie an increase in tall vegetation. A short, variable 5–20 cm sward, depending on the bird species, is required during the egg-laying period. The maintenance of such a biotope relied on traditional agriculture, especially mowing and cattle grazing. The cessation of these activities occurred because keeping cattle and other domestic animals became economically unprofitable, and the establishment of a strict nature protection regime in the territory in 1987 unwisely precluded any human intervention. As a result, neighbouring reedbeds encroached onto wet grassland, and scrub and young trees (*Betula pendula*, *Pinus sylvestris* and *Salix cinerea*) appeared. Fortunately the semi-natural hydrology of the site remained unaffected during this period.

Recently, specific measures have been undertaken to restore the wet meadow biotopes. These include reinstating grazing and mowing, and burning.

Restoration management for breeding waders

- Preliminary management in March 1993 involved the uncontrolled burning of approximately 7 ha of grass and reedbed (Figure 1). Subsequent burns were under controlled conditions (see below).

- In March 1995, another approximately 20 ha of grass was burned (Figure 1). The burning was done immediately after the snow melt (ie before the arrival of waders) in favourable wind conditions. Three people conducted the burn in the presence of the fire-brigade. This was followed by clearance, using chainsaws, of trees and shrubs from the entire grassland area.

- In August 1995, approximately 10 ha was burned, and approximately 10 ha mown for hay and left ungrazed (Plate 1, Figure 1). Additionally, the soil surface along the edges of the reedbeds was rotovated using a tractor, to a depth of 20 cm, to prevent reedbed expansion; in total about 5 ha was treated (Plate 2).

- In April 1996, a further 5 ha of wet grassland was burned (Figure 1).

- From 1996, horse grazing was introduced. Grazing by 10–15 animals took place from May to August.

Otars Opermanis

Plate 1
In August 1995 10 ha of rank vegetation were mown for hay.

Otars Opermanis

Plate 2
In August 1995 areas were cleared of rank vegetation by burning (right) and rotovation (left).

These animals were allowed to roam the whole wetland area. A fence was erected in 1995 to contain grazing animals (Figure 1). However, observations show that horses feed mainly in the drier central and northern part along the road. The wet grasslands along the edges mostly remain ungrazed.

- In July 1997, mowing took place on approximately 10–15 ha (Figure 1). Mowing took place after 15 July to avoid damaging nests and young birds, but there is a perception amongst farmers that this produces poorer quality fodder. The mowing, as well as horse grazing, was possible due to an agreement between a local farm and the Riga Environmental Protection Board.

- The number of breeding waders was monitored annually from 1990 until 1997 (except for 1991). Counts were performed 3–5 times per season from late April to early June.

Figure 1 Management undertaken at Vecdaugava during its restoration, 1993–96.

Spring 1993   **Spring 1995**

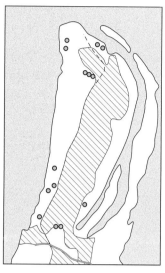

Summer 1995

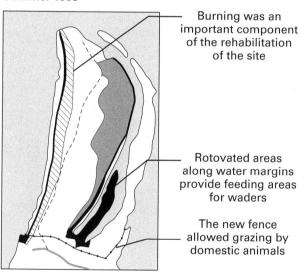

Burning was an
important component
of the rehabilitation
of the site

Rotovated areas
along water margins
provide feeding areas
for waders

The new fence
allowed grazing by
domestic animals

Spring 1996   **Summer 1997**

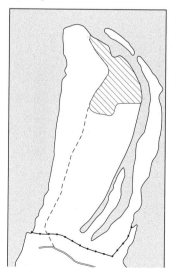 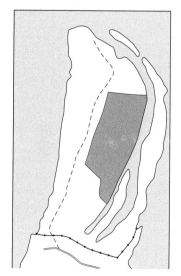

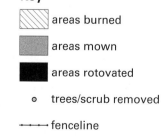

Key

[hatched] areas burned

[grey] areas mown

[black] areas rotovated

o trees/scrub removed

•—• fenceline

Benefits

- Breeding numbers of *Vanellus vanellus*, *Limosa limosa* and *Tringa totanus* had significantly decreased since the mid-1980s, with the lowest levels being reached from 1992 to 1994 (Figure 2). Since the 1995 breeding season, wader numbers have been increasing. This can be attributed to the restoration and improved conservation management of the site.

- During the early part of the management period breeding was not recorded for some species. *Limosa limosa* probably did not breed in 1994. *Philomachus pugnax* ceased to breed in 1992 (the site formerly supported up to five breeding females). However, in 1997, a lek of 13 males returned to the site.

- Burning of old grass and reeds has been the most frequently used management technique on the site. This method initially produces very open areas, but changes occur rapidly in May when vegetation begins to develop, and very soon islands of taller vegetation appear. Burning provides excellent nesting sites for *Vanellus vanellus*, which need very short vegetation or none at all. However, nesting of other species (eg *Tringa totanus* and *Limosa limosa*) can be delayed because of their requirement for taller vegetation. Burning is a good technique especially if alternative management is not possible owing to financial reasons.

- Approximately 10 ha of the grassland was mown in 1995 and left ungrazed. By the following spring, during the egg-laying period, the sward was about 15 cm in height, leaving only scattered shorter patches. In this area, higher breeding densities of *Limosa limosa* and *Tringa totanus* were recorded. *Gallinago gallinago* also bred, but numbers remained stable. *Vanellus vanellus* was not present in the mown but ungrazed area, preferring areas with shorter vegetation.

- Rotovation of reedbed edges created ideal feeding conditions for wader species, and areas treated in this way were also used by *Vanellus vanellus* for nesting.

- The removal of trees and scrub from within and around the wet grassland area in 1995 improved wader nesting success by removing perches for predatory birds, eg Corvidae. In 1994 all *Vanellus vanellus* clutches failed to hatch, owing to predation, but in the season following bush and tree removal, 10 nests out of 15 hatched young.

Figure 2 Numbers of key breeding waders at Vecdaugava, 1990–97. Black bar – minimum number. Hatched bar – maximum number. Note that the site was not surveyed in 1991.

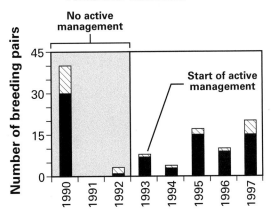

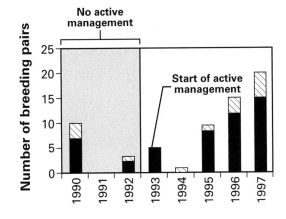

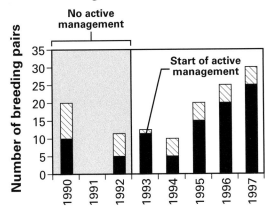

References and further reading

Ingelög, T, Andersson, R and Tjernberg, M (1993) *Red Data Book of the Baltic Region*. Swedish Threatened Species Unit, Uppsala.

Opermanis, O (1995) Recent changes in breeding bird fauna at the seacoast of the Gulf of Riga. In M G H Healy and J P Doody (Eds), *Directions in European Coastal Management*, pp 361–368. Samara Publishing, Cardigan.

Strazds, M, Priednieks, J, Vaverins, G (1994) Latvijas putnu skaits. *Putni daba* 4: 3–19. {In Latvian]

Case Study Author/Consultant: Otars Opermanis (Museum of Zoology, University of Latvia)

Marais de la Vacherie

Case Study 11

France

Techniques

Water management

Grasslands management

Main management objectives

- To maintain and restore wet grassland

- To act as a demonstration site for the maintenance of nature conservation interests in wetlands using extensive farming systems

- To increase the numbers of species of conservation concern (those on Annex I of EU Birds Directive, in the French Red Data book, or in the EU Habitats Directive), specifically breeding birds such as *Limosa limosa, Tringa totanus, Vanellus vanellus, Chlidonias niger, Anas querquedula*; migratory species such as *Limosa limosa, Philomachus pugnax* and *Pluvialis apricaria*; and wintering waterfowl such as *Anas acuta, Anas penelope* and *Anas crecca*; but also the mammal *Lutra lutra*.

Location

6 km north of Baie de l'Aiguillon, 25 km north of La Rochelle, in the Commune de Champagné-les-Marais, France. 46°20'N 01°07'W.

Area

The 800 ha site includes 290 ha of wet grassland under NGO control (Ligue pour la Protection des Oiseaux – LPO) and forms part of the Marais Poitevin, a larger complex of wet grassland once about 80 000 ha in extent but with only 15 000 ha remaining.

Wet grassland type

Wet grassland is made up of *Ranunculo–Oenanthetum* (C15.52) and exists within a mosaic of brackish marsh and aquatic communities.

Soil

Clay of fluvial and marine origin.

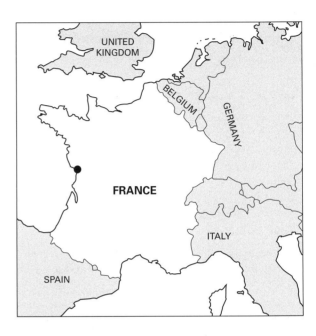

Hydrology

Marais de la Vacherie is a drained marsh made up of land claimed from saltmarsh since the Middle Ages and until the 1960s. The water regime is dependent upon precipitation that falls between September and April. This winter precipitation is evacuated as quickly as possible to the sea. During the summer period (May to August) water formerly entered the drainage channel network by gravity from the River Vendée and was used to irrigate arable crops in the former wet grassland areas. Today, owing to intensive irrigation upstream of the Marais de la Vacherie, the summer water supply is much reduced, often to the degree that drainage channels around the remaining wet grasslands dry out.

Circulation of water is through drainage channels with hydraulic control systems, and out to the sea through tidal non-return flaps, preventing seawater from flowing back into the drainage channel system.

Climate

Mean annual precipitation: 778 mm (La Rochelle)

Average air temperature:

Winter (January) 5.7°C

Summer (July) 19.3°C

Annual average number of days with frost: 26.

Average water deficit of 357 mm between March and October.

Designations

The area is designated as a Zone National d'Intérêt Florisitique et Faunistique (ZNIEFF) but this affords no legal protection. Additionally, the site is a designated SPA and a candidate SAC. The area is part of the French IBA No 49 (Marais Poitevin avec Baie de l'Aiguillon) which covers 57 830 ha.

Tenure/ownership

The LPO owns 255 ha of the site and a further 35 ha are privately owned but subject to an agreement between the owner and the LPO. The resulting 290 ha are let under management agreements to tenant farmers (Figure 1).

Mechanisms

The area falls within an Environmentally Sensitive Area scheme, the uptake of which is voluntary (see Case Study 5). The prescriptions of the ESA control cattle grazing, fertiliser inputs, mowing dates and drainage channel maintenance, but do not control water level management. This is achieved by additional management agreements between the LPO and tenant farmers.

Background

The site was formerly part of the Parc Naturel Régional de Marais Poitevin (Regional Natural Park), created in 1979. The aim of French Regional Natural Parks is to integrate development with the needs of the environment. Despite this, over the period 1980–95 the availability of both EU and national grant aid for drainage and conversion to arable agriculture led to widespread loss of the wet grassland resource within the Park. Between 1980 and 1995 three-quarters of the resource within the Natural Park, some 33 000 ha of wet grassland, was destroyed. The extent of the loss of semi-natural biotope eventually led to the descheduling of the Park in 1996.

With the failure of the legislation and natural park designation, it became clear to the LPO that the best way of safeguarding the remaining 15 000 ha of wet grassland in the area was land purchase and implementation of an agri-environment support system. The LPO has purchased land since 1989, and by 1997 a total of 255 ha (plus an additional 35 ha bought by a LPO member) was being rented back to tenant farmers. The LPO encouraged dairy and beef tenant farmers to take on the role of managing the land for nature conservation by providing financial incentives. This was the precursor to ESA in France (see also Case Study 5), which began in 1991. Financial help by LPO

has been the key to maintaining traditional forms of wet grassland management in this disadvantaged rural area. The incentives provided are indirect by lowering the standard rent by €76–108 ha⁻¹yr⁻¹. The LPO management agreements include the prescription of maintaining high water levels in the drainage channels. ESA prescriptions in wetlands in France do not yet include this requirement. The financial incentives from the ESA contract, which has a highest tier payment of €259–305 ha⁻¹yr⁻¹, can be combined with the LPO agreement. This provides reasonable support for the farmers and ensures better management for wet grassland wildlife.

Though modest, rent reductions do help the agricultural economy of the area and allow the maintenance of the wet grassland nature conservation interest. The LPO scheme on 290 ha costs the organisation between €22 100 and €30 950 per annum depending on annual drainage tax costs.

Figure 1 Location of LPO landholdings at Marais de la Vacherie.

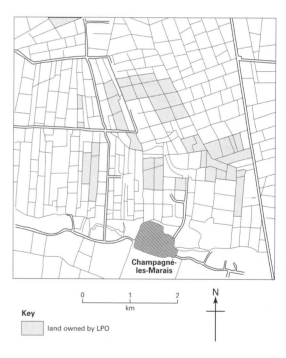

Key

land owned by LPO

Water management

- The existing hydraulic control system of sluices has isolated the wet grassland blocks allowing independent raised water level management in winter and spring (Plate 1). This system maintains water approximately 80 cm above the level of the local Water Management Organisation – a body made up of local landowners within the drainage basin. The system used to allow summer water intake by gravity from the River Vendée but this is no longer possible due to over abstraction elsewhere in the catchment.

- Initially, after the drop in river water level, drainage channels surrounding the wet grasslands were filled in summer with groundwater pumped from 15 m below the ground surface. This practice has now been halted due to recent salinity increases in the groundwater (≥ 5 g l^{-1}) caused by infiltration of sea water into the aquifer following the over-abstraction of freshwater in the area. As a result the surrounding drainage channels are now dry from July to October which is far from ideal.

- High water level management in winter and spring involves total or partial flooding of wet grassland and depressions to a depth of 10–60 cm, ie about 40% of the grassland. In spring only the depressions are flooded (10–40 cm), ie 10–20% of the grassland. In summer the depressions are completely dry from mid-July to mid-October, until the first significant autumn rains. Being able to maintain water within the drainage channels depends on surface water from the rivers. Unfortunately, no provision of summer water is now possible because of the excessive development of irrigation on neighbouring agricultural land and the increase in salinity (4–5 g l^{-1}) of groundwater in the marsh.

Plate 1
Installing water control structures at Marais de la Vacherie has allowed the water levels on LPO land to be maintained 80 cm higher than surrounding land when necessary.

J J Blanchon, LPO

Grassland management

- Grazing is let to local farmers with a limit on the density of stock (cattle and horses) in spring.

- A maximum of 1.5 cattle ha^{-1} from 15 March to 15 June is allowed. In practice, cattle normally arrive on the site in April because of access difficulties. A more favourable regime for breeding waders and *Chlidonias niger* would be densities of 1 cow ha^{-1} with a delay in grazing until at least 15 May.

- Controlled grazing early in the season prevents grass from growing too tall for breeding waders. Wet depressions are grazed later in the season.

- No fertiliser or pesticide use is allowed.

- One fifth of all fields are mown every year..

Benefits

- Raised water level conditions (Plates 2 and 3) have greatly benefited wetland wildlife. The site supports wetland breeding birds such as *Limosa limosa*, *Tringa totanus*, *Vanellus vanellus*, *Chlidonias niger*, *Anas querquedula*, *Himantopus himantopus*, *Ciconia ciconia* and *Ardea purpurea*. Breeding birds, especially waders, have responded to improved management (Table 1). Some species are breeding in nationally important numbers (Table 2).

- During the winter and migration periods the site is also important for *Limosa limosa* (2500–5000), *Numenius phaeopus* (1000–2500), *Philomachus pugnax* (1000), *Anser anser* (300), *Anas acuta* (250–500) and *Platalea leucorodia* (5–10). Recent winters have also seen maxima of 20 000 *Vanellus vanellus* and 1000 *Pluvialis apricaria*.

- Plant species of high conservation value (eg *Ranunculus ophioglossifolius*, *Cerastium dubium* and *Trifolium michelianum*) have benefited from the reintroduction or maintenance of traditional management.

- Additionally the site has a number of wider functions:

    - providing flood storage capacity
    - acting as a buffer zone and improving local water quality
    - supporting and enhancing cattle production, maintaining land prices and reducing land abandonment
    - encouraging ecotourism
    - demonstrating good agricultural and water level management in an SPA.

Plate 2
Before restoration, flooding was rarely observed at Marais de la Vacherie during the winter and spring.

Plate 3
After restoration, flooding to depths of 60 cm was made possible, greatly enhancing the value of Marais de la Vacherie to wetland wildlife.

Table 1 Numbers of breeding pairs of birds at Marais de la Vacherie.

Species	1990	1994	1997	1998
Limosa limosa	0	3	6	6
Tringa totanus	1–2	7	12–15	8–10
Vanellus vanellus	0	15–16	40–50	25
Himantopus himantopus	0	15–17	0	6–9
Chlidonias niger	0	17	0	10–12
Tadorna tadorna	0	1	0	2–3
Anas platyrhynchos	2	6	?	?
Anas querquedula	0	2	2	2–3
Ciconia ciconia	0	1	1	2

Table 2 Comparison of the numbers of pairs of breeding birds in the Marais de la Vacherie with the Marais Poitevin and the rest of France.

Species	Number of pairs breeding in Marais Vacherie, 1997	Number of pairs breeding in Marais Poitevin, 1997		Number of breeding pairs in France 1995–96	
	No. pairs	No. pairs	% found in the the Marais de la Vacherie	No. pairs	% found in the Marais de la Vacherie
Limosa limosa	6	26–29	23	165	4
Tringa totanus	12–15	87–99	14–15	1400	1
Vanellus vanellus	40–50	348–393	11–13	18 000	<0.5
Ciconia ciconia	1	13	8	420	<0.5

References and further reading

Blanchon, J J, Delaporte, P and Egreteau, C (1993) *Protection and restoration of migratory stop–overs for the spoonbill.* Unpublished LPO report. [In French]

Deceuninck, B and Mahéo, R (1997) *Nesting waders of France – synthesis of 1995–1996 national survey.* Unpublished report by Ministère de l'Environment, Wetlands International and LPO. [In French]

Dubois, P J, Mahéo, R and Hötker, H (1991) Waders breeding on wet grasslands in France. *Wader Study Group Bulletin* 61 Supplement: 27–31.

LPO (1996) *Management of coastal aquatic habitats for the spoonbill on migration and other associated birds.* Proceedings of the 23rd Eurosite nature management workshop, 1996.

Seriot, J (1996) Protection of the black tern *Chlidonias niger,* in the west of France. *Ornithos* 3: 103–134. [In French]

Case Study Authors/Consultants: J J Blanchon, A Duncan, C Egreteau and J J Terrisse (LPO).

Alúvium rieky Moravy

(Morava River Floodplain), Slovakia

Case Study 12

Techniques

Mowing
Wet grassland restoration

Main management objectives

- To achieve conservation management of biodiverse meadows

- To restore arable land in the floodplain to biodiverse meadows

- To benefit breeding birds which inhabit the floodplain meadows, particularly *Crex crex* and *Ciconia ciconia*.

Location

The Morava River Floodplain is located north of Bratislava in western Slovakia.
48°10' to 48°41'N, 16°50' to 16°58'E.

Area

The Morava floodplain supports the largest complex of species-rich floodplain meadows in central Europe, with an area of 2823 ha.

Wet grassland type

Meadow communities from the alliance *Cnidion dubii* (C37.23) are the most common in the floodplain area, of which two types are represented:

- the mesophyllous *Cnidio–Violetum pumilae*, which is regularly flooded for a short time in the spring

- the wet *Gratiolo–Caricetum praecoxis-suzae*, which is maintained by a higher ground water table and longer-term flooding.

Soil type

Alluvial soils and meadow soils are most common. The alluvial soils are mostly loamy clay or clay and predominate in the regularly flooded riparian zone up to a width of approximately 1 km. In more elevated parts of the floodplain, where floods are only temporary, meadow soils dominate (Racko and Bedrna 1994).

Hydrology

The Morava River is one of the largest tributaries of the Danube River, with a mean discharge of 109 m^3s^{-1} and channel width of 70 m. Its length is 328 km and the river basin is approximately 26 000 km^2. Maximal river discharges are in March and April due to mountain snow melt. In summer months, discharges are conditioned by heavy precipitation and the floodwaters of the Danube which can affect up to 32 km upriver. In the past, the river meandered naturally in its own sediments, which allowed the water to flood the surrounding area when discharges exceeded 210 m^3s^{-1} (Farkas 1995). Regulation and flood protection measures developed since 1935 now allow the riverbed to conduct discharges of about 440 m^3 s^{-1}. The present floodplain area is embanked and only 20% of its original area remains.

Climate

Dry and warm.
Mean annual precipitation: 600 mm.
Mean air temperature:
Winter (January) –2°C
Summer (July) 20°C.

Designations

Ramsar site and part of a Protected Landscape Area (IUCN category V). Also part of IBA No 009 of former Czechoslovakia, which covers 7000 ha of the floodplains of the confluence of the Rivers Dyje and Morava.

Tenure/ownership

Communist policies from 1945 to 1989 favoured large-scale agricultural production under collective or state ownership, but since then a process of re-privatisation has begun. The process is not complete, but it is possible to distinguish three types of ownership:

- co-operative farms which rent the land from small private owners

- private companies which bought former state farms

- private owners, ie individuals and families.

Mechanisms

Two projects have been developed which aim to determine techniques to manage existing meadows for conservation and restore arable land in the floodplain to biodiverse meadows:

- A pilot research project was financed by the GEF Biodiversity Protection Project in 1994–95 to determine the most appropriate management techniques for biodiverse meadows and to establish best practice for the conversion of arable land back to biodiverse meadows.

- A second project was approved in September 1997 as a part of the Strategic Action Plan Implementation Programme of the Danube Environmental Programme, and financed for three years by the EU PHARE Environmental Programme for the Danube River Basin. The project is focused on the restoration of biodiverse meadows on 150 ha of arable or abandoned land and on supporting the management of 1000 ha of degraded meadows by direct financial incentives to farmers.

Background

The study area is situated within the former Iron Curtain zone which was closed until 1990, the river forming the border between the Slovak Republic and Austria in the lower part, and between the Slovak and Czech Republics in the upper part. For thousands of years the inhabitants of this region practiced low-intensity land management, thereby enhancing and sustaining biodiversity. In the past 50 years, there has been an intensification of agriculture, river regulation, drainage and other destructive activities such as gravel extraction in the floodplain. The results of this have been a changed environment, loss of native plant and animal species and an increase in non-native species. Intensive agriculture has caused soil erosion, an increase in pollution in the Morava River and a decrease in species richness. For example, 500 ha of

meadows in the middle of the present Ramsar site were ploughed for arable land during the communist period 1960–89, with fertilisers and herbicides regularly applied. Although some fields are still actively farmed, most have been abandoned and are being invaded by weeds including alien plant species, especially *Aster novi-belgii* agg.

The Morava floodplain consists mostly of a mosaic of forest, wetland and grassland biotopes (Plate 1). There have been 215 bird species recorded in the floodplain, including 118 breeding species (Kalivodová *et al* 1994). The floodplain also supports more than 850 plant species. Banásová *et al* (1998) recorded 540 plant species, 12% of which were endangered or rare.

Viera Banásová

Plate 1
Floodplain meadows and associated biotopes along the Morava River.

Mowing

- A field experiment was conducted between 1994 and 1997 in order to analyse the effects of mowing on wet grassland vegetation. The results showed that many of the species most characteristic of the *Cnidion venosi* community were favoured by regular cutting, with less desirable species disadvantaged. Table 1 demonstrates the responses to cutting on a twice yearly basis of a representative range of plant species found in the dry variant of *Cnidion* community.

- A system of financial compensation for the loss of profit caused by delaying mowing has been proposed as a consequence of these recommendations.

Wet grassland restoration

- Field trials were initiated in 1994 in order to establish effective wet grassland restoration techniques for arable land in the Morava

Table 1 Impact of mowing twice a year on species composition of the *Cnidio-Violetum* community in the Morava River floodplain.

Negative impact on	Positive impact on
Poa palustris	*Iris pseudacorus*
Agrostis stolonifera	*Carex praecox*
Ranunculus repens	*Allium angulosum*
Glechoma hederacea	*Taraxacum officinale*
Carex acutiformis	*Festuca arundinacea*
Poa trivialis	*Plantago lanceolata*
	Alopecurus pratensis
	Ranunculus acris

Table 2 Composition of meadow seed mixture collected from the Morava River floodplain.

Species	Percentage representation by weight
Alopecurus pratensis	33
Serratula tinctoria	14
Centaurea jacea	14
Galium boreale	7
Clematis integrifolia	7
Inula salicina	7
Sanguisorba officinalis	7
Galium verum	3
Lythrum salicaria	3
Plantago lanceolata	3
Allium angulosum	3

floodplain. The trials involved comparing transplanted turves with sowing a seed mixture and monitoring the development of the subsequent vegetation.

- Permanent plots were ploughed in an area which had been used to grow arable crops for many years. In autumn 1994, turves were cut (0.5 m² to a depth of 0.15 m) from a nearby source meadow supporting a *Cnidion venosi* community and transplanted (in 10 x 10 cm samples) into the experimental plots.

- Seeds from meadow species were collected and stored indoors overwinter. These were sown in May 1995, in the ratio shown in Table 2, into plots that had been freshly ploughed.

- Plots from both experiments were mown at the end of June and September in 1995 and in July 1996 and 1997.

Benefits

- Meadows are the most abundant and valuable ecosystem of the Morava River floodplain. They make up the largest complex (approximately 2800 ha) of *Cnidion venosi* plant communities in central Europe and can support more than 30 species of higher plant per m² (Seffer *et al* 1995), including the following species listed in the Red Data Book of Slovakia (Maglocky and Ferakova 1993): *Ophioglossum vulgatum, Viola pumila, Gratiola officinalis, Plantago altissima, Iris sibirica, Leucojum aestivum, Cnidium dubium, Clematis integrifolia, Allium angulosum, Cerastium dubium, Gentiana pneumonanthe, Lathyrus pannonicus* and *Lathyrus palustris*. The Morava meadows are also important

feeding and nesting places for rare and endangered bird species with 88 bird species associated with the meadows (Kalivodová *et al* 1994), including 50 pairs of the globally threatened *Crex crex* and the largest *Ciconia ciconia* colony in Europe (80 pairs). Nevertheless, floodplain meadows are among the most endangered ecosystems in central Europe as a result of river regulation and land drainage.

- The mowing research led to the following conclusions and management recommendations:

  - mowing (with crop removal) is necessary for conserving the floristic diversity of the meadows, and the first annual cut has the greatest positive impact on the preservation of diversity
  - the minimum frequency of mowing is once every three years for mesophyllous floodplain meadows and once every two years for wet types with a predominance of grass and *Carex* species
  - meadows should be mown from the centre out to the edges, or in strips or in small blocks, to protect nesting birds (see Case Study 4)
  - the timing of mowing is important and depends on the management objectives. For agriculture, it is advantageous to mow during the flowering of the dominant grass species in June, because the nutritional value of the biomass is high. To maintain high meadow plant diversity, however, it is better to mow after the seeds of the dominant species are ripe, which is in July. For the protection of breeding birds with flightless young, it is optimal to mow in early August. Thus, in meadows with high plant diversity or nesting bird interest the

first yearly cut should be delayed until early August as this will conserve nesting birds and allow ripening of most of the flowering meadow species. Areas cut may be varied annually in order to maximise biodiversity over a larger area.

- The results of the wet grassland re-creation trials are shown in Figures 1 and 2 and demonstrated that:

  - turf transplantation was an effective means of rapidly establishing meadow vegetation, with a high and stable number of meadow species present from the outset (including three nationally rare species), and, after the initial disturbance caused by transplantation in 1995 a relatively low proportion of adventitious weed species (Figure 1). The plots exhibited a mean of 90% cover by meadow species in the second year after transfer
  - restoration by seeding was also successful, the number of meadow species increasing between 1995 and 1998 and the number of weed species declining slightly (Figure 2). However, an important factor in the enrichment of diversity in the sown plots was the colonisation of new meadow species from nearby species-rich vegetation
  - turf removal had little long-term impact on the donor meadow. The 0.5 m² gaps rapidly

revegetated such that after two years there was no significant difference between the colonised vegetation and the surrounding meadow community.

- The results of the field experiments provided the basis for a programme of restoration and aftercare management summarised in Table 3. This was begun in 1998 and is designed to restore 150 ha of arable land to meadow by using a combination of turf transplantation and seed introduction, and mowing management.

- The restoration of arable land to managed meadows will decrease soil erosion and inputs of organic nutrients into ground and surface waters.

- Restoration will also increase the biodiversity of the area and improve the biotope for many rare plant and animal species. For example, the middle section of the Morava river floodplain, which was affected by intensive agriculture, represents a gap in the distribution of *Crex crex* and other rare bird species. The higher plant diversity in species-rich meadows is more than 30 species m⁻² which far exceeds the diversity of arable land or abandoned fields invaded by alien plants.

- Local farmers recognise the economic benefits of ecologically sustainable meadow systems, and are keen to co-operate with the project, which is essential for the long-term viability of the scheme.

Figure 1 Meadow and weed species diversity in turf transplantation plots in the four years after transplantation.

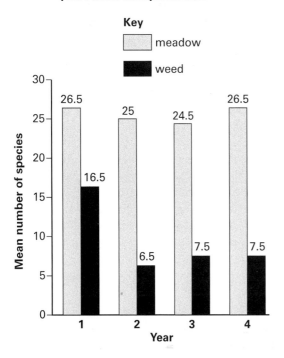

Figure 2 Meadow and weed species diversity in seed-sown plots in the four years after sowing.

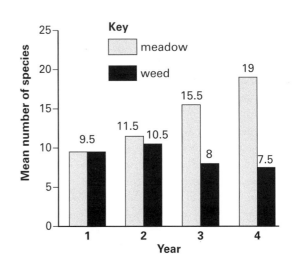

Table 3 Plan for restoring arable land to species-rich meadows on the Morava River floodplain.

Year 1

Spring/summer

- selection of seed and turf source areas

- harvesting of seeds by mowing for hay at three different times to ensure most meadow species are included.

Autumn

- ploughing to prepare soil

- distribution of seeds/hay from the summer harvesting on the soil surface

- creation of "islands of high diversity" by transfer of turf from meadows of ecological quality to encourage colonisation of species into surrounding areas. The size of the islands will be 2 x 8 m (each consisting of 2 m^2 of turf taken from donor meadows, scattered in 0.5 m^2 blocks). Islands will be distributed on 100 m centres (ie 1 per hectare).

Year 2

- hay from the previous autumn will be removed in spring

- restored areas will be mown approximately three times, although the frequency of mowing will depend on the rate and extent of weed invasion with greater infestation necessitating more cutting

- in the event of poor meadow seed germination an additional input of seeds will be undertaken.

Year 3

- restored areas will be mowed and hay removed at least twice a year

- any plots heavily invaded by weed species will be re-seeded.

References and further reading

Balatova-Tulackova, E (1969) Contribution to the knowledge of the Czechoslovakian *Cnidion venosi* meadows. *Vegetatio* 17: 200–207. [In German]

Banásová, V, Jarolímek, I, Otahelová, H and Zaliberová, M (1998) Inundation grasslands of the Morava river, Slovakia: plant communities and factors affecting biodiversity. In C B Joyce and P M Wade (Eds) *European wet grasslands: biodiversity, management and restoration*, pp 111–136. John Wiley and Sons, Chichester.

Farkas, J (1995) Restoration measures on Morava river. Proceedings from conference *Revitalization of Morava and Dyje Floodplains*, pp 2–5. Union for Morava River, Distelverein, DAPHNE, Mikulov.

Kalivodová, E, Feriancova-Masarova, Z and Darolova, A (1994) Birds of the floodplains of the River Morava, *Ekologia Bratislava* 13 (Suppl. 1): 189–199.

Maglocky, S and Ferakova, V (1993) Red list of ferns and flowering plants (Pteridophyta and Spermatophyta) of the flora of Slovakia. *Biológia Bratislava* 48/4.

Racko, J and Bedrna, Z (1994) Soils in the floodplain of Lower Morava. *Ekologia Bratislava* 13 (Suppl. 1): 5–13.

Seffer, J, Stanová, V and Vicenikova, A (1995) *Management and Restoration of Meadows in Morava River Floodplains*. Unpublished report by DAPHNE Centre for Applied Ecology, Bratislava.

Stanová V, Cierna M and Seffer, J (1997) *Strategy For Sustainable Agriculture in the Lower Part of the Záhorie Region*. Unpublished report by DAPHNE Center for Applied Ecology, Bratislava.

Case Study Authors/Consultants: Dr Jan Seffer and Viera Stanová
(DAPHNE Centre for Applied Ecology, Bratislava).

Niva Reky Lužnice

(Lužnice River Floodplain), Czech Republic

Technique

Reinstatement of cutting management

Main management objectives

- To assess the feasibility of restoring abandoned flood-meadows to their former characteristic plant communities

- To determine the potential of restoring plant species diversity to former higher level

- To determine the time taken for unmanaged grasslands when restored to return to high conservation and agricultural value.

Location

The study area was located between the villages of Dvory nad Lužnice and Hlamky, approximately 20 km SSE of Třeboň in South Bohemia, 5 km north of the Austrian border, in the Czech Republic. 48°51'N 14°55'E.

Area

The Lužnice River supports approximately 1000 ha of floodplain grasslands in the Czech Republic with a further 300 ha in Austria.

Wet grassland type

The following wet grassland types are present:

- *Alopecurus pratensis* grasslands (C38.2)

- *Festuca rubra–Sanguisorba officinalis* grasslands (C38.2)

- *Deschampsia caespitosa* grasslands (C37.213)

These exist alongside *Carex* (C53.21) and *Phalaris arundinacea* stands (C53.16).

Soil

The floodplain is dominated by alluvial soils. Younger soils occur near the river channel and comprise unconsolidated sand and occasional organic layers. Older soils with deeper soil profiles have a better-developed organic horizon and occur further from the main channel. Gleysols have developed in depressions and ox-bows where clay and organic matter has

accumulated during flooding, or near the terrace where seepage occurs.

Hydrology

The Lužnice river has a relatively natural hydrological regime. The study area is characterised by a lack of river engineering and exhibits many meanders and ox-bows as well as pool and riffle sequences. The floodplain varies from 150 m to 1000 m in width and river water quality is generally good, despite past pollution (Prach *et al* 1996). Flood events usually occur annually, particularly in spring when snow melts in the headwaters. The water table in the vicinity of the study area fluctuates considerably in the course of a year, often with a brief period of surface flooding in March–April, before falling up to 1.5 m below ground level by August–October.

Climate

The climate has a somewhat continental character.
Mean annual precipitation: 656 mm
Average air temperature:
Winter (January) –2.4°C
Summer (July) 16.8°C.

Designations

The study area is included within the Třeboň Basin Biosphere Reserve (IUCN category IX) and Ramsar site, and the Třeboň Landscape Protected Area. It is also a part of the Upper Lužnice National Nature Reserve, an area of 414 ha declared in 1994 (IUCN category IV). Furthermore the Lužnice floodplain was designated as a Territorial System of Ecological Stability (TSES) by the Czech Government. The TSES involves land-use analysis and the identification, protection and appropriate management of the most valuable ecosystems within the Czech Republic. As a consequence of the improved management of the floodplain region, the threat of channelisation has been removed and the volume of nutrients has decreased in recent years (Drbal and Rauch 1996). At present certain activities are prohibited within the floodplain, including the conversion of grassland to arable land, the use of pesticides, artificial fertilisers and slurry wastes, new building activities and the introduction of non-native plants and animals. However, there are still significant problems in conserving the wet grasslands, the most serious being the decline of hay-making. Unfortunately, the floodplain has little economic value at present and therefore government subsidy is required in order to stimulate appropriate management.

Tenure/ownership

The situation is complex and confused. Parts of the Lužnice floodplain are privately owned and parts are state-owned, and the status of some areas is unclear. A system of land re-privatisation is underway.

Mechanisms

The experimental programme of meadow restoration in the Lužnice floodplain was undertaken by the Academy of Sciences of the Czech Republic and the University of South Bohemia and was initiated through a project funded by the UNESCO Man and Biosphere programme. The experiment aimed to establish the feasibility of restoring abandoned grasslands in the Lužnice floodplain and to provide guidelines for the restoration and management of other European floodplain grasslands.

Background

The Lužnice river and its floodplain have been studied by the Academy of Sciences of the Czech Republic (and its former equivalent body) since 1986 because:

- it is considered to be representative of small rivers in central Europe

- it displays a high biodiversity (Prach *et al* 1996), supporting a mosaic of wetland, grassland and forest biotopes.

The river drains a total of 422 500 ha, including most of

the Třeboň basin, a large depression infilled with sand, gravel and clay sediments of Cretaceous to Miocene age (Janda 1994) with a mean altitude of 410 to 470 m. The flat landscape of the basin is characterised by extensive forests and wetlands, including more than 500 artificial fish ponds, mires, valley bogs, acidic fens and floodplain grasslands.

Grasslands were first created in the Lužnice floodplain in the 12th century (Janda 1994) and by the 20th century grasslands that were annually cut for hay and straw dominated the floodplain landscape (Prach *et al* 1996). Up to the 1950s, these grasslands were generally used for hay-making, but for the next 40 years, owing to communist policies, were subject to a range of agricultural practices, including intensive cultivation (Prach 1992). This resulted in changes in meadow management, often with substantial inputs of both organic and inorganic fertilisers, or a decrease in the frequency of mowing (Prach 1992, Joyce 1994). Less accessible parts of the floodplain, and those within an Iron Curtain exclusion zone, were abandoned. Consequently, many formerly diverse meadows have been replaced by species-impoverished communities dominated by *Urtica dioica* and *Phalaris arundinacea* (Plate 1). Since the end of communism in 1989, land ownership and management have been in a state of flux, and much of the floodplain has been unmanaged. However, the biodiversity value of the Lužnice floodplain grasslands was recently recognised by their inclusion amongst the ten most ecologically important complexes of floodplain grasslands in the Czech Republic (Straškrabová *et al* 1996).

Reinstatement of cutting management

- The section of floodplain grassland in which the experiment was undertaken had been left unmanaged for approximately 20 years. *Phalaris arundinacea* dominated over much of the area, with *Urtica dioica* in the more elevated parts.

- In 1989 a 150 m long transect between the river bank and the terrace was established (Plate 2). Cutting was reinstated to mimic the traditional management regime by mowing a 5 m wide strip of vegetation along the transect and removing the crop.

- Cutting was undertaken three times a year in 1989–91 and twice a year for the next two years because of the insufficient increase in biomass later in the 1992 and 1993 seasons. Meadows need to be regularly cut to avoid rapid degradation to monotonous swards of competitively vigorous herb species. Cutting also prevents the invasion of alien species.

Chris Joyce

Plate 1
Neglected Lužnice River floodplain grassland dominated by *Urtica dioica*.

Chris Joyce

Plate 2
Cutting has been reinstated to the Lužnice River floodplain within this experimental transect.

- Sampling was undertaken for five years (until 1994) and comprised three variables:

  - a measure of the number of plant species in each 1 m² plot along the transect
  - a visual estimate of the percentage cover of each species present in the plots
  - above-ground biomass samples (from randomly selected plots of 0.5 m x 0.5 m) in both the cut transect and adjacent uncut vegetation. Biomass was sorted to living and dead portions, dried at 90°C and weighed.

  Further details are in Straškrabová and Prach (1998).

- This monitoring programme gave an indication of the benefits of reinstating cutting management in relation to three key plant community variables, namely species diversity, community composition and production.

Benefits

- Rapid changes were observed between 1989 and 1994 with respect to species diversity (Table 1). The number of species per square metre almost doubled after one year and attained a level consistent with nearby regularly managed flood-meadows (Plate 3), which average 8.6 species m⁻², after two years of regular cutting.

- The increase in the number of species along the whole transect was similarly pronounced, reaching almost three times the number recorded before management was reinstated (Table 1).

- Restoration of the cutting regime induced rapid changes in vegetation cover (Table 2). The dominant species typical of abandoned meadows, namely *Phalaris arundinacea* and *Urtica dioica*,

decreased considerably during the monitoring period and species typical of the regularly managed meadows in the Lužnice floodplain (*Alopecurus pratensis, Deschampsia caespitosa, Poa* spp, and *Ranunculus repens*) increased.

- Instead of a dominance of *Phalaris arundinacea* over the major portion of the transect, the vegetation began to differentiate as a result of varied moisture conditions reflected by elevation. *Carex* communities prevailed in the lowest elevation (the wettest part of the moisture gradient), with *Deschampsia caespitosa* followed by *Alopecurus pratensis* as elevation increased and moisture decreased. In the highest elevation, species appeared that are characteristic of the driest flood-meadows in the Lužnice floodplain, eg *Avenula pubescens, Holcus lanatus* and *Festuca rubra* (Prach 1992, Prach *et al* 1996).

- After four years of cutting management the above-ground biomass of the mown grassland, at the time of the first annual harvest in early June, was significantly greater than the biomass of the adjacent uncut vegetation (Figure 1). At the time of the second cut of the year, the biomass of the uncut vegetation was naturally greater than the mown grassland. The higher biomass of the mown sward at the first harvest was partly caused by the earlier growth of *Alopecurus pratensis* in comparison with *Phalaris arundinacea*, the two dominant species of the respective stands.

- Cutting also gradually decreased the amount of dead biomass (Figure 1), apparently enabling new species of shorter stature and lower competitive ability to establish.

- Estimates of productivity were obtained by adding the biomass values obtained at the time of each harvest in the cut grassland and comparing the

Table 1 Mean number of species m⁻² and the total number of species along the whole transect across the Lužnice River floodplain. After Prach *et al* (1996).

	1989	1990	1991	1992	1993	1994
Mean no of species m⁻²	4.0	7.3	8.9	6.9	8.1	8.2
Total no of species	28	48	61	71	79	70

Table 2 Mean percentage cover of principal species along the transect across the Lužnice River floodplain following the reinstatement of regular cutting management in 1989 (after 20 years without management). After Prach *et al* (1996).

Species	Average cover (%)					
	1989	1990	1991	1992	1993	1994
Alopecurus pratensis	14.4	20.3	16.3	26.5	26.8	30.4
Deschampsia caespitosa	0	0	0.4	0.6	1.6	1.7
Phalaris arundinacea	28.0	35.1	12.3	4.4	1.0	0.9
Poa spec. div.	0	0.7	1.5	2.5	2.9	4.7
Ranunculus repens	0	5.8	10.8	29.2	42.4	43.5
Urtica dioica	18.4	7.8	2.0	0	0	0

Chris Joyce

Plate 3
Regularly cut meadows in the Lužnice floodplain can be exceptionally diverse botanically. The plate shows approximately one square metre of vegetation.

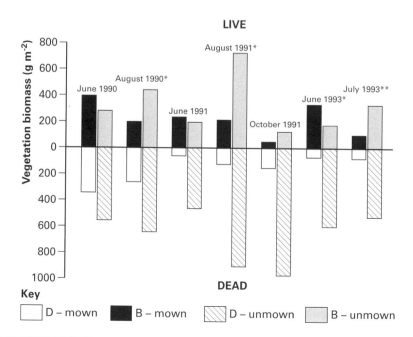

Figure 1
Changes in living and dead biomass of mown and unmown stands in three years during the experiment in the Lužnice River floodplain. Apart from the wet year of 1991 the productivity of the mown variant was higher than the unmown one.
Significant differences between mown and unmown variants are indicated: * *P*<0.05, ** *P*<0.01, *** *P*<0.001
(Straškrabová and Prach 1998). Reproduced with permission of John Wiley and Sons, Chichester.

total with the maximum biomass of the uncut vegetation (Table 3). It is evident that, except for the wet year of 1991, the production of the cut meadow was higher than that of the uncut vegetation, indicating that the regular cutting supports the productivity of the grassland.

- The change from *Phalaris arundinacea* stands to *Alopecurus pratensis* meadow is also desirable from an agricultural perspective, as *Alopecurus pratensis* is more palatable to livestock and is one of the most productive grassland species in the Lužnice area (Prach *et al* 1996).

- The preliminary results from this study suggest that following 20 years of abandonment, five years was a sufficient period for the restoration of the characteristic flood-meadow plant community in the Lužnice floodplain. Unfortunately, at present, there are no economic incentives that would persuade local agriculturists to re-establish regular cutting over the whole area of floodplain grassland. If they were to do so, they could have, relatively rapidly, the most productive meadows in the region, which are also of value from ecological and biodiversity perspectives.

Table 3 Approximate annual production of above-ground biomass estimated for the mown and unmown variant in the elevated part of the Lužnice River floodplain section. From Straškrabová and Prach (1998), reproduced with permission of John Wiley and Sons, Chichester.

| Year | Above ground biomass (g dry mass m^{-2}) | |
	Mown	Unmown
1990	593	436
1991	495	701
1993	444	344

References and further reading

Drbal, K and Rauch, O (1996) Water chemistry. In K Prach, J Jenik and A R G Large (Eds) *Floodplain ecology and management. The Lužnice River in the Trebon Biosphere Reserve, Central Europe*, pp 47–51. SPB Academic Publishing, Amsterdam.

Janda, J (1994) Třeboň Basin Biosphere Reserve. In J Jeník and M F Price (Eds) *Biosphere reserves on the crossroads of central Europe*, pp 66–80. Man and Biosphere Programme, Empora Publishing, Prague.

Joyce, C B (1994) Effects of land-use changes on the Lužnice floodplain grasslands in the Czech Republic. In R J Haggar and S Peel (Eds) *Grassland management and nature conservation*, pp 299–301. Occasional Symposium No 28, British Grassland Society, Reading.

Prach, K (1992) Vegetation, microtopography and water table in the Lužnice River floodplain, South Bohemia, Czechoslovakia. *Preslia, Praha* 64: 357–367.

Prach, K, Jeník, J and Large, A R G (Eds) (1996) *Floodplain ecology and management. The Lužnice River in the Třeboň Biosphere Reserve, Central Europe*. SPB Academic Publishing, Amsterdam.

Straškrabová , J and Prach, K (1998) Five years of restoration of alluvial meadows – a case study from central Europe. In C B Joyce and P M Wade (Eds) *European wet grasslands: biodiversity, management and restoration*, pp 295–303. John Wiley and Sons, Chichester.

Straškrabová , J, Prach, K, Joyce, C and Wade, M (Eds) (1996) Floodplain meadows – ecological functions, contemporary state and possibilities for restoration. *Příroda* 4, 1–176. [In Czech, with English summary]

Case Study Author/Consultant: Dr Karel Prach (University of South Bohemia).

Hornborgasjön

(Lake Hornborga), Sweden

Technique

Wet grassland restoration

Main management objective

- To restore Hornborgasjön to a wetland supporting open water, reedbed and wet grassland plant and animal communities with associated high biodiversity.

Location

Between Skara, Falköping and Skövde, 150 km north-east of Gothenburg, Skaraborg County, Sweden. 58°20'N 13°34'E.

Area

Total area of wetland: 4124 ha
Total area of wet grassland: approximately 600 ha.

Wet grassland type

Two grassland associations are represented:

- *Deschampsia caespitosa* grassland associations (C37.213) cover 400 ha

- *Alopecurus geniculatus* grassland associations (C37.242) cover 150 ha

These exist alongside *Carex* swamp associations (C53.21) which cover 50 ha.

Soil

Peat soil predominates in flat areas, some areas have exposed glacial gravels.

Hydrology

The current hydrological regime, established by the restoration scheme, has raised the water level by 85 cm, and allows for spring flooding as well as low water situations during summer and winter. The lake now has a maximum seasonal fluctuation of approximately 1.7 m. The following levels occur:

> Extreme high water 120.84 m above sea-level
> Normal high water 120.47 m above sea-level
> Average 119.88 m above sea-level
> Normal low water 119.59 m above sea-level
> Lowest low water 119.12 m above sea-level.

Climate

Typically continental climate with a moderate temperature range between summer and winter.
Mean annual precipitation: 560 mm
Average air temperature:
Winter (December–February) –2.8°C
Summer (June–August) 15°C
Average period of ice cover: 1 December–15 March.

Designations

Ramsar site and State Nature Reserve (IUCN category IV). Recognised as Swedish IBA No 014.

Tenure/ownership

2600 ha owned by the state and managed by the Swedish Environmental Protection Agency (EPA), the rest (approximately 1500 ha) is owned by individual farmers or communally by nearby residents.

Mechanisms

The restoration project was entirely state-funded. Subsequent management also uses state funds channelled through the EPA which is responsible for managing the lake and its environs. Some income is derived from visitors to the site (up to €62 000 per year). Additionally, there is some state support for graziers managing wet grassland on the site.

Background

Hornborgasjön is a large post-glacial lake, some 10 000 years old. Successive agricultural drainage projects between 1805 and 1935 lowered the lake water level and reduced the extent of wet grassland around the lake. The remaining shallow open water was steadily invaded by *Phragmites australis*, *Carex* and *Salix* scrub until, by the mid-1960s, little open water remained. Drainage and land use changes reduced the value of the wet grassland for birds, especially breeding waders. Ambitious plans to restore the lake were proposed in 1965 and have recently been completed.

The restoration plan aimed to raise the lake water level by 0.85 m. In order to achieve this a 3 km bund was built around the western boundary to protect neighbouring arable farmland (Figure 1). Water levels were slowly raised between 1992 and 1995. Approximately 800 ha of invasive *Betula* and *Alnus* woodland and *Salix* scrub were cut and 1200 ha of reedbed was burnt and/or chopped using specially designed amphibious machinery.

The reserve supports the only remaining Swedish breeding colony of *Podiceps nigricollis* (110 pairs in 1997). Additionally, although maximum water levels have only just been achieved, *Chlidonias niger* has returned to breed on the lake (65 pairs in 1997). The management of the reedbeds has provided improved feeding conditions for many birds and, despite a marked reduction in overall cover of this biotope, the reedbeds now support increased numbers of many species such as *Botaurus stellaris*, *Circus aeruginosus* and *Acrocephalus arundinaceus*.

Wet grassland restoration

- An initial feasibility study was undertaken in the 1960s and regularly updated during the lengthy project planning phase. Inputs were made by experts in the fields of limnology, ornithology, agronomy and hydrology.

- The Swedish EPA acquired 1700 ha of the surrounding land prior to restoration.

- A 3 km bund was constructed by removing peat down to the subsoil and keying in a bund of clay-rich moraine material (Plate 1). Along the inner side of the bund an erosion-secure layer of limestone was applied. On the outer side peat was used to create a shallow slope rendering the bund almost invisible when viewed from a distance. Additionally, a geotextile was used as added protection for the bund.

- A simple concrete sluice was installed within the bund. Lake levels are kept as natural as possible and the sluice is used only to lower the water level

Jan Johansson

Plate 1 The 3 km bund prevents flooding of neighbouring farmland and includes an outflow sluice which allows manipulation of the Hornborgasjön water level.

after extreme spring floods. With hindsight it is recognised that this structure is over-engineered and does little to encourage natural flow dynamics and features in the area downstream.

- Grazing from early May to late October with 1–1.5 cattle ha^{-1} is the main management technique over most of the wet grassland area. Other grazing animals used are sheep and horses. Pigs are also used on an experimental basis to create early successional communities in wet grasslands.

- Cattle are invariably commercial breeds but the Swedish EPA also owns some traditional domestic breeds, which are considered beneficial as they are able to graze later into the autumn than commercial varieties without losing condition. Economic support through 'Environmental support for biodiversity', a Swedish agri-environment scheme, is important as it encourages continued cattle grazing by farmers on the site.

- Hardy traditional breeds of sheep owned by the Swedish EPA were used during the restoration phase to eliminate encroaching *Salix* and *Betula* trees on drier restored meadows.

- A herd of about 25 Icelandic ponies is used where heavy grazing pressure is required to reduce tussocks of *Carex elata*, *Carex acuta* and *Deschampsia caespitosa*. These ponies are hardy enough to graze year-round.

- Small numbers of pigs of traditional domestic breeds are also used in selected small plots during the late summer. Pigs churn up the soil creating rotovated areas that are attractive to wading birds and create conditions suitable for plants such as *Bidens cernua*, *Bidens tripartita* and *Alisma plantago-aquatica* which in turn produce seed for passage wildfowl.

- Some of the restored meadows are now cut for silage using special machinery and are aftermath grazed using traditional breeds of cattle and pigs.

- Hay is also mown in mid or late July on about 20 ha of wet grassland, the timing in late summer preventing damage to nesting birds. It is planned that hay cutting will increase as *Carex* swamp communities develop following the raising of water levels through restoration. Tractors with low-pressure flotation tyres are used for mowing, and the hay is used for supplementary feeding of cattle and sheep in the winter.

- Mechanical treatment and burning are used to accompany the more traditional techniques detailed above. Heavy rotovators are used to eliminate tussocks and scrub in areas inadequately grazed. These are set above ground level to avoid damaging root systems as this could lead to soil

erosion. Carefully controlled burning was used in selected areas during the restoration phase and could be used again to manage the grassland.

- Costs totalled €9.2 million (in 1992), including €2.5 million in compensation payments, €1.8 million in bund and sluice construction and a similar sum spent on vegetation clearance.

Benefits

- The restoration scheme has increased the amount of wet grassland biotope around the lake from 50 ha to approximately 600 ha (Figure 1, Plate 2).

- Positive effects of the restoration of the Hornborgasjön wetland include dramatic increases in the number of wildfowl and waders using the area.

- Breeding wildfowl have shown dramatic increases

Figure 1 Biotope distribution (a) before and (b) after restoration management at Hornborgasjön. Raising water levels and treating swamp vegetation has effectively increased the amount of open water and allowed the creation of large amounts of wet grassland in peripheral, former arable areas.

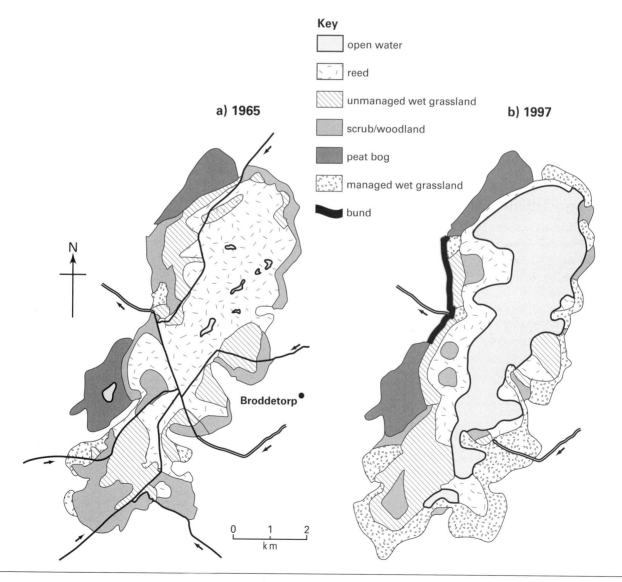

Key
- open water
- reed
- unmanaged wet grassland
- scrub/woodland
- peat bog
- managed wet grassland
- bund

a) 1965

b) 1997

N

Broddetorp

0   1   2
km

Plate 2
Restoration has created a diverse mosaic of wetland biotopes and has greatly expanded the amount of wet grassland on the site.

Jan Johansson

on the site largely as a result of the increase in the availability of open water. *Anas clypeata* and *Anas querquedula*, two species closely associated with wet grassland, have also shown considerable increases (Table 1).

- Breeding waders that utilise wet grassland have also shown marked increases in population (Table 1). Restored wet grassland provides breeding habitat for *Vanellus vanellus, Tringa totanus* and *Gallinago gallinago*. Since restoration, *Calidris alpina* (1–2 pairs) and *Philomachus pugnax* (15 females)

have returned as breeding species. Passage waders such as *Calidris alpina, Calidris canutus, Calidris ferruginea* and *Pluvialis squatarola* have also benefited.

- The lakeside wet grasslands continue to provide an important migration stopover site for flocks of migrating *Grus grus*. Up to 15 000 use the site during the spring, with smaller numbers passing through in autumn.

Table 1 Breeding figures for wetland birds at Hornborgasjön during the different phases of restoration (data from Hornborga Fältstation).

Species	1981 Pre-restoration	1986 Early restoration	1991 Start of intensive restoration (water levels raised)	1996 Final water level achieved
Anas clypeata	9	15	32	65
Anas querquedula	6	11	25	45
Calidris alpina	0	3	2	2
Tringa totanus	9	8	30	60
Philomachus pugnax	0	10	20	12
Numenius arquata	–	6	7	14
Porzana porzana	14	10	11	8
Grus grus	5	8	13	15
Chlidonias niger	2	5	13	45

References and further reading

Hertzman, T and Larsson, T (1997) *Hornborgasjön – from an ocean of reeds to a kingdom of birds*. Swedish EPA report 4694, Stockholm. [In Swedish]

Hertzman, T and Larsson, T (1999) *Lake Hornborga, Sweden – the return of a bird lake*. Wetlands International Publ. 50, Wageningen, Netherlands.

Case Study Author/Consultant: Tomas Hertzman (Swedish Environmental Protection Agency).

River Brede Floodplain

Denmark

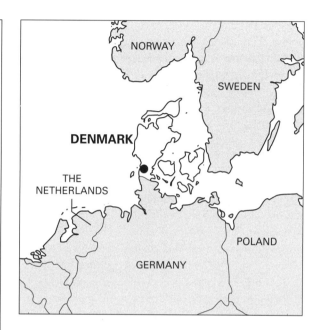

Technique

Physical restoration of floodplain wet grassland

Main management objectives

- To enhance floodplain biotopes, specifically wet grassland utilised for grazing

- To re-establish former biodiversity in both river channel and floodplain

- To improve physical characteristics and water quality in streams

- To reduce nutrient and ochre pollution of the watercourses

- To provide/improve opportunities for outdoor recreation.

Location

Southern part of Jutland, 20 km north of the Danish–German border, Denmark. 55°02' to 55°13'N, 08°42' to 09°10'E.

Area

Total area of catchment: 47 300 ha
Area of raised groundwater level: 1000 ha
Area of wet grassland: 175 ha.

Wet grassland type

Grazing marshes and hay meadows characterised by *Deschampsia caespitosa* (C37.21) and containing *Alopecurus geniculatus* and *Poa trivialis* predominate, with transitional tall herb meadows supporting *Cirsium oleraceum*. In the wettest areas, grasslands with tall *Carex* species occur.

Soil

The western end of the catchment is typified by fine material (silt and clay) deposited by the Wadden Sea. Further inland the catchment is dominated by a sandy till with overlying peat.

Hydrology

Most of the River Brede flows through an outwash plain deposited by meltwater during the last Ice Age. On the edge of the Brede catchment there are several bogs. The whole river system upstream of Bredebro is naturally characterised by very iron-rich groundwater and the ochre content of watercourses has increased greatly in recent decades owing to oxidation following drainage. The River Brede catchment contains more than 1000 km of streams which flow through an outlet at the Ballum Floodgate into the Wadden Sea. Mean discharge of the River Brede is 6 m^3 sec^{-1} and maximum recorded discharge is 40 m^3 sec^{-1}.

Climate

Mild, humid coastal climate.
Mean annual precipitation: 800 mm
Average air temperature:
Winter (January) 1.1°C
Summer (July) 15.2°C.

Designations

Part of the catchment is an IBA.

Tenure/ownership

The majority of the area is in private ownership. All streams wider than 2 m are managed by the county regional water and nature authority.

Mechanisms

- Environmentally Sensitive Areas scheme administered by the County Council using EU funds

- The Strategy for River Valleys (County of Sønderjylland)

- an EU LIFE project provides additional support.

Background

In the 1950s, the main watercourses, the River Brede and Lobæk Brook, were channelised and their beds lowered to increase their water discharge capacity (Plate 1). Weirs were constructed to expend energy and prevent the river from meandering. These measures enabled the river valleys to be drained and in this way floodplain meadows could be used more effectively for agricultural production. Often the meadows continued to be used for harvesting hay and grazing.

Cultivation of the meadows along the river valley first started with the mechanisation of agriculture in the 1960s. At that time Denmark aimed to be self-supporting in terms of food, and there was political and economic support for enhancing agricultural efficiency. For a number of years farmers obtained good yields from river valley soils, but drainage and soil treatment eventually resulted in the collapse of soil structure through oxidation and subsequent difficulties in cultivation. At the same time, iron compounds in the soil became oxidised and ochre leaked into the watercourses.

During the 1980s the catchment also suffered from sewage and industrial waste pollution. These problems were addressed by investment in new sewage treatment plants, strict licensing to reduce inputs and an efficient regulatory system. Despite these measures the ecological quality of many streams remained low.

Most streams had been regulated and a number of valuable wetland ecosystems and flood storage areas had been destroyed.

Improved drainage of the meadows and slopes of the river valleys also led to surges of water entering the river, resulting in more frequent flooding of the lower reaches of the valley. Additionally, nutrients (mostly nitrogen and phosphorous) from agricultural land were flowing through the watercourses and out into the Wadden Sea, where they enhanced algal growth. Previously these nutrients were largely taken up by the natural buffer zone (floodplain wetlands such as wet grassland) and did not reach the watercourses.

Until recently, the priority function of streams in Denmark was to drain excess precipitation as quickly as possible from farmland and urban areas. During the 1980s, attitudes began to change and concern about the environment led to additional and quite different demands being made on streams. In recent years, Denmark has devoted considerable resources to projects aimed at environmental improvement and enhancing possibilities for outdoor recreation, justified in part by the undesirability of agricultural surpluses. Now the requirement for streams and their riparian zones are that they must also:

- have a diverse flora and fauna

- be a natural part of the landscape

- be aesthetically and recreationally attractive.

Restoration of the River Brede catchment began in 1991. In 1993 the EU LIFE Programme granted funds to establish a demonstration project on river and catchment restoration. The aim was to improve

County of Sønderjylland

Plate 1
Before restoration between Løgumkloster and Bredebro. The River Brede was channelised in 1957. The floodplain experienced a lower water table and as a result flooding was reduced and floodplain functions impaired.

understanding of ecosystem diversity, the impact of human activities on biodiversity, and the restoration of natural functions and biodiversity. The project involved three rivers, one of which was the Brede (the other two were the Rivers Cole and Skerne, both in England).

Catchment planning and regulations

- Prior to undertaking construction work, catchment-wide plans and regulations were prepared including:

    - a water quality plan for surface water in the catchment including discharge limits for sewage plants and treatment of sewage from farms and isolated houses in the catchment
    - a water abstraction and groundwater protection plan, allowing minimal abstraction of surface water
    - water quality objectives for the stream, which were determined according to the then new Environmental Protection Act (1991)
    - regulations for stream maintenance that balance requirements for stream run-off and the needs of wildlife
    - legal requirements for a minimum 2 m buffer strips along all Danish streams. Wider buffer strips would be preferable, but drainage interests often prevent this. Cultivation within these buffer zones is illegal and can result in prosecution.

Physical restoration

- Restoration design was aided by preliminary examination of old maps and aerial photographs and existing information on the local geology and the stream hydrograph. After a levelling survey of the stream and its surroundings, the hydraulic consequences of different restoration approaches were determined using computer-based hydraulic models.

- The basic restoration approach was to re-establish the natural riffle–pool sequence in the river channel, with a riffle 2–3 times the channel width in length, at intervals of 5–7 times channel width. Five typical cross sections have been adopted (Figure 1, Plate 2).

- Restored channel stretches crossed the old streambed at many points to allow the recolonisation of stream flora and fauna.

- At the downstream end of each restored stretch a temporary sediment trap was installed which limits the downstream damage caused by restoration work. Sediment traps consist of a 50–100 m stretch which is 1 m deeper and 2 m wider than the norm; the water slows and drops suspended sediment. A large sediment trap between Bredebro and the outlet of the river collects 3000 m^3 of sediment per year.

- Approximately 25 km of the Brede have been restored in this manner to date, and the project is ongoing. A 2.6 km stretch was restored in 1991 at a cost of €230 000.

Benefits

- Raising stream beds during re-meandering raises groundwater levels creating wet floodplain biotopes, specifically wet grassland and shallow pools in the riparian zone.

- Several hectares of wetland and shallow lakes have been created along the Slotsbækken tributary near Løgumkloster in order to reduce ochre discharge into the River Brede. Simply re-flooding adjacent meadows prevents the oxidation of iron-rich deposits.

- River wildlife has benefited from the restoration process. Aquatic vegetation, especially emergent species, has benefited from shallower bank profiles.

- Flooding frequency has increased and the groundwater level has risen in floodplain grassland areas.

- Monitoring of the populations of breeding and migratory birds is currently in place but it is too early to describe fully the benefits of the restoration project on the numbers of wetland birds using the floodplain.

- The project has created ideal conditions for the recolonisation of *Lutra lutra*, which occurs in nearby rivers.

- A reduction in water-borne pollutants by interaction with floodplain vegetation is expected.

- The restoration of streams benefits both the individual landowner and society as a whole. Experience from the Brede project has shown that conflicts between landowners and environmental interests can be reduced. The landowners involved have indicated that it is particularly important in some cases that land redistribution occurs. With re-meandering, land on either side of a previously straightened river can be swapped so that the river is still the property boundary. If a landholding is primarily within the previously drained floodplain, land swaps to include some higher ground may be needed to ensure farming viability.

Figure 1 River restoration process implemented along the River Brede to return natural functioning to the floodplain.

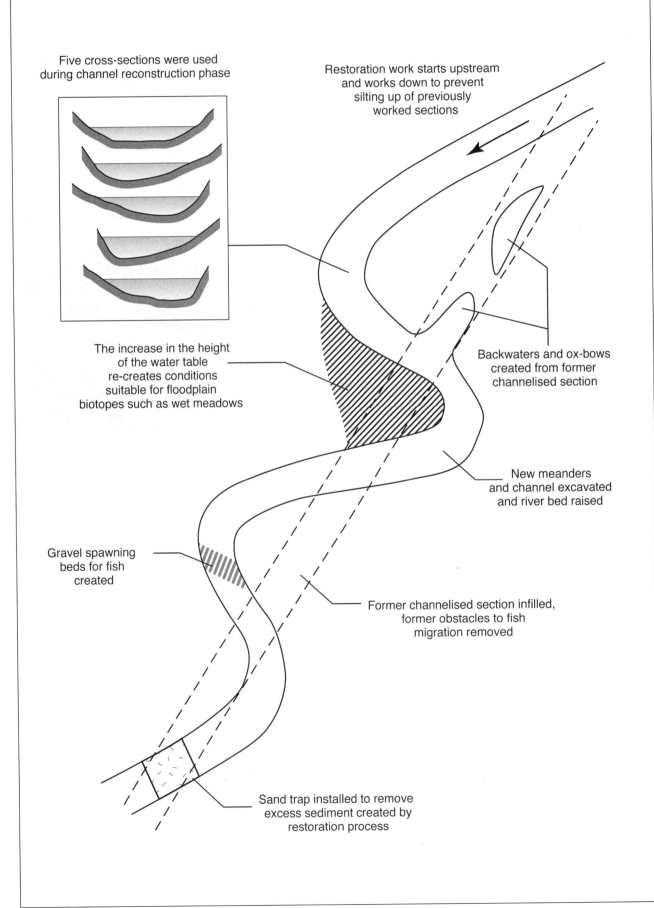

Five cross-sections were used during channel reconstruction phase

Restoration work starts upstream and works down to prevent silting up of previously worked sections

The increase in the height of the water table re-creates conditions suitable for floodplain biotopes such as wet meadows

Backwaters and ox-bows created from former channelised section

New meanders and channel excavated and river bed raised

Gravel spawning beds for fish created

Former channelised section infilled, former obstacles to fish migration removed

Sand trap installed to remove excess sediment created by restoration process

Plate 2 After restoration; elevation of the channel bottom and greater channel roughness has resulted in raised water levels and active floodplains.

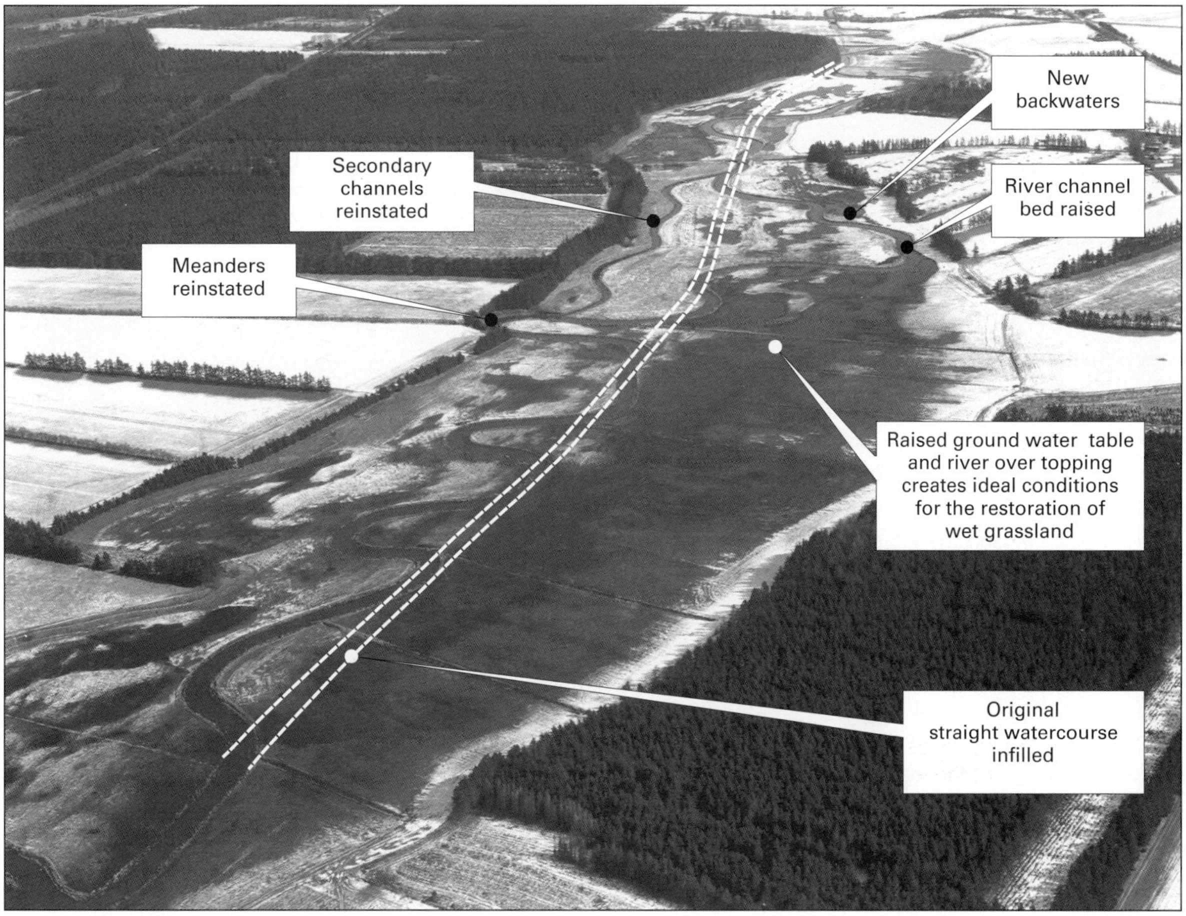

New backwaters

Secondary channels reinstated

River channel bed raised

Meanders reinstated

Raised ground water table and river over topping creates ideal conditions for the restoration of wet grassland

Original straight watercourse infilled

County of Sønderjylland

References and further reading

Hansen, H O (Ed) (1996) *River restoration – Danish experience and examples*. National Environment Research Institute, Denmark.

Nielsen, M B (1995) Restoration of streams and their riparian zones – South Jutland, Denmark. In M Eiseltová and J Biggs (Eds) *Restoration of stream ecosystems – an integrated catchment approach*, pp 30–44. IWRB, Slimbridge.

Nielsen, M B (1996a) Lowland stream restoration in Denmark. In A Brookes and F D Shields (Eds) *River channel restoration*, pp 269–289. John Wiley and Sons, Chichester.

Nielsen, M B (1996b) River restoration: report of a major EU Life demonstration project. *Aquatic Conservation: Marine and Freshwater Ecosystems* 6: 187–90.

Case Study Authors/Consultants: Mogens Bjørn Nielsen and Rikke Schultz (County of Sønderjylland, Denmark).

Donauaue bei Pfatter

Floodplain of the River Danube, Germany

Techniques

Physical restoration of floodplain topography and hydrology
Low-intensity floodplain management

Main management objectives

- Maintaining and improving habitat for breeding waders and wildfowl

- Maintaining and improving important plant communities associated with naturally functioning floodplain with varying relief, including specialist plants of bare mud and shingle mound communities.

Location

Between the villages of Pfatter and Wörth on the banks of the Danube River, 20 km south-east of Regensburg, eastern Bavaria, Germany.
48°57'N 12°19'E.

Area

Wetland area: approximately 450 ha.
Wet grassland area: approximately 340 ha.
Experimental area: 29.3 ha.

Wet grassland type

The following wet grassland types are represented:

- *Sanguisorbo–Silaetum* lowland hay meadow (C38.2) the most important and endangered plant community of the floodplain

- *Arrhenetheretum–Alopecuretosum* lowland hay meadow (C38.2)

- *Ranunculus repens* grassy flood-sward (C37.242)

- remnants of *Brometum alluviale* occur (C34.324).

Remainder of wetland area consists of tall herbs, *Salix* scrub, old watercourses and remnants of floodplain forest.

Soil

Sands, gravels, and loamy soils and alluvial bare mud.

Hydrology

The Danube and associated floodplain have been greatly modified by river regulation including channelisation for navigation, construction of embankments for flood control, and the construction of major dams for hydroelectric projects. Floodplain area has been reduced as a result. This has prevented natural hydrological and geomorphological processes from operating. Isolation of the floodplain by embankments from the main river has lost the hydrological connectivity between the two environments vital for the ecological well-being of the site. Variability in the water levels at the site has been reduced from up to 5.6 m to as little as 0.4 m.

Climate

Mean annual precipitation: approximately 650 mm
Average annual air temperature variation: 20°C.

Designations

Nature Reserve (IUCN category IV) and SPA. The site is part of the German (FDR) IBA No 097 (Donau-Tal) which covers 15 600 ha.

Tenure/ownership

Mostly private, but the NGO Landesbund für Vogelschutz (LBV) owns the 29.3 ha experimental area.

Mechanisms

Land purchase and research costs were met by funding from the EU (50%), the Bavarian Ministry of Environment (20%), the Nature Protection Fund (15%) and LBV (15%).

Background

Much of the floodplain of the Danube has been adversely affected by development to provide access to shipping and hydroelectric power. Traditional land use was extensive grazing (1–3 cattle ha^{-1}) and mowing. Two annual cuts of hay were taken in June/July and September. Embankment has allowed the conversion to intensive agriculture of many former floodplain areas.

Under a natural flooding regime the river formerly created a varied floodplain topography with deep depressions separated by shingle mounds and bars. The depressions used to remain wet for most of the year while higher patches were well-drained and drier. This varied relief is exceptionally important and supports a diverse flora and fauna.

Today less than 10% of Bavaria's floodplain ecosystems function naturally. This has resulted in a loss of bare ground and its associated flora owing to modified hydrology. There have also been declines of plants associated with typical floodplain meadows and the xeric grassland on shingle mounds. In 1988 the LBV in co-operation with the EU and the Bavarian Ministry for Environment undertook a series of measures to restore a 25 ha area of floodplain grassland.

Physical restoration of floodplain topography

- A 25 ha area of former arable and intensive grassland has been restored. Depressions were created and shingle mounds formed (Figure 1). Approximately half the area is made up of these shingle mounds.

- The re-created shingle mounds were seeded in the autumn using seed collected by hand from natural xeric grasslands elsewhere along the Danube. Species introduced in this way included: *Allium angulosum, Peucedanum officinale, Filipendula vulgaris* and *Cirsium tuberosum*. Seed was spread at low density to allow seeds present in the seedbank and naturally colonising species to germinate as well.

Figure 1 Location, management and infrastructure of Donauaue bei Pfatter reserve. The insert diagram shows the re-modelled relief of the shingle ridges and wet depressions.

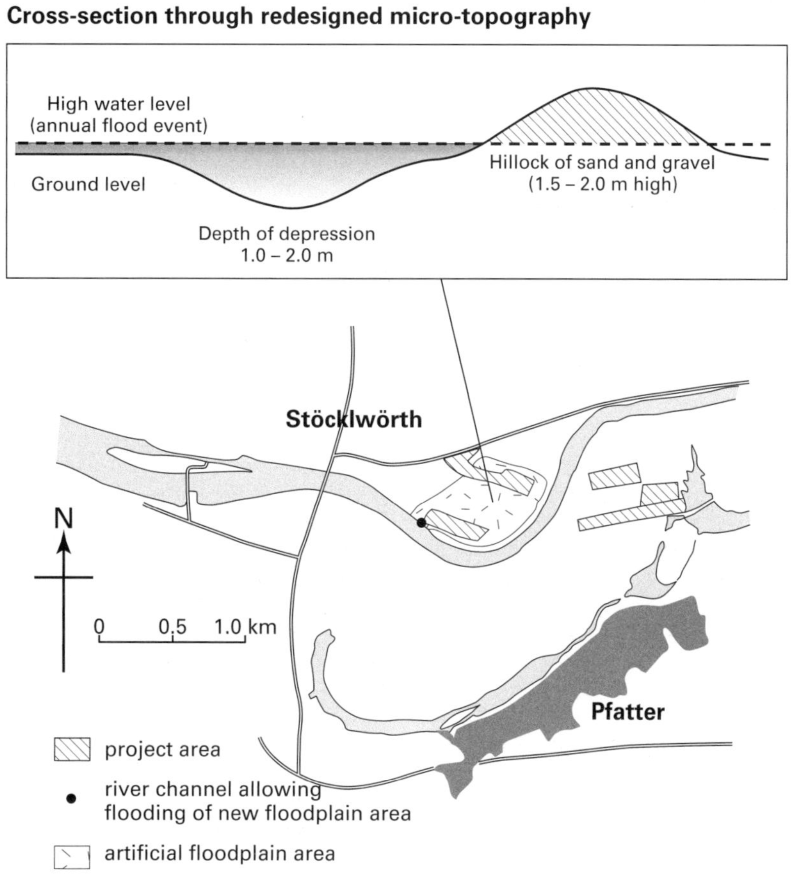

Cross-section through redesigned micro-topography

■ *Sanguisorbo–Silaetum* grassland was seeded using a specially created mixture of grasses and herbs. This mixture was composed of a commercial seed mix to which the following characteristic target species were added; *Sanguisorba officinalis*, *Silaum silaus*, *Bromus racemosus*, *Lotus uliginosus*, *Trifolium hybridum* and *Galium verum*. The eventual mix contained 60–70% of the target species.

■ Areas contiguous with the existing semi-natural grassland resource were left to revegetate naturally.

Artificial flooding

■ Natural flooding had become rare as a consequence of engineering work for shipping and hydroelectricity generation at Straubing and Geisling. To counter this effect the newly designed floodplain topography was connected to the river through a reconstructed river channel. This channel allows the restored area to be flooded whenever the river rises more than 0.4 m from its mean level.

■ Flooding of the restored site is nearly annual, with flood peaks in March/April and June/July.

■ The flooded area totals 50 ha and is restricted to depressions in the grassland. In exceptional floods (every 100 years or so), the shingle mounds will also be submerged.

Flood meadow management

■ Meadows are cut mechanically twice a year in July and September using agricultural equipment. Mowing is let at no cost to neighbouring farmers, but several restrictions apply. For example, no fertilisers are allowed and mowing must take place after the bird breeding season. There are currently

no plans to reinstate grazing.

■ *Salix* scrub is invading certain areas and is removed by hand to maintain open areas for breeding waders. Some areas of *Salix* are maintained, however, as habitat for *Luscinia svecica* and *Remiz pendulinus*.

Benefits

■ Donauaue bei Pfatter is the most important site for *Tringa totanus* in Bavaria, supporting 4 pairs. The site also currently supports breeding waders such as *Numenius arquata* (12 pairs), *Vanellus vanellus* (10 pairs) and *Limosa limosa* (4 pairs). Wet areas created by topographical restoration provide ideal feeding conditions for young wildfowl and wader chicks (Plate 1).

■ Other important breeding birds include *Ciconia ciconia* (1 pair), *Alcedo atthis*, *Anas clypeata* (2 pairs) and *Circus aeruginosus* (1 pair).

■ Migrant birds utilising the site during spring and autumn include nationally important numbers of *Philomachus pugnax* and *Anas querquedula*.

■ Re-creation of shingle mound biotope and subsequent re-seeding provide areas where the scarce dry grassland *Brometum alluviale* community can re-establish. This benefits many of the rare associated species, for example *Allium scorodoprasum*, *Allium angulosum*, *Cirsium tuberosum*, *Euphorbia salicifolia*, *Linum austriacum*, *Thalictrum lucidum* and *Verbascum blattaria*.

■ Meadow restoration provides habitat for a number of scarce species requiring seasonally flooded riparian wet grassland and associated wetland biotopes, for example *Alisma lanceolata*, *Butomus*

Plate 1 The re-modelled topography created wet areas that provided ideal feeding conditions for young wildfowl and waders such as *Tringa totanus* chicks.

Plate 2 Bare, muddy margins which are devoid of competitors are required by a suite of scarce plant species including *Limosella aquatica*.

umbellatus, Inula brittanica, Peucedanum officinale and *Senecio fluviatilis.*

- Reinstatement of the flooding regime and subsequent revival of a bare muddy margin biotope benefits scarce plant species such as *Cyperus fuscus, Lindernia procumbens, Scirpus maritimus* and *Limosella aquatica*, that require wet mud substrates devoid of competitors (Plate 2).

References and further reading

Leibl, F (1994) Comments on the bird community, and the influence of habitat management on the avifauna, of the Stöcklwörth nature reserve. *Jber. OAG Ostbayern* 21 S: 23–39. [In German]

Case Study Author/Consultant: Bernd Raab (Landesbund für Vogelschutz).

Appendix 1 Glossary

Terms in italics are included in the Glossary

above sea level (asl)   height above mean sea-level, used as a datum for calculating height of land.

abstraction   extraction of surface or groundwater for domestic, agricultural or industrial use.

aftermath   grass re-growth after cutting a crop of *hay* or *silage* which can subsequently be used for grazing or as a second grass crop.

agri-environment scheme   schemes for farmers which provide incentives for positive environmental management, eg restoration of arable land to wet grassland.

allochthonous   applied to material that originates elsewhere.

alluvium   the sedimentary deposits resulting from the action of rivers, including those laid down in river channels, *floodplains*, estuaries, lakes and deltas; also alluvial.

alvar   a plant community consisting typically of mosses and herbs growing on a steppe-like, shallow, alkaline soil overlying limestone.

association   an assemblage of plants living in close interdependence that exhibit similar habitat and growth requirements, with usually one or more dominant species.

biodiversity   the variety of living organisms and the ecological complexes of which they are a part. This includes diversity within species, between species and of ecosystems. It is a concept which applies at all levels, from landscapes and ecosystems down to individual species and their gene pools.

biomass   a quantitative measurement or assessment of animal and/or plant matter.

biotope   an area in which the main environmental conditions and organisms adapted to them are uniform.

bog   an area of wet acid peat dominated by *Sphagnum* mosses forming typically in areas with high precipitation.

boulder clay   an unsorted and usually unstratified glacial deposit of rock flour, often containing coarser, ice-transported material ranging in size from sand to boulders. Also called *till*.

bovine   pertaining to cattle.

brackish   water that is intermediate in salinity between fresh water and sea water.

broad   a shallow, flooded medieval peat working in East Anglia (UK).

brood   collectively, the young hatched from a single clutch of eggs.

brown earth   brown friable soil with no visible layering, often highly calcareous. The high calcium carbonate content helps to retard leaching.

browse	of livestock, to feed on tender portions of trees and shrubs.
bund	an artificial embankment keyed into the substrate and used to retain water.
callow	a low-lying wet meadow liable to flooding adjacent to an Irish river.
catchment or catchment area	the total area from which a single river collects water (in the USA the term 'watershed' is used in this context).
climax	the terminal community in ecological succession that maintains itself, more or less unchanged, for a long period of time under the prevailing climatic and edaphic conditions.
community	any group of organisms occupying a common environment. The term is a general one, see *association*.
CORINE	a standardised classification system for European *biotopes*. Most CORINE *biotopes* are defined in terms of their constituent plant communities.
corncrake	*Crex crex*.
Cretaceous	the third and final period of the Mesozoic era beginning about 135 million years ago.
Culm grassland	local name given to unimproved *pastures* which support a distinctive flora on the underlying Carboniferous sandstones, slates and shales (Culm measures) of northern Devon and north-east Cornwall, UK, which give rise to acidic, poorly draining soils most conspicuously in the many valley bottoms of this region.
culvert	a channel for carrying water under a structure such as a road or railway.
detritivores	organisms that feed on the material formed through the breakdown and decay of animals and plants.
diaspore	any spore, seed or fruit or other portion of a plant which, after dispersal, is capable of producing a new plant.
discharge	the rate of flow of a river or stream at a particular point.
drainage channel	engineered linear waterbody intended to drain areas of wet grassland or facilitate water movement around them and to act as 'wet fences' for livestock.
dung	excrement of animals.
equine	a collective term for horses and ponies.
euryhaline	organisms adapted to a wide range of salinity.
eutrophic	applied to *biotopes*, especially wetlands (eg *fens*) that have an excess of nutrients; also eutrophication.
evapotranspiration	the loss of moisture from soil and wetland vegetation by means of direct evaporation and transpiration from vegetation.
ewe	female sheep.

fen	waterlogged ground with a peat soil that may be alkaline, neutral or slightly acid – in contrast to *bog* in which the soil is very acid.
fen meadow	mire grassland association (ie on peat) similar to typical wet grassland but with more short *Carex, Juncus* and moss species.
flexi-pipe	flexible PVC pipe used to make cheap sluice structures.
flood meadow	wet grassland in a *floodplain* cut for hay or silage and subject to periodic flooding.
floodplain	that part of a river valley adjacent to the channel over which a river flows in times of flood. It is a zone of low relief and gentle gradients and composed of *alluvium* which generally buries the rock floor of the valley to variable depths; often characterised by high *biodiversity* and production.
flood-sward	a stretch or expanse of grass that is frequently inundated.
fly-strike	a damaging infestation of *Sarcophaga* larvae, which feed on the skin and tissues of sheep.
flyway	migration route used by birds.
fodder	food material (eg *hay* and *silage*) used to feed livestock through the winter.
footdrain	small drainage channel in grasslands designed to assist water distribution and flow.
foot-rot	a bacterial infection (*Fusiformis nodosus*) affecting the feet of sheep.
forage	harvested grass or hay.
forb	any herbaceous plant other than a grass or a grasslike plant such as *Carex*.
formation	one or more plant communities which exhibit comparable structures within a climatic region.
gley	a soil that is permanently or periodically waterlogged and therefore anaerobic, characterised by blue-grey colours.
geotextile	strong fabrics typically made of synthetic fibres and used in civil engineering, eg in stabilising embankments along rivers or roads.
grazier	a farmer who keeps cattle or sheep on grazing land.
grazing marsh	wet grassland used during summer months for grazing livestock, usually cattle.
groundwater	underground water that is retained in the soil and in pervious rocks.
habitat	the local environment occupied by individuals of a particular species.
hay	grass and associated vegetation cut and dried for fodder.
haying	the process of mowing and storing hay.
hydrograph	a graph showing the *discharge* of a stream as a function of time at a given point along the stream.

hydrophyte	a plant that grows wholly or partly immersed in water.
lek	a display ground where male birds gather to attract mates.
levee	a naturally formed elevated bank bordering the channel of a river which stands above the level of the *floodplain*.
ley	land temporarily under grass.
liver fluke	a trematode worm that infects the bile-duct of sheep and cattle.
loam	an easily worked permeable soil comprising an almost equal mix of sand and silt but with less than 30% clay.
manure	any organic substance, especially *dung*, applied to land to make it more fertile.
marsh	ground that is waterlogged, the summer water level being normally at or near the soil surface. The soil has an inorganic (ie mineral) basis, usually silt or clay, in contrast to fen which is organic (ie peat).
meadow	grassland cut for *hay* or *silage*.
mesophyllous/mesophilous	(1) applied to plants or plant communities associated with neutral soil conditions. (2) pertaining to constant moderately moist conditions.
mesotrophic	applied to *biotopes*, especially wetlands (eg fens) that contain moderate amounts of nutrients and are therefore moderately productive.
Miocene	a geological epoch of the Tertiary period extending from about 26 million years ago to about 7 million years ago.
mire	a synonym for peatland used to describe both *bog* and *fen*.
mole drain	narrow drainage tunnels made in sub-soil by a cylindrical implement attached to a blade. When dragged through the soil the slit made by the blade closes but the tunnel remains open.
moraine	general term to describe landforms composed of glacial drift.
ochre	naturally occurring iron oxides, typically with yellow or red pigmentation.
ox-bow	a crescent-shaped waterbody occurring on a river *floodplain* having once been part of a river meander that has been cut through by the river and abandoned.
pasture	grassland that is regularly grazed by livestock.
peat	organic soil, often deep, composed of partly decomposed plant material. It forms under anaerobic conditions in waterlogged areas such as *fens* and *bogs*.
pen	a small enclosure for livestock, eg cows and sheep.
plagioclimax	any plant *community* with a more or less stable composition and in equilibrium under existing conditions but which, as a result of human intervention, has not achieved the natural *climax*, eg grassland under continuous pasture.

poaching	excessive trampling by livestock causing removal of vegetation cover and exposure of soil surface.
podzol	a type of soil formed in cool, seasonally humid climates where leaching is a dominant process.
polder	low-lying land claimed from wetland (eg *saltmarsh* or sea).
Ramsar site	site designated as a Wetland of International Importance under the Ramsar Convention. This requires signatory countries to protect internationally important wetlands, particularly those used by migratory waterfowl. The convention was signed in Ramsar, a town in Iran in 1975.
rank	coarsely overgrown, typically of grasslands.
reedbed	a large often monospecific stand of tall emergent grass or grass-like species, usually *Phragmites australis*.
rehabilitation	the act of bringing back into good condition or function.
rendzina	a soil with dark grey or black organic surface layers developed over soft light calcareous material derived from chalk, limestone or marl.
reprivatisation	the process by which land acquired by the state is returned, often to the original landowner.
restoration	the act of bringing back to a (supposed) former state.
riffle	a depositional bar on the channel floor of a river comprising a collection of sedimentary particles formed into a characteristically rippled surface.
riparian	of, or inhabiting, a riverbank or margin.
rotovate	to cultivate the soil by means of a rotovator, a motorised soil-tilling machine.
saltmarsh	coastal *biotope* with a characteristic salt-tolerant flora, influenced by regular tidal inundation.
scrub	low trees and bushes collectively.
sere	a series of temporary communities (seral stages) that develop a successional sequence in a given area and lead to a *climax* community.
shallows	a shallow part of a body of water, for example a lake or river.
silage	cut grass preserved in a succulent state for fodder under air-tight, acid conditions.
siliceous	that which contains an abundance of silica.
spillway	a channel that carries away surplus water, as from a dam.
splash-flooding	land flooded at, or just above, ground level.
stakeholder	a person who has an interest or concern with a particular issue or business.

store cattle	cattle normally between one and two years old that can either be bullocks/steers (castrated males) or cows. Store cattle may be sold either in the autumn for fattening indoors or in the following spring for subsequent finishing on grass.
suckler cows	cows accompanied by calves, reared for beef.
swamp	an area usually saturated with water but in which the soil surface is not deeply submerged. Often dominated by just one or two species of plant.
sward	above ground vegetative components of grassland.
terrace	a horizontal flat area of ground, often one of a series in a slope.
till	see *boulder clay*.
topping	mechanical cutting aimed at removing tall, coarse or excessive vegetation.
turf	the layer of low, dense grassland comprising the above ground portions and the upper roots and rhizomes with attached soil particles (plural 'turves'; see *sward*).
tussock	a bunchy clump of grasses, sedges or rushes.
underdrainage	in-field infrastructure to facilitate drainage, usually in the form of subterranean clay or plastic pipes.
valley pasture	permanent grassland situated in a *floodplain* that is regularly grazed by livestock.
washland	a river floodplain surrounded by artificial embankments into which the river is diverted in times of flood in order to alleviate further flooding downstream. In the USA, the term is synonymous with water meadow.
water meadow	grassland along the *floodplain* of a river where the growth of herbage is stimulated by periodic flooding, often by artificial means using channels and sluices. It is termed a washland in the USA.
water table	the upper surface of the zone of saturation in a soil or rock formation.
weedwiper	device that delivers herbicide to plants without spraying, so can be used selectively on tall, rank plants, leaving the sward undamaged.
wildfowl	members of the order Anatidae (ducks, geese and swans).
withy bed	a plot of land in which a shrubby species of willow *Salix viminalis* and hybrids is grown. This species is noted for its long narrow leaves and very flexible twigs which are much valued for basket making.
xeric	inhabiting places where water supply is limited, or where conditions, eg excess of salts, make it difficult for plants to take in water.
xerophilous	liking dry conditions, usually referred to plants and vegetation communities.

Appendix 2 Abbreviations used in the text

asl	above sea-level
ass.	association
BA	Broads Authority
BGS	British Grassland Society
CORINE	Information system on the Co-ordination of Information on the Environment
EA	Environment Agency
EIA	environmental impact assessment
EN	English Nature
EOS	Estonian Ornithological Society
EPA	Environmental Protection Agency
ESA	Environmentally Sensitive Area
EU	European Union
FRCA	Farming and Rural Conservation Agency
GEF	Global Environment Facility
IBA	Important Bird Area
IUCN	International Union for Conservation of Nature and Natural Resources (World Conservation Union)
IWRB	International Waterfowl and Wetlands Research Bureau
LBV	Landesbund für Vogelschutz
LPO	Ligue pour la Protection des Oiseaux
MAFF	Ministry of Agriculture, Fisheries and Food
NABU	Naturschutzbund Deutschland
NGO	non-governmental organisation
NHA	Natural Heritage Area
PHARE	Poland and Hungary: Assistance to the Restructuring of the Economy
RDB	Red Data Book
REPS	Rural Environment Protection Scheme
RIZA	Institute for Integrated Water Management and Waste Water Treatment (Netherlands)
RSPB	Royal Society for the Protection of Birds
SAC	Special Area of Conservation
SAC	Scottish Agricultural College
SPA	Special Protection Area
SPEC	Species of European Conservation Concern
TSES	Territorial System of Ecological Stability
UK	United Kingdom
UNESCO	United Nations Educational, Scientific and Cultural Organisation
WWF	Worldwide Fund for Nature
ZNIEFF	Zone National d'Intérêt Floristique et Faunistique.

Appendix 3 Bird species of European conservation concern (SPECs) occurring in wet grassland in north and central Europe

Listed by country (after Tucker and Heath 1994 and Tucker and Evans 1997).

Species	SPEC category	Austria	Belarus	Belgium	Bulgaria	Croatia	Czech Republic	Denmark	Estonia	Finland	France	Germany	Hungary	Italy	Latvia
Ardea purpurea	3	✓			✓	✓	✓				✓	✓	✓	✓	
Ciconia ciconia	2	✓	✓	✓	✓	✓	✓	✓	✓		✓	✓	✓	✓	✓
Cygnus columbianus	3			✓	✓			✓			✓	✓			
Cygnus cygnus	4			✓	✓			✓	✓	✓	✓	✓			✓
Anser brachyrhynchus	4			✓				✓							
Anser erythropus	1				✓	✓									
Anas acuta	3	✓	✓		✓			✓	✓	✓	✓		✓	✓	✓
Anas querquedula	3	✓	✓	✓	✓	✓	✓	✓	✓	✓	✓	✓	✓		✓
Circus cyaneus	3		✓	✓	✓	✓	✓	✓	✓	✓	✓	✓	✓	✓	✓
Falco tinnunculus	3	✓	✓	✓	✓	✓	✓	✓	✓	✓	✓	✓	✓	✓	✓
Aquila pomarina	3		✓		✓	✓	✓		✓				✓		✓
Aquila clanga	1		✓												✓
Aquila heliaca	1				✓	✓							✓		
Coturnix coturnix	3	✓	✓	✓	✓	✓	✓	✓	✓	✓	✓	✓	✓	✓	✓
Porzana porzana	4	✓	✓	✓	✓			✓	✓	✓		✓	✓	✓	✓
Crex crex	1	✓	✓	✓	✓	✓	✓	✓	✓	✓	✓	✓	✓	✓	✓
Grus grus	3		✓				✓	✓	✓	✓	✓	✓			✓
Calidris alpina	3		✓	✓				✓	✓	✓	✓	✓	✓		✓
Philomachus pugnax	4		✓					✓	✓	✓	✓	✓	✓		✓
Gallinago media	2		✓						✓	✓					✓
Limosa limosa	2	✓	✓	✓				✓	✓	✓	✓	✓	✓		✓
Numenius tenuirostris	1				✓	✓							✓	✓	
Numenius arquata	3	✓	✓	✓				✓	✓	✓	✓	✓	✓		✓
Tringa totanus	2	✓	✓	✓	✓	✓	✓	✓	✓	✓	✓	✓	✓	✓	✓
Larus canus	2	✓	✓	✓				✓	✓	✓	✓	✓	✓		✓
Chlidonias niger	3		✓		✓	✓	✓	✓	✓	✓	✓	✓	✓	✓	✓
Tyto alba	3	✓	✓	✓	✓	✓	✓	✓			✓	✓	✓	✓	✓
Athene noctua	3	✓	✓	✓	✓	✓	✓	✓			✓	✓	✓	✓	✓
Asio flammeus	3	✓	✓	✓			✓	✓	✓	✓	✓	✓	✓		✓
Alauda arvensis	3	✓	✓	✓	✓	✓	✓	✓	✓	✓	✓	✓	✓	✓	✓
Hirundo rustica	3	✓	✓	✓	✓	✓	✓	✓	✓	✓	✓	✓	✓	✓	✓
Anthus pratensis	4	✓	✓	✓				✓	✓	✓	✓	✓			✓
Saxicola rubetra	4	✓	✓	✓	✓	✓	✓	✓	✓	✓	✓	✓	✓	✓	✓
Saxicola torquata	3	✓		✓	✓	✓	✓	✓			✓	✓	✓	✓	
Locustella naevia	4	✓	✓	✓		✓	✓	✓	✓	✓	✓	✓	✓		✓
Acrocephalus paludicola	1		✓									✓	✓		✓

SPEC categories

1 Species of global conservation concern – classified as globally threatened, conservation dependent or data deficient.

2 Concentrated in Europe but with an unfavourable conservation status.

Lithuania	Moldova	Netherlands	Norway	Poland	Portugal	Republic of Ireland	Romania	Russia	Slovakia	Slovenia	Spain	Sweden	Switzerland	Ukraine	UK	Species
	✓	✓		✓	✓		✓	✓	✓		✓		✓	✓		*Ardea purpurea*
✓	✓	✓		✓	✓		✓	✓	✓	✓	✓		✓	✓		*Ciconia ciconia*
		✓				✓	✓							✓	✓	*Cygnus columbianus*
✓		✓	✓	✓		✓	✓					✓		✓	✓	*Cygnus cygnus*
		✓	✓			✓									✓	*Anser brachyrhynchus*
		✓					✓			✓		✓				*Anser erythropus*
✓		✓	✓	✓			✓	✓	✓		✓	✓	✓	✓	✓	*Anas acuta*
✓	✓	✓	✓	✓	✓	✓	✓	✓	✓	✓	✓	✓	✓	✓	✓	*Anas querquedula*
✓	✓	✓	✓	✓	✓	✓			✓	✓	✓	✓		✓	✓	*Circus cyaneus*
✓	✓	✓	✓	✓	✓	✓	✓	✓	✓	✓	✓	✓	✓	✓	✓	*Falco tinnunculus*
✓	✓			✓			✓	✓	✓					✓		*Aquila pomarina*
	✓			✓			✓	✓						✓		*Aquila clanga*
	✓						✓	✓	✓					✓		*Aquila heliaca*
✓	✓	✓	✓	✓	✓	✓	✓	✓	✓	✓	✓	✓	✓	✓	✓	*Coturnix coturnix*
✓	✓	✓	✓	✓			✓	✓	✓	✓	✓	✓	✓	✓	✓	*Porzana porzana*
✓	✓	✓	✓	✓		✓	✓	✓	✓	✓	✓	✓	✓	✓	✓	*Crex crex*
✓		✓	✓				✓	✓				✓		✓		*Grus grus*
✓		✓	✓	✓		✓		✓				✓			✓	*Calidris alpina*
✓		✓	✓	✓				✓				✓		✓	✓	*Philomachus pugnax*
✓			✓	✓				✓				✓		✓		*Gallinago media*
✓		✓	✓	✓		✓	✓	✓	✓		✓	✓		✓	✓	*Limosa limosa*
							✓	✓						✓		*Numenius tenuirostris*
✓		✓	✓	✓		✓	✓	✓	✓	✓	✓	✓	✓	✓		*Numenius arquata*
✓	✓	✓	✓	✓	✓	✓	✓	✓	✓	✓	✓	✓		✓	✓	*Tringa totanus*
✓	✓	✓	✓	✓		✓		✓	✓			✓	✓		✓	*Larus canus*
✓	✓	✓		✓			✓	✓	✓		✓	✓		✓		*Chlidonias niger*
✓	✓	✓		✓	✓	✓	✓		✓	✓	✓		✓	✓	✓	*Tyto alba*
✓	✓	✓		✓	✓		✓	✓	✓	✓	✓		✓	✓	✓	*Athene noctua*
✓	✓	✓	✓	✓			✓	✓	✓		✓	✓		✓	✓	*Asio flammeus*
✓	✓	✓	✓	✓	✓	✓	✓	✓	✓	✓	✓	✓	✓	✓	✓	*Alauda arvensis*
✓	✓	✓	✓	✓	✓	✓	✓	✓	✓	✓	✓	✓	✓	✓	✓	*Hirundo rustica*
✓	✓	✓	✓			✓	✓	✓	✓			✓	✓	✓	✓	*Anthus pratensis*
✓	✓	✓	✓	✓	✓	✓	✓	✓	✓	✓	✓	✓	✓	✓	✓	*Saxicola rubetra*
	✓	✓	✓	✓	✓	✓	✓		✓	✓	✓		✓	✓	✓	*Saxicola torquata*
✓	✓	✓	✓	✓		✓	✓	✓	✓	✓	✓	✓	✓	✓	✓	*Locustella naevia*
✓				✓				✓						✓		*Acrocephalus paludicola*

3   Not concentrated in Europe but with an unfavourable conservation status
4   Concentrated in Europe and with a favourable conservation status

Appendix 4 International instruments relating to European wet grassland management.

After Tucker and Evans c1997.

Instrument	Objectives	Obligations
Global conventions 'Biodiversity Convention' – Convention on Biological Diversity. 26 contracting parties (including EU) and 12 signatories from Europe.	To ensure the conservation of biodiversity, the sustainable use of its components and the fair and equitable sharing of the benefits arising out of the utilisation of genetic resources.	To prepare national Biodiversity Action Plans for conservation and sustainable use of nation's biological resources and to integrate these into other relevant plans, programmes and policies. To promote the protection of ecosystems, natural habitats and the maintenance of viable populations of species in natural surroundings, and to rehabilitate and restore degraded ecosystems and promote the recovery of threatened species for example by implementation of Biodiversity Action Plans or other management strategies.
'Ramsar Convention' – Convention on Wetlands of International Importance especially as Waterfowl Habitat. 32 European states are signatories.	To stem the loss of wetlands and to ensure their conservation and wise use.	To designate suitable wetlands for inclusion within a 'List of wetlands of international importance'. To formulate and implement planning so as to promote the conservation of 'listed' wetlands and as far as possible the wise use of all wetlands. To promote the conservation of wetlands and wildfowl in general by establishing nature reserves and adequately wardening them.
'Bonn Convention' – Convention on the Conservation of Migratory Species of Wild Animals. 20 European states and the EU are contracting parties, one European state is a signatory.	The conservation and effective management of terrestrial, marine and avian species over the whole of their migratory range.	To undertake research activities in relation to migratory species. To adopt strict protection measures for endangered migratory species listed in Appendix I of the Convention. To conclude agreements for the conservation of migratory species with unfavourable conservation status' or those which would benefit significantly from international co-operation (listed in Appendix II of the Convention).
'World Heritage Convention' – Convention concerning the Protection of the World Cultural and Natural Heritage. 31 European states are signatories.	To ensure the protection of natural and cultural areas of outstanding universal values as a duty of the international community as a whole, by granting collective assistance.	To ensure the identification, protection, conservation, presentation and transmission to future generations of the cultural and natural heritage situated on the territory of each party state.
Pan European Conventions 'Bern Convention' – Convention on the Conservation of European Wildlife and Natural Habitats. 29 European countries, as well as the EU, have ratified the Convention.	To conserve wild flora and fauna and their natural habitats, especially those species that would benefit from co-operation of several states.	To take appropriate and necessary legislative and administrative measures to ensure the conservation of habitats of the wild flora and fauna, especially those specified in Appendices I and II of the Convention, and the conservation of endangered natural habitats.

Appendix 4 (cont)

'Espoo Convention' – Convention on Environmental Impact Assessment in a Transboundary Context. A total of 28 European countries are signatories.	To promote the environmental assessment of proposed activities whose impacts have the potential to affect more than one state. To improve the methodology of such assessments, and improve mechanisms of co-operation between states, so as to minimise and mitigate the transboundary environmental impacts of economic activities.	As a minimum requirement contracting parties should undertake EIAs at the project level where a proposed activity is likely to cause significant adverse transboundary impacts. The general public of the affected areas of other contracting parties' territory should be allowed access to the consultation process equal to that of the general public of the state which originates the proposed activity.
EU instruments		
'Birds Directive' – Council Directive 79/409/EEC on the conservation of wild birds. All 15 EU member states are signatories.	Conservation of all species of naturally occurring birds in the wild state in the European territory of the member states (excluding Greenland).	To classify as Special Protection Areas (SPAs) the most suitable territories for the conservation of bird species listed in Annex I of the Directive, taking into account their protection requirements in the area. To take similar measures for regularly occurring migratory species not listed in Annex I, paying particular attention to the protection of wetlands, particularly to wetlands of international importance. To ensure that the SPAs form a coherent whole which meets the protection requirement of the species in the area where the Directive applies. SPAs will form part of the Natura 2000 network (see *Habitats Directive* below). To avoid significant disturbance and habitat deterioration in SPAs with respect to Annex I and regularly occurring migratory species for which the areas have been designated. To assess the implications for an SPA of any plan or project likely to have a significant effect thereon (either directly or in combination with other plans or projects) and which is not directly connected with or necessary to the management of the site. Having carried out an assessment, only to allow such plans or projects to proceed if they will not have an adverse effect on the integrity of the site or, if there will be an adverse effect, only to allow the plan or project to proceed in the absence of alternative solutions and for imperative reasons of overriding public interest. If a plan or project which damages the integrity of an SPA is allowed to proceed, member states must take all compensatory measures necessary to ensure the overall coherence of the Natura 2000 network To avoid pollution or deterioration of habitats outside SPAs.

153

Appendix 4 (cont)

'Habitats Directive' – Council Directive 92/43/EEC on the conservation of natural habitats of wild fauna and flora. All 15 EU member states are signatories.	To contribute towards ensuring biodiversity through the conservation of natural habitats and of wild fauna and flora (in the EU) through measures that maintain or restore, at favourable conservation status, natural habitats and species of wild fauna and flora of EU interest in the European territory of the member states. These measures shall take account of economic, social, cultural and regional requirements.	To create a coherent ecological network (Natura 2000) of Special Areas of Conservation (SACs) setting the minimum standard for biodiversity conservation in the EU. To establish, in each member state, the conservation status of habitats and species listed in the Annexes (especially priority habitats and species as defined in Article 1), and to provide the means to monitor the further evolution of their conservation status. Each member state should propose a list of sites indicating which of the priority natural habitat types and species (listed in Annexes 1 and 2) are hosted by the site. The EU will then establish and adopt a draft list of sites of community importance, in agreement with each member state and drawn from the lists provided by each member state. As soon as possible after June 1998 and before June 2004, each member state shall designate the listed sites as SACs, establishing priority for designation in the light of relative importance of each site for the maintenance or restoration, at a favourable conservation status, of a natural habitat type in Annex I or a priority species in Annex II, and for the coherence of Natura 2000, and in the light of the threats of degradation or destruction to which each site is exposed. To avoid significant disturbance and habitat deterioration in SACs with respect to habitats and species for which the areas have been designated. To assess the implication for any SAC of any plan or project likely to have a significant effect thereon (either directly or in combination with other plans or projects) and which is not directly connected with or necessary to the management of the site. Having carried out an assessment only to allow such plans or projects to proceed if they will not have an adverse effect on the integrity of the site or, if there will be an adverse effect, only to allow the plan or project to proceed in the absence of alternative solutions and for imperative reasons of overriding public interest. If a plan or project which damages the integrity of an SPA is allowed to proceed, member states must take all compensatory measures necessary to ensure the overall coherence of the Natura 2000 network
'Agri-environment Regulation' – Council regulation 2078/92/EEC on agricultural production methods compatible with protection of the environment and maintenance of countryside.	Protection of the farmed environment through payments to farmers for farming practices which protect and manage the countryside.	Member states submit plans to the EU for multi-annual programmes, determined at national or regional levels, covering all territories. Schemes for paying farmers for extensification of livestock or arable, maintenance of the countryside, organic farming and public access are prepared and administered by national governments.

References and further reading

ADAS (1996a) *Botanical monitoring of grassland in the Broads ESA, 1987–1994*. Report to Ministry of Agriculture, Fisheries and Food. HMSO, London.

ADAS (1996b) *Environmental monitoring in the Broads ESA, 1987–1995*. Report to Ministry of Agriculture, Fisheries and Food. HMSO, London.

Alcock, M R and Palmer, M A (1985) *A standard method for the survey of ditch vegetation*. Chief Scientist Team (CST) Notes 37. Nature Conservancy Council, Peterborough.

Alderson, L and Small, R (1997) Rare breeds, natural choices. *Enact* 5 (4): 4-7.

Ausden, M and Treweek, J (1995) Grassland. In W J Sutherland and D A Hill (Eds) *Managing habitats for conservation*. Cambridge University Press, Cambridge.

Baattrup-Pedersen, A, Riis, T, Hansen, H O and Friberg, N (in prep) Restoration of a Danish headwater stream: short term changes in plant species abundance and composition (submitted to *Aquatic Botany*).

Babbs, S, Cook, A S and Durdin, C (1997) *Broads ESA Wintering Waterfowl Survey 1996/1997*. Unpublished report. RSPB, Norwich.

Bailey, R G, José, P V and Sherwood, B R (Eds) (1988) *United Kingdom Floodplains*. Westbury, West Yorkshire.

Bakker, J P (1989) *Nature management by grazing and cutting*. Kluwer Academic, Dordrecht.

Balatova-Tulackova, E (1969) Contribution to the knowledge of the Czechoslovakian *Cnidion venosi* meadows. *Vegetatio* 17: 200–207. [In German]

Banásová, V, Jarolímek, I, Otahelová, H and Zaliberová, M (1998) Inundation grasslands of the Morava river, Slovakia: plant communities and factors affecting biodiversity. In C B Joyce and P M Wade (Eds) *European wet grasslands: biodiversity, management and restoration*, pp 111–136. John Wiley and Sons, Chichester.

Barkman, J, Moravec, J, and Rauschert, S (1986) Code of phytosociological nomenclature. *Vegetatio* 67(3): 145–195.

Beintema, A J (1983) Meadow birds as indicators. *Environmental Monitoring and Assessment* 3: 391-398.

Bejcek, P and Stastný, K (1996) Vertebrates of the Lužnice floodplain. In K Prach, J Jeník and A R G Large (Eds) *Floodplain ecology and management. The Lužnice River in the Třeboň Biosphere Reserve, central Europe*, pp 113-124. SPB Academic, Amsterdam.

Benstead, P, Drake, M, José P, Mountford, O, Newbold, C and Treweek, J (1997) *The wet grassland guide. Managing floodplain and coastal wet grasslands for wildlife*. RSPB, Sandy.

Berendse, F, Oomes, M J M, Altena, H J and de Visser, W (1994) A comparative study of nitrogen flows in two similar meadows affected by different groundwater levels. *Journal of Applied Ecology* 31: 40–48.

Berendse, F, Oomes, M J M, Altena, H J and Elberse, W Th (1992) Experiments on the restoration of species-rich meadows in The Netherlands. *Biological Conservation* 62: 59–65.

Berlin, G (1998) *Semi-natural meadows in southern Sweden – changes over time and the relationship between nitrogen supply and management*. Department of Ecology, University of Lund.

Blake, S and Foster G N (1998) The influence of grassland management on body size in Caribidae (ground beetles) and its bearing on the conservation of wading birds. In C B Joyce and P M Wade

(Eds) *European wet grasslands: biodiversity, management and restoration*, pp 163–172. John Wiley and Sons, Chichester.

Blanchon, J J, Delaporte, P and Egreteau, C (1993) *Protection and restoration of migratory stop-overs for the spoonbill*. Unpublished LPO report. [In French]

Boer, T E den (1995) *Meadowbirds: facts for conservation*. Technical report 16. Vogelbescherming, Zeist. [In Dutch with English summary]

Brooks, A (1980) *Hedging: a practical conservation handbook*. 2nd Edition. British Trust for Conservation Volunteers, Reading.

Brooks, A and Agate, E (1997) *Waterways and wetlands: a practical handbook*. 3rd Edition. British Trust for Conservation Volunteers, Wallingford.

Byczkowski, A and Kicinski, T (1984) Surface water in the Biebrza river drainage basin. *Polish Ecological Studies* 10 (3–4): 271–299.

Callaway, T (1998) Restoration of lowland wet grassland at Pulborough Brooks RSPB Nature Reserve. In R G Bailey, P V José and B R Sherwood (Eds) *United Kingdom Floodplains*, pp 459–63. Westbury, West Yorkshire.

Callaway, T and Glover, J (1993) *Management plan – Pulborough Brooks RSPB reserve*. Unpublished report. RSPB, Sandy.

Claßen, V A, Hirler, A and Oppermann, R (1996) Impact of mower type on the flora and fauna of meadows in north-east Poland, with reference to amphibians and white storks. *Naturshutz und Landschaftsplanung* 28 (5): 139–144. [In German]

Collar, N J, Crosby, M J and Stattersfield, A J (1994) *Birds to Watch 2: the world list of threatened birds*. BirdLife International, Cambridge.

Council of the European Communities (1992) Council Directive 92/43/EEC of 2 April 1992 on the Conservation of Natural Habitats and of Wild Fauna and Flora. (The Habitats Directive). *Official Journal of the European Communities* L206.

Cowx, I G and Welcomme, R L (Eds) (1998) *Rehabilitation of rivers for fish*. Fishing News Books, Oxford.

Crofts, A and Jefferson, R G (Eds) (1999) *The lowland grassland management handbook*. 2nd Edition. English Nature/The Wildlife Trusts.

Décamps, H and Tabacchi, E (1994) Species richness in vegetation along river margins. In P S Giller, A G Hildrew and D G Raffaelli (Eds) *Aquatic ecology: scale, pattern and process*, pp 1–20. Blackwell Scientific Publications, Oxford.

Deceuninck, B and Mahéo, R (1997) *Nesting waders of France – Synthesis of 1995–1996 national survey*. Unpublished report by Ministère de l'Environment, Wetlands International and LPO. [In French]

Dister, E, Gomer, D, Obrdlik, P, Petermann, P and Schneider, E (1990) Water management and ecological perspectives of the Upper Rhine's floodplains. *Regulated Rivers: Research and Management* 5: 1–16.

Drake, M (1998) The important habitats and characteristic rare invertebrates of lowland wet grassland in England. In C B Joyce and P M Wade (Eds) *European wet grasslands: biodiversity, management and restoration*, pp 137–150. John Wiley, Chichester.

Drbal, K and Rauch, O (1996) Water chemistry. In K Prach, J Jeník and A R G Large (Eds) *Floodplain ecology and management. The Lužnice River in the Třeboň Biosphere Reserve, Central Europe*, pp 47–51. SPB Academic Publishing, Amsterdam.

Dubois, P J, Mahéo, R and Hötker, H (1991) Waders breeding on wet grasslands in France. *Wader Study Group Bulletin* 61 Supplement: 27–31.

Dyrcz, A, Kozikowska, Z, Palczynski, A, Raczynski, J and Witkowski, J (1985a) The problems of nature protection and peatland management in the valley of the Biebrza river. *Polish Ecological Studies* 11 (1): 107–121.

Dyrcz, A, Okulewicz, J and Witkowski, J (1984) Bird communities of the Biebrza valley. *Polish Ecological Studies* 10 (3–4): 403–423.

Dyrcz, A, Okulewicz, J and Witkowski, J (1985b) Changes in bird communities as the effect of peatland management. *Polish Ecological Studies* 11 (1): 79–85.

Eurosite (1996) *Management plans for protected and managed semi-natural areas.* Report of Eurosite Working Group. Eurosite, Wimeraux.

Fabritius, H (1995) Meadow birds in the Mijzenpolder and the Eilandspolder – connections with management, 1986–1993. *Graspieper* 15: 25–32. [In Dutch with English summary]

Farkas, J (1995) Restoration measures on Morava river. Proceedings from conference *Revitalization of Morava and Dyje Floodplains,* pp 2–5. Union for Morava River, Distelverein, DAPHNE, Mikulov.

Fischer, S F, Poschlod, P and Beinlich, B (1996) Experimental studies on the dispersal of plants and animals on sheep in calcareous grasslands. *Journal of Applied Ecology* 23: 1206-1222.

Geerts, R H E M, Ketelaars, J J M H, Oomes, M J M, Korevaar, H and van der Werf, A K (1996) Reintroduction of grassland species. In *Annual Report 1995 – AB-DLO,* pp 65–68. AB-DLO, Wageningen.

George, M (1992) *The Land Use, Ecology and Conservation of Broadland.* Packard Publishing Ltd, Chichester.

Gilbert, G, Gibbons, D W and Evans, J (1998) *Bird monitoring methods: a manual of techniques for key UK species.* RSPB, Sandy.

Girard, N (1992) *Extensive rearing of horses for the management of nature reserves.* Office National Chase, Paris. [In French]

Green, R E, Tyler, G A, Stowe, T J and Newton, A V A (1997) A simulation model of the effect of mowing of agricultural grassland on the breeding success of the corncrake (*Crex crex*). *J. Zool. London* 243: 81–115.

Grimmett, R F A and Jones, T A (1989) *Important Bird Areas in Europe.* International Council for Bird Preservation, Cambridge.

Hansen, H O (Ed) (1996) *River restoration – Danish experience and examples.* National Environment Research Institute, Denmark.

Hawke, C J and José, P V (1996) *Reedbed management for commercial and wildlife interests.* RSPB, Sandy.

Haycock, N E, Burt, T P, Goulding, K W T and Pinay, G (1997) *Buffer zones: their processes and potential in water protection.* Proceedings of the International Conference on Buffer Zones, September 1996. Samara Publishing, Tresaith.

Heath, M F and Evans, M I (in press) *Important bird areas in Europe.* 2nd Edition. BirdLife International, Cambridge.

Heery, S (1991) The plant communities of the grazed and mown grassland of the River Shannon Callows. *Proceedings of the Royal Irish Academy* 91B: 1–19.

Heery, S (1993) *The Shannon Floodlands: a natural history of the Shannon Callows.* Tir Eolas, Kinvara.

Hellawell, J M (1991) Development of a rationale for monitoring. In F B Goldsmith (Ed) *Monitoring for conservation and ecology,* pp 1-14. Chapman and Hall, London.

Hertzman, T and Larsson, T (1997) *Hornborgasön – from an ocean of reeds to a kingdom of birds.* Swedish EPA report 4694, Stockholm. [In Swedish]

Hertzman, T and Larsson, T (1999) *Lake Hornborga, Sweden – the return of a bird lake.* Wetlands International Publ. 50, Wageningen, Netherlands.

Hirons, G, Goldsmith, B and Thomas, G (1995) Site management planning. In W J Sutherland and D A Hill (Eds) *Managing habitats for conservation,* pp 22–41. Cambridge University Press, Cambridge.

Holve, H (1996) *The Broads Natural Area Profile*. English Nature and the Broads Authority, Norwich.

Hooijer, A (1996) *Floodplain hydrology: an ecologically oriented study of the Shannon Callows, Ireland*. PhD thesis – Vrije Universitiet, Amsterdam, Netherlands.

Hötker, H (1991) Waders breeding on wet grassland in the countries of the European Community – a brief summary of current knowledge on population densities and population trends. In H Hötker (Ed) *Waders breeding on wet grassland. Wader Study Group Bulletin* 61. Wader Study Group, Tring.

Ingelög, T, Andersson, R and Tjernberg, M (1993) *Red Data Book of the Baltic Region*. Swedish Threatened Species Unit, Uppsala.

IUCN (1998) *Guidelines for re-introductions*. Prepared by the IUCN/SSC Re-introduction Specialist Group. IUCN, Gland, Switzerland and Cambridge, UK.

Janda, J (1994) Třeboň Basin Biosphere Reserve. In J Jeník and M F Price (Eds) *Biosphere reserves on the crossroads of central Europe*, pp 66–80. Man and Biosphere Programme, Empora Publishing, Prague.

Jefferson, R G and Grice, P V (1998) The conservation of lowland wet grassland in England. In C B Joyce, and P M Wade (Eds) *European wet grasslands: biodiversity, management and restoration*, pp. 31-48. John Wiley and Sons, Chichester.

José, P (1988) The *hydrochemistry of backwaters and deadzones*. PhD thesis. Loughborough University of Technology.

Joyce, C B (1994) Effects of land-use changes on the Lužnice floodplain grasslands in the Czech Republic. In R J Haggar and S Peel (Eds) *Grassland management and nature conservation*, pp 299–301. Occasional Symposium 28, British Grassland Society, Reading.

Joyce, C B and Wade, P M (Eds) (1998) *European wet grasslands: biodiversity, management and restoration*. John Wiley and Sons, Chichester.

Kalivodová, E, Feriancova-Masarova, Z and Darolova, A (1994) Birds of the floodplains of the River Morava. *Ekologia Bratislava* 13 (Suppl. 1): 189–199.

Kaljuste, T (1994) Matsalu – valuable wetland and bird paradise. *WWF Baltic Bulletin* 1: 7–10.

Kirby, P (1992) *Habitat management for invertebrates: a practical handbook*. RSPB, Sandy.

Kminiak, M (1994) Amphibians in the alluvium of the Morava River. *Ecology Bratislava* 13: 77–88.

Kovalenko, E P, and Taskaev, V I (1987) Water resource use in the Pripyat River basin. *Problemy Polessia* 11: 168–170. [In Russian]

Kozulin, A V, Nikiforov, M E, and Pareiko, O A (1995) Goose migration in Belarus. *IWRB Goose Research Group Bulletin* 6: 20–24.

Kozulin, A V, Nikiforov, M E, Mongin, E A, Pareiko, O A, Samusenko, I E, Cherkas, N D, Shokalo, S I and Byshnev, I I (1997) Waterfowl migration in Belarus. *Belovezhskaya pushcha Forest Biodiversity Conservation*: 262–280.

Lane, A (1992) *Practical conservation: grasslands, heaths and moors*. Hodder and Stoughton, London.

Leibak, E and Lutsar, L (Eds) (1996) *Estonian coastal and floodplain meadows*. Kirjameeste Kirjastus, Tallinn.

Leibl, F (1994) Comments on the bird community, and the influence of habitat management on the avifauna, of the Stöcklwörth nature reserve. *Jber. OAG Ostbayern* 21 Supplement: 23–39. [In German]

LPO (1996) *Management of coastal aquatic habitats for the spoonbill on migration and other associated birds*. Proceedings of the 23rd Eurosite nature management workshop, 1996.

Mägi, E, Kastepold, T and Lotman, A (in press) Ornithological monitoring and wetland management in Matsalu. In A Kuresoo (Ed) *Bird numbers 1995. Bird monitoring for conservation*.

Proceedings of the 13th International Conference of EBCC, Pärnu.

Maglocky, S and Ferakova, V (1993) Red list of ferns and flowering plants (Pteridophyta and Spermatophyta) of the flora of Slovakia. *Biológia Bratislava* 48/4.

Manchester, S, Treweek, J, Mountford, O, Pywell, R and Sparks, T (1998) Restoration of a target wet grassland community on ex-arable land. In C B Joyce and P M Wade (Eds) *European wet grasslands: biodiversity, management and restoration*, pp 277–294. John Wiley, Chichester.

Mitsch, W J and Gosselink, J G (1993) *Wetlands*. 2nd Edition. Van Nostrand Reinhold, New York.

Müller, H S (1997) *Institutional criteria and guidelines for successful wetland restoration*. Workshop on a Wetland Restoration Project in the Danube River Basin – Bratislava. December 1997, pp 1–16.

Muller, S, Dutoit, T, Alard, D and Grévilliot, F (1998) Restoration and rehabilitation of species-rich grassland ecosystems in France: a review. *Restoration Ecology* 6: 94–101.

Nagy, B (1990) Orthopteroid insects (Orthoptera, Montidea, Blattodea, Dermaptera) of the Batorliget Nature Reserves (NE Hungary). In S Marhumka (Ed) *The Batorliget Nature Reserves – after fifty years. Volume I.* Hungarian Natural History Museum, Budapest.

Nairn, R G W, Herbert, I J and Heery, S (1988) Breeding waders and other wet grassland birds of the River Shannon Callows. *Irish Birds* 3: 521–537.

NCC (1988) *Site management plans for nature conservation – a working guide*. Nature Conservancy Council, Peterborough.

Newbold, C and Mountford, O (1997) *Water level requirements of wetland plants and animals*. English Nature Freshwater Series 5. English Nature, Peterborough.

Newbold, C, Honnor, J and Buckley, K (1989) *Nature conservation and the management of drainage channels*. The Association of Drainage Authorities and the Nature Conservancy Council, Peterborough.

Nielsen, M B (1995) Restoration of streams and their riparian zones – South Jutland, Denmark. In M Eiseltová and J Biggs (Eds) *Restoration of stream ecosystems – an integrated catchment approach*, pp 30–44. IWRB, Slimbridge.

Nielsen, M B (1996a) Lowland stream restoration in Denmark. In A Brookes and F D Shields (Eds) *River channel restoration*, pp 269–289. John Wiley and Sons, Chichester.

Nielsen, M B (1996b) River restoration: report of a major EU Life demonstration project. *Aquatic Conservation: Marine and Freshwater Ecosystems* 6: 187–90.

Niemann, S (1995) *Habitat management for corncrakes*. Unpublished report. RSPB, Sandy.

Nilson, E, Kannukene, L, Truus, L, Ratas, U, Puurmann, E and Tobias, M (1997) Biological diversity. In U Ratas and E Nilson (Eds) *Small islands of Estonia*, pp 131–179. Institute of Ecology, Tallinn.

NRA (1995) *Yare Catchment Management Plan*. National Rivers Authority, Norwich.

Oates, M and Bullock, D (1997) Browsers and grazers. *Enact* 5 (4): 15–18.

Ojaste, I (in press) Breeding bird fauna of Hullo Bay, Vormsi. Linnarad 1998. [In Estonian].

Oomes, M J M (1992) Yield and species density of grasslands during restoration management. *Journal of Vegetation Science* 3: 271–274.

Oomes, M J M (1997) Management of the groundwater-table and changes in grassland production, nutrient availability and biodiversity. In *Management for Grassland Biodiversity*. Proceedings of EGF Occasional Symposium, 1997. Warszawa-Lomza, Poland.

Oomes, M J M and Mooi, H (1981) The effect of cutting and fertilizing on the floristic composition and production of an *Arrhenatherion elatioris* grassland. *Vegetatio* 47: 233-239.

Oomes, M J M, Olff, H and Altena, H J (1996) Effects of vegetation management and raising the water-table on nutrient dynamics and vegetation change in a wet grassland. *Journal of Applied Ecology* 33: 576–588.

Opermanis, O (1995) Recent changes in breeding bird fauna at the seacoast of the Gulf of Riga. In M G H Healy and J P Doody (Eds) *Directions in European Coastal Management*, pp 361–368. Samara Publishing, Cardigan.

Palczynski, A (1984) Natural differentiation of plant communities in relation to hydrological conditions of the Biebrza valley. *Polish Ecological Studies* 10 (3–4): 347–385.

Palmer, M A, Bell, S L and Butterfield, I (1992) A botanical classification of standing waters in Britain: applications for conservation and monitoring. *Aquatic Conservation: Marine and Freshwater Ecosystems* 2: 125–143.

Parmenter, J (1995) *The Broadland Fen Resource Survey*. Volumes 1–5. BARS 13a–f. Broads Authority and English Nature, Norwich.

Pasternak-Kuśmierska, D (1984) Changes in species structure and density of meadow sward under the influence of inorganic fertilization. *Ekologia Polska* 32: 613–627.

Pollard, E and Yates, T J (1993) *Monitoring butterflies for ecology and conservation*. Chapman and Hall, London.

Pork, K (1985) The floodplain plant communities of the Kasari River, their utilisation and conservation. In E Kumari (Ed) *Matsalu – a wetland of international importance*, pp 88–112. [In Estonian with English summary]

Prach, K (1992) Vegetation, microtopography and water table in the Lužnice River floodplain, South Bohemia, Czechoslovakia. *Preslia, Praha* 64: 357–367.

Prach, K and Straškrabová, J (1996) Meadows in the Lužnice river floodplain in the Třeboň Biosphere Reserve – potential for restoration. In J Straškrabová, K Prach, C Joyce and M Wade (Eds) (1996) Floodplain meadows – ecological functions, contemporary state and possibilities for restoration. *Příroda* 4: 163-168. [In Czech]

Prach, K, Jeník, J and Large, A R G (Eds) (1996) *Floodplain ecology and management. The Lužnice River in the Třeboň Biosphere Reserve, central Europe*. SPB Academic Publishing, Amsterdam.

Puurmann, E and Ratas, U (1995) Problems of conservation and management of the west Estonian seashore meadows. In M G Healy and J P Doody (Eds) *Directions in European Coastal Management*, pp 345–349. Samara Publishing, Cardigan.

Puurmann, E and Ratas, U (1998) The formation, vegetation and management of sea-shore grasslands in west Estonia. In C B Joyce and P M Wade (Eds) *European Wet Grasslands: biodiversity, management and restoration*, pp 97–110. John Wiley and Sons, Chichester.

Racko, J and Bedrna, Z (1994) Soils in the floodplain of Lower Morava. *Ekologia Bratislava* 13 Suppl. 1: 5–13.

Rebassoo, H-E (1985) Plant communities of sea-shore meadows in Matsalu. In E Kumari (Ed) *Matsalu – a wetland of international importance*, pp 77–87. [In Estonian with English summary]

Rey Benayas, J M and Scheiner, S M (1993) Diversity patterns of wet meadows along geochemical gradients in central Spain. *Journal of Vegetation Science* 4: 103-108.

Reyrink, L A F (1988) Bird protection in grassland in the Netherlands. In J R Park (1988) *Environmental management in agriculture. European perspectives*, pp 159 – 169. Bellhaven Press, London & New York.

Ružička, M (Ed) (1994) Ecological potential of floodplain area of the river Morava. *Ecology Bratislava* 13: 1–216.

SAC (1990) *Farm Management Handbook*. Scottish Agricultural College, Auchincruive.

Seffer, J, Stanova, V and Vicenikova, A (1995) *Management and restoration of meadows in Morava river floodplains*. Unpublished report by DAPHNE Centre for Applied Ecology, Bratislava.

Self, M, O'Brien, M, and Hirons, G (1994) Hydrological management for waterfowl on RSPB lowland wet grassland reserves. *RSPB Conservation Review* 8: 45–56.

Seriot, J (1996) Protection of the black tern *Chlidonias niger*, in the west of France. *Ornithos* 3: 103–134. [In French]

Sheppard, R and Green, R E (1994) Status of the Corncrake in Ireland in 1993. *Irish Birds* 5 (2): 125–138.

Simpson, D and Gee, M (1997) Setting up a grazing project. *Enact* 5 (4): 23–26

Smith, I R, Wells, D A and Welsh, P (1985) *Botanical survey and monitoring methods for grasslands.* Focus on Nature Conservation No. 10. Nature Conservancy Council, Peterborough.

Spellerberg, I F (1992) *Evaluation and assessment for conservation. Ecological guidelines for determining priorities for nature conservation.* Chapman and Hall, London.

Stanova V, Cierna M and Seffer, J (1997) *Strategy for sustainable agriculture in the lower part of the Záhorie region.* Unpublished report by DAPHNE Center for Applied Ecology, Bratislava.

Straškrabová, J and Prach, K (1998) Five years of restoration of alluvial meadows – a case study from central Europe. In C B Joyce and P M Wade (Eds) *European wet grasslands: biodiversity, management and restoration*, pp 295–303. John Wiley and Sons, Chichester.

Straškrabová, J, Prach, K, Joyce, C and Wade, M (Eds) (1996) Floodplain meadows – ecological functions, contemporary state and possibilities for restoration. *Příroda* 4, 1–176. [In Czech, with English summary]

Strazds, M, Priednieks, J, Vaverins, G (1994) Latvijas putnu skaits. *Putni daba* 4: 3–19. [In Latvian]

Tallowin, J R B and Mountford, J O (1997) Lowland wet grasslands in ESAs. In R D Sheldrick (Ed) *Grassland management in the 'Environmentally Sensitive Areas'.* Proceedings of the BGS Conference held at the University of Lancaster, 23–25 September 1997. Occasional Symposium 32, British Grassland Society.

Thomas, G J (1982) Autumn and winter feeding ecology of waterfowl around the Ouse Washes, England. *Journal of Ecology* 197: 131–172.

Thomas, G J, Allen, D A and Grose, M P B (1981) The demography of the flora of the Ouse Washes, England. *Biological Conservation* 21: 197–228.

Tickner, M B and Evans, C E (1991) The management of lowland wet grasslands on RSPB reserves. Unpublished report. RSPB, Sandy.

Tockner, K, Scheimer, F, Baumgartner, C, Kum, G, Weigand, E, Zweimüller, I and Ward, J V (1999) The Danube restoration project: species patterns across connectivity gradients in the floodplain. *Regulated Rivers: Research and Management* 15: 245–258.

Truus, L (1998) Influence of management cessation on reedbed and floodplain vegetation on the Kloostri floodplain meadow in the delta of the Kasari River, Estonia. *Proceedings of the Estonian Academy of Sciences, Biology and Ecology* 47: 58–72.

Truus, L and Tõnisson, A (1998) The ecology of floodplain grasslands in Estonia. In C B Joyce and P M Wade (Eds) *European wet grasslands: biodiversity, management and restoration*, pp 49-60. John Wiley, Chichester.

Tubridy, M (1987) *The heritage of Clonmacnois.* Unpublished report. Environmental Sciences Unit, Trinity College, Dublin.

Tucker, G M and Evans, M I (1997) *Habitats for birds in Europe: a conservation strategy for the wider environment.* BirdLife International, Cambridge.

Tucker, G M and Heath, M F (1994) *Birds in Europe: their conservation status.* BirdLife International, Cambridge.

Usher, M B (Ed) (1986) *Wildlife conservation evaluation.* Chapman and Hall, London.

Voznyachuk, L N, Kopisov, Y G, Kononov, A N and Mahnach, A S (1972) Geological structure, relief and climate of Polessie region. *Problemy Polessia* 1: 38–108. [In Russian]

Weaver, D J (1995) Broads ESA *Breeding Wader Survey* 1995: *Report of Results*. Unpublished report. RSPB, Norwich.

Welch, H (Ed) (1996) *Managing water – conservation techniques for lowland wetlands*. RSPB, Sandy.

Williams, G and Hall, M (1987) The loss to arable agriculture of coastal grazing marshes in south and east England, with special reference to east Essex. *Biological Conservation* 3: 243–253.

Wolseley, P A, Palmer, M A and Williams, R (1984) *The aquatic flora of the Somerset Levels and Moors*. Nature Conservancy Council, Peterborough.

Yurkevich, I D, Kruganova, E A, Burtis, N A and Petrucguk, N I (1975) Pripyat floodplain meadows. *Problemy Polessia* 4: 3–28. [In Russian]

Other RSPB management handbooks

The wet grassland guide: managing floodplain and coastal wet grasslands for wildlife by Phil Benstead, Martin Drake, Paul José, Owen Mountford, Chris Newbold and Jo Treweek. RSPB. 1997. ISBN 0 903138 86 7. £17.95.

Reedbed management for commercial and wildlife interests by C J Hawke and P V José. RSPB. 1996. ISBN 0 903138 81 6. £14.95.

The new rivers and wildlife handbook edited by Diana Ward, Nigel Holmes and Paul José. RSPB. 1994. ISBN 0 903138 79 9. £19.95.

Gravel pit restoration for wildlife by John Andrews and David Kinsman. RSPB. 1990. ISBN 0 903138 60 3. £12.00.

Also available

European wet grasslands: biodiversity, management and restoration edited by C B Joyce and P M Wade. John Wiley and Sons, Chichester. 1998. ISBN 0 471976 19 9. £70.00.

UK floodplains edited by R G Bailey, P V José and B R Sherwood. Westbury Press, Otley, West Yorkshire. 1998. ISBN 1 841103 000 7. £35.00.

Bird monitoring methods: a manual of techniques for key UK species by G Gilbert, D W Gibbons and J Evans. RSPB. 1998. ISBN 1 901930 03 3. £17.95.

Index

The alphabetical arrangement is letter by letter. Numbers in *italics* refer to photographs. Numbers in **bold** refer to figures and tables.